Language and Nationalism

Language and Nationalism

Two Integrative Essays

Joshua A. Fishman

Ferkauf Graduate School of Humanities and Social Sciences
Yeshiva University

NEWBURY HOUSE PUBLISHERS / ROWLEY, MASSACHUSETTS

NEWBURY HOUSE PUBLISHERS, INC.

Language Science
Language Teaching
Language Learning

68 Middle Road, Rowley, Massachusetts 01969

Library of Congress Card Number: 72-149036
ISBN: 912066-15-6

Cover design: Philip L. Abbott

Printed in the U.S.A.

First printing: February 1973
Second printing: November 1975

It is easy for speakers of English, secure in the imperialism or even
colonialism of their language—conquering and settling, as it were, whole
vocabularies of German, French, Latin and Arabic—to scorn what
appears to be puerile or at least pedantic defensive linguistics. Secure in
the farflung domain of our language, we cannot really understand the
desperate defensiveness of those who stand against us. Is not language,
after all, merely a means of communication, and, as such, to be judged
merely in pragmatic terms? If a better means is available, should it not
be adopted? Can there be any real virtue in maintaining inefficient,
obsolescent, or even obsolete languages? Surely serious men of affairs
have more important tasks than to worry about the origins of words,
their esoteric meanings, their linguistic "purity." To the defenders of
other languages, the case appears quite differently .... (They) have
found in those languages not merely a means of communication but the
genius of their nationhood. And not alone among the non-European
languages has this been the case.

(Polk, 1970)

דאָס בוך גיב איך איבער

מײַן מאַמען און מײַן מאַמע־לשון

Foreword

That nationalism is a powerful force in the modern world is by now a well-worn cliché. What we need are some powerful analytic models to give a degree of order and coherence to the numerous and varied phenomena that are often subsumed under this label. There is the nationalism underlying anti-colonial struggles, such as those in Algeria, Vietnam, or Angola; the nationalism of separatist movements, whether in Biafra, Bangladesh, or French Canada; the nationalism of the Afrikaners that demands apartheid in South Africa; the clashing nationalisms in the Middle East that block resolution of the Arab-Israeli conflict; the competing nationalisms that create continuing tensions in such multi-ethnic states as Belgium, Yugoslavia, or Cyprus; the emerging nationalism that helps to unify such multi-ethnic states as India; the revolutionary nationalism of China or Cuba; the counterrevolutionary nationalism of Greece; the nationalism of smaller states that has helped to break down the image of a monolithic world Communism; the nationalism of the great powers that has limited the effectiveness of the United Nations as a peacekeeping force. Perhaps most fascinating, at least for the American observer, is the nationalism of Black Americans—an almost classical case of the emergence of national consciousness in a group that, only a few short years ago, very few scholars would have described as a nationality.

The Black American movement is one of three nationalist movements (the others being the Yiddish secularist and the Hebrew Zionist) that Dr. Fishman cites in his Preface as ones that he has witnessed at first hand and that he has wanted to understand more deeply. The present volume does indeed provide considerable insight into these movements and new perspectives on them, placing them in relationship to other nationalist movements that have arisen over a wide range of times and places. Dr. Fishman's analytic model, which offers a coherent framework for the varied examples of nationalism cited in the last paragraph (and which, incidentally, would exclude some of these examples from the definition of nationalism), seems to fit these three movements very well. Yet, by a remarkable *tour de force*, these cases—which clearly provided the emotional impetus for his work and which the work, in turn, illuminates—are barely mentioned in the text and only rarely in the footnotes. His broad overview draws, with an impressive display of scholarship, on numerous historical examples, but not on those personally closest to him. Thus, on the one hand, Dr. Fishman is emotionally involved in the issues he discusses—an involvement that both feeds his interest in nationalism and enhances his insight into it; on the other hand, by a conscious decision, he distances himself from the problem as he proceeds to derive and apply generalizations.

Closeness and distance is one of several interrelated polarities that characterize this book and make it a unique contribution to the study of nationalism. Another pair of often polar approaches that Dr. Fishman's analysis bridges and combines is that of the historian and that of the social scientist. The book is primarily a social-scientific contribution: it is highly analytical and aims toward deriving general propositions. At the same time, it is heavily historical, both in its attempt to trace the historical development of nationalism and its various manifestations, and in its use of historical cases to illustrate general propositions and the specific forms they have taken.

The value of combining social-scientific and historical approaches is readily apparent, for example, in Dr. Fishman's discussion of the role of social change in promoting nationalism. He analyzes nationalism as a response to both the problems and the opportunities created by social change—to the heightened need for reestablishing group identity in the face of rapid change and to the heightened awareness that group membership can serve as a basis for exclusion from or inclusion in the benefits accompanying such change. In doing so, he gives historical content to various analytical dimensions, such as the two sources of attachment—sentimental and instrumental—to a political system or nationalist movement which I have distinguished in my own work on nationalism.[1] At the same time, he provides an analytical handle for understanding the contradictions inherent in nationalism: that it makes extensive use of the institutions and

---

[1]Cf. Herbert C. Kelman, "Patterns of Personal Involvement in the National System: A Social-psychological Analysis of Political Legitimacy," in *International Politics and Foreign Policy* (rev. ed.) ed. J. N. Rosenau (New York: Free Press, 1969), 276-288.

techniques of mass society while seeking to counteract the alienating conditions fostered by that society; that it flourishes in urban centers while searching for the rural roots of the national culture and often espousing an anti-urban ideology; and that it promotes modernization while locating ethno-cultural authenticity in continuity with the distant past. These built-in tensions of nationalist ideology may account for its enormous power, as a potentially constructive as well as destructive force.

Overlapping the two polarities I have described so far—distance vs. closeness of the focal object and social science vs. history as the disciplinary approach—is that of the perspectives from which the phenomena of nationalism are examined. Again, Dr. Fishman combines two perspectives that are often antagonistic: that of the critical analyst and that of the sympathetic observer. In keeping with his stance as a social scientist, he applies his analytic tools to revealing, for example, the myth-making efforts by which nationalist movements create a noble and authentic past around which a population can be mobilized, the often arbitrary processes of integration and differentiation—minimizing some differences and maximizing others—by which the boundaries between in-group and out-groups are defined, and the self-fulfilling prophecies by which national unity and resistance to transnational integration are promoted. Both the first part of the book, which deals with the nature of nationalism in general, and the second, which focuses on language, demonstrate that the supposedly natural bases for defining a national group or selecting a national language are usually the end-points of social processes that are functional for the advancement of a nationalist movement or political state, that are deliberately fostered by the relevant elites, and that are heavily buttressed by rationalizations.

Yet at the same time it is clear that, in his critical analysis, Dr. Fishman is not merely exposing the myths and rationalizations that underlie nationalist movements and their roles in language planning. He is sympathetic to the efforts of various groups to achieve ethno-cultural integration, to define and authenticate their group identity, and to utilize language as a vehicle for unity and authenticity. Though these efforts—inevitably—involve some convenient myths and arbitrary boundaries, they are grounded not only in basic human needs, but also in genuine ethno-cultural values and bonds. Dr. Fishman clearly sees the emergence of national consciousness as a process combining deliberate creation and genuine discovery. He brings to his analysis of this process a warm understanding of individual and group needs for finding roots and a deep appreciation of the emotional, esthetic, and practical significance of a group's unique cultural products—and particularly of its language—in confirming its sense of rootedness.

There is, finally, one other polarity that this book bridges: that between political and cultural definitions of nationalism. Unlike many current writers, Dr. Fishman does not define nationalism as a primarily political ideology, linked to the establishment or enhancement of a nation-state. Rather, he presents it as an ideology designed to unify a group and to promote its interests by organizing that group around a more inclusive ethno-cultural identity and elaborating its unique beliefs, values, and behaviors. The push toward an independent political state is a possible and in fact rather frequent outcome of nationalist ideology but it is not, in Dr. Fishman's usage, a defining characteristic of that ideology. This definition does justice to those efforts at ethno-cultural mobilization—historical and contemporary—that are not directed toward an independent state, while at the same time illuminating the role of ethno-cultural mobilization as a powerful political force. Although my own work has proceeded in the opposite direction—starting out with nationalism as a political ideology with major ethno-cultural inputs (rather than as an ethno-cultural ideology with major political outcomes)—I see a great deal of virtue in Dr. Fishman's approach. It does seem to cut through much of the confusion and ambiguity that characterize the literature on nationalism. It provides a far better handle than most analyses, for example, in accounting for the recent development of a nationalist movement among Black Americans.

Dr. Fishman's approach is, of course, ideally suited to highlighting the relationship between nationalism and language, since language is both a major focus and tool of ethno-cultural integration. The analysis illuminates the relationship in both directions. Its major purpose is to clarify the role of language and language planning by exploring nationalist influences on these processes. No less important, however, is its contribution to our understanding of nationalism itself by exploring the ways in which language and language planning give shape and expression to it. Even our understanding of a nationalist movement like that of Black Americans, in which language does not play an obviously central part (as it does, for example, among French Canadians), can be enhanced by an analysis of the sentimental and instrumental implications of the group's linguistic patterns. I feel personally indebted to Dr. Fishman for introducing me to his analysis of language as an aid to understanding nationalism and for encouraging me, despite my lack of background in the field of sociolinguistics, to explore the relationship between the two.[2] Perhaps the best way I can express my gratitude is by passing the word to other students of nationalism and urging them to begin their exploration of language and nationalism with the present volume.

HERBERT C. KELMAN
Harvard University
June, 1972

[2]See Herbert C. Kelman, "Language as an Aid and Barrier to Involvement in the National System," in *Can Language be Planned? Sociolinguistic Theory and Practice for Developing Nations*, ed. J. Rubin and B. H. Jernudd (Honolulu: University Press of Hawaii, 1971), 21-51.

Preface

A very few concerns have been at the forefront of my awareness in preparing the two essays that constitute this monograph. The first of these has been to gain sociohistorical and cross-national perspective with respect to language planning, a process which several colleagues and I are currently investigating via a variety of empirical and quantitative social science methods (Fishman, in press a).* I have previously tried to locate my sociological inquiries within their broader human contexts (Fishman et al. 1966), Fishman et al. 1968, Fishman et al. 1971). As one initially trained in historical research and much engrossed in the lessons of history to this very day, I frankly tend to see the best problems of the sociology of language as those that are closely linked to historical developments of lasting social significance (Fishman in press b, Fishman 1971).

Language planning, like all planning, usually entails both a *direction* toward which movement is desired as well as an overall *justification* for movement in the specified direction. The planners and planning agencies, the detailed and daily processes of planning, and the cross-pressures, bargaining, and compromises to which they are commonly subjected, all of these interact in movement toward overarching goals which may well involve not only language but other areas of nationality functioning as well. A common link between the direction of language planning and the direction of other planning efforts in many countries may be the nationalist ideological underpinnings that they may all share.

---

*Abbreviated bibliographic references only (author, year, and page numbers when appropriate) are mentioned within parentheses in the text proper. Fuller bibliographic details concerning each item mentioned are given in the Bibliography beginning on page 147.

Nationalist ideologies are often so broadly formulated that there remains room for wide differences of opinion as to how they should be implemented. In addition, nationalist goals are frequently amended or supplemented by more timely and more precise goals. Nevertheless, nationalist theories and philosophies are often sufficiently pervasive and persistent that they provide important constraints, tendencies, and rationales for future planning, even after their own initial and most marked goals are attained or replaced. The past is frequently an influential modifier of present and future ingenuity and nationalism has been one of the most common and lasting interpretive links between the past, present, and future of nationalities. As a result I have kept before me the hypothesis that nationalist builders and planners (who may differ in ever so many ways) tend to turn to and return to nationalist philosophies in the pursuit of their strivings, in the language arena as in others.

In the pages that follow, I would like to examine the extent to which the language planning that has been pursued in many localities and in many periods has been guided by nationalism, i.e., by "the social movements, attitudes and ideologies which characterize the behavior of nationalities engaged in the struggle to achieve, maintain or enhance their position in the world (Wirth 1936)." In order to do so, however, it seemed desirable, first of all, to become familiar with the formations and the transformations of nationalism itself, and second, to examine how and why language so commonly comes to be one of the ingredients in nationalist goals and programs. If these first two topical clusters can profitably be viewed as revealing sufficient regularity across-time and across-nations, then our consideration of the impact of nationalism on language planning per se would be all the more revealing.

However, if I have hoped, not just on this occasion but also again and again, that history could inform my social science ("The contribution of history is *perspective*. This is no small matter." Landes and Tilly 1971, p. 2), I have hoped equally much that social science would inform my history. One of the truly esthetic experiences afforded by modern quantitative social science is encountered in its striving for parsimony in all explanatory efforts. I have, accordingly, asked myself whether nationalism, early and late, East and West, could not advantageously be viewed as a recurring constellation along a small number of parameters. As in all factor analytic explorations the dimensions themselves might be more or less orthogonally related to each other. Furthermore, as in all such efforts to gain conceptual parsimony, different instances of the phenomenon under study (here the flowering of nationalism and language planning) could receive widely different loadings on the dimensions derived. As a result, neither a Procrustean bed nor an endless array of unique cases has appealed to me, and I have wondered whether I, an outsider to the normal pursuit of social history, could steer an enlightening course between the two and yet arrive at a goal rather more characterized by the canon of parsimony than by its absence.

In all frankness, yet another goal has been in my awareness, at least from time to time, and the fact that it has not always been visible to me has not blinded me to the possibility that, after all, it might have been the most important of all, if only because it combined emotional and intellectual tension. I have witnessed three nationalist movements myself, at first hand so to speak (the Yiddish secularist, the Hebrew Zionist, and the Black American), and I have dearly wanted to understand them better and, above all, to understand why I respond to them as I do. Nevertheless, I have decided to do so by engaging in a once removed, twice removed, thrice removed mode of analysis, in the hope that the wider canvas would illumine the narrower, while the narrower passion would drive me on to examine one hidden corner after another in the broader picture.

I have not been unaware of the fact that my topic, the nationalist impact on language planning, is (both emotionally and intellectually) not a popular one, particularly among American scholars. Nationalism is often viewed as a perversion, language planning as either impossible or undesirable. The rich, the white, and the safe have always been more than a little suspicious of problems particularly prevalent among the poor, the colored, and the endangered—even when they have deigned to help them, to guide them, or even to serve them. If even a historian of recent Black nationalism could conclude from his labors that other people have gladly left their ethnic ties behind them but "only the Negro has had to invent a spurious nationalism to cope with his extraordinary position," then what seems to be lacking is not so much sympathy as empathy, not so much knowledge as perspective, not so much information as understanding. If we listen only to each other we hear constant references to the "excesses" of nationalism. However, without at all condoning them, we must grant that excesses occur in connection with every cause in which men believe strongly. Are we then to condemn dedications and convictions, or merely to pray for their greater mutual toleration? If we also listen to the third world we hear:

> This I know: we of Indonesia and the citizens of many countries of Asia and Africa have seen our dearest and best suffer and die, struggle and fail, and rise again to struggle and fail again—and again be resurrected from the very earth, and finally achieve their goal. Something burned in them; something inspired them. They called it nationalism. We who have followed and have seen what they built, but what they destroyed themselves in building—we, too, call their inspiration and our inspiration, nationalism. For us there is nothing ignoble in that word. On the contrary, it contains for us all that is best in mankind and all that is noblest (Sukarno, cited in Snyder 1964, p. 337).

Hearing this, it has seemed to me, we must not ask if the passion is "good," if it is "justified," if it is based on "valid arguments." Rather we must ask "why does it occur, and when, and how can its obvious power be most productively channeled?"

The literature on nationalism—both that produced by nationalists per se, as well as that of those commenting upon the phenomenon from the sidelines—is voluminous. If one also attempts to follow this literature, as I have, in several languages and over a span of half a century or more, the task is literally endless as well as thankless. In order to remain afloat on this ocean of words—an ocean in which I, as a normal quantifier, first had to learn to swim—I have emphasized those writings dealing with language and only sampled those more generally or specifically (directionally) oriented. The major amount of time and freedom required for an undertaking of this kind was made available to me by the International Division of the Ford Foundation and by the East-West Center. To them, and most particularly to the colleagues with whom I have worked on language planning research under Ford Foundation auspices since 1968 (Das Gupta, Jernudd, Ferguson, and Rubin), and to all of the participants in the May 1969 Consultative Meeting on Language Planning Processes (see Rubin and Jernudd 1971) who so helpfully and encouragingly commented on an earlier version of this monograph, go my sincere thanks for their assistance and their stimulation. Their patience and their support will be repaid, at least in part, and my own hopes for this monograph will be realized, if now, on the basis of some of the dimensions that it suggests, the *empirical* measurement and description of nationality beliefs, actions, attitudes and emotions can be more fully related to corresponding differentials with respect to language behavior and behavior toward language (of which language planning is but one example).

JOSHUA A. FISHMAN
Jerusalem, June 1971.

Contents

Part I

The Nature of Nationalism

"For, whosoever is of such mean reason that he thinks his birthplace the most delightful under the sun, will also prefer his own vulgar tongue, that means his mother tongue, to all others . . . . But we, whose Fatherland is the world, as for the fish the sea . . . we have found out that there are many places and cities, and we believe more noble and more delightful ones, than Tuscany and Florence from which I derive and of which I am a citizen; and that many nations and peoples use a more delightful and useful language than the Italians."

Dante Alighieri, in his *De Vulgari Eloquentia,* Book I, section 6.

"As you speak the French language by nature, it is reasonable that you should be the subject of the King of France. I quite agree that the Spanish language should belong to the Spaniard and the German to the German. But the whole region of the French language must be mine."

Henry IV, to deputies of newly acquired provinces, according to Pierre Nathieu in his *Histoire de Henri IV,* 1631.

"Has a nationality anything dearer than the speech of its fathers? In its speech resides its whole thought domain, its tradition, history, religion and basis of life, all its heart and soul. To deprive a people of its speech is to deprive it of its one eternal good . . . With language is created the heart of a people."

Johann G. Herder, in his *Briefe zu Beförderung der Humanität,* 1783.

"Indeed, we can hardly conceive a more glorious object, a more sublime spectacle, than a nation . . . who could form and highly refine a language, write elaborate works on its grammars and compose hymns and prayers while their brethren in other parts of the world could hardly think it possible to represent the elementary sounds in their speech by visible characters."

A Hindu, *Bengal Magazine,* 1875-76, 4, 367.

"Up, ye Slovaks, still is living our true Slovak language while our loyal hearts are beating for our nation. Living, living, yes and deathless is the Slovak spirit. Hell and lightning, hell and lightning rage in vain against us."

Slovak National Anthem

"To have a state composed of peoples who speak the same language, or to make only those peoples who speak the same language an independent state seems more natural and most desirable."

Ziya Gökalp in *Turk Yurdu*, 1914.

The Nature of Nationalism

PRELIMINARY DEFINITIONS

The basic concepts in any discussion of nationalism deal primarily with transformations in sociocultural integration on the one hand, and, secondarily, with transformations in political-operational integration, on the other hand. In view of the long and varied history of interest in both of these phenomena in scientific as well as in lay circles (sociocultural collectivities and their supposedly distinctive characteristics having been commented upon by Herodotus and other ancient scholars, commentators, and leaders) it is not at all surprising that usage varies considerably, both from language to language as well as from period to period. The definitions that follow are not motivated by any conviction as to their purported terminological superiority, but rather, in order to indicate the usage that will be followed in the present discussion.[1]

Nationality

The designation nationality will be employed to indicate sociocultural units that have developed beyond primarily local self-concepts, concerns, and integrative bonds. The term stands in contrastive juxtaposition to others such that it presupposes at least a level of sociocultural integration more elementary (i.e., simpler, smaller, more particularistic, more localistic) than the one it designates, namely *ethnic group*,[2] if not also a level of sociocultural integration that is more advanced (i.e., larger, more inclusive, more complex, although still characterized to some extent by ethnicity). Although the term "nationality" can be traced back over a century in its present usage (see, e.g., Acton, 1907; originally published 1862) it first came to be "widely applied during the first quarter of this century in connection with the well-known political problem of reconciling the sovereignty of states with the autonomy of ethnic groups" (Znaniecki 1952, p. xiv).

In connection with the prevalent use just referred to, the term "nationality" is neutral with respect to the existence or nonexistence of a corresponding political unit or polity. Indeed, it is precisely because the human populations encompassed by the referents of *nationality* and *polity* need *not* be isomorphic that it becomes possible to more clearly pursue the issue of the circumstances under which sociocultural groups (i.e., groups distinguished by customs and values pertaining to their daily and all-encompassing goals and behaviors) do or do not have or seek polities of their own.

If the term is *not* intended to denote absence or presence of control over a polity (although it is not meant to rule out political activity toward that or other ends, viz. Akzin 1964), it *is* intended to denote a more advanced degree and inclusive scope or scale of effective organization and of elaborated beliefs, values, and behaviors than those that obtain in the case of ethnic groups per se. The organization–behavior–ideology interactions referred to focus *directly* upon the preservation, strengthening, and guided development of the presumably distinctive customs and values of nationality, and, only *indirectly* (in order to safeguard the above) upon whatever political, economic, religious, or other social systems may be considered necessary for that purpose.

Nationalism

The more inclusive organization and the elaborated beliefs, values, and behaviors which nationalities develop on behalf of their avowed ethnocultural self-interest constitute the referents of the terms nationalism.[3]

Some few writers, among them Wuorinen (1950), prefer the terms national consciousness or nationality consciousness, particularly when referring to less militant manifestations of conscious ethnicity than those for which they reserve the term nationalism. However, it seems to me that the further introduction of strength or saliency considerations into a notion which already, in part, depends on such considerations for its differentiation from ethnicity per se may be more troublesome than helpful for the purposes of initial nonquantitative discussion. In addition, of course, nationality consciousness would seem to refer at best only to the cognitive aspects of nationalism rather than to their more complex cognitive, conative (valuational and affective), and overt realizations.

Far more prevalent are those who tie the term nationalism either to the pursuit of political independence, or, thereafter, to the maximization of interpolity economic (or other) advantage. In this connection I believe Baron's approach (1947) to be more productive, in that it considers nationalism to be essentially conscious or organized ethnocultural solidarity which may or may not then be directed outside of its initial sphere toward political, economic, and religious goals. In Parsonian terms one might say that while nationalism derives from the pattern maintenance and integrative subsytems of general social systems, the interdependence of subsystems is such that it also commonly interacts with the adaptation and goal attainment subsystems as well. Since politically independent territoriality *is* so common a goal in the modern era, I have proposed that the cluster of behaviors-beliefs-values pertaining specifically to *its* acquisition, maintenance, and development be separately designated as *nationism* (Fishman 1968a).

Nation

In our discussions that follow the term *nation* will primarily refer to any independent political-territorial unit which is largely or increasingly under the control of a particular nationality.[4] In order not to anticipate the subsequent discussion in detail, I will only suggest at this juncture that the term may be usefully contrasted with such terms as *state, polity,* or *country* which do not necessarily denote either independence vis-à-vis external control or the pre-dominance of a single nationality vis-à-vis internal control. The past two hundred years have undeniably witnessed the eclipse of several multinationality states and the appearance of larger numbers of polities whose leaders have aspired to reach the goal of single-nationality nations. As Znaniecki observes, "the conception of 'national land' . . . is rooted first in the old idea of 'patria' or 'fatherland' and is obviously connected with the myth of common origin" (1952, p. 96). This means whereby nationalism and nationism both strive to confirm this myth (i.e., their efforts to produce a better fit between the theory of common ancient origin and the reality of common current interdependence) and the role of language in these efforts, constitute the story I wish to tell.

RECURRENT COMPONENTS OF NATIONALISM

Having decided to define *nationalism* as the organizationally heightened and elaborated beliefs, attitudes, and behaviors of societies acting on behalf of their avowed ethnocultural self-interest, it is clear that for such societally organized goal activity to occur it is first necessary for populations to become convinced that they possess in common certain unique ethnocultural characteristics, and that these similarities, over and above obvious local variations and subgroup differences, are of *importance* to them. Neither of these traits (*recognition* of common ethnocultural characteristics and *conviction* with respect to their overriding importance) is part of the biologically given nature of mankind. Neither of them has existed in all ethnically different groups at all times. Indeed, such organized and heightened affiliative beliefs, attitudes, and behaviors among larger populations that are not exposed to messages or contacts from outside their immediate environments are seemingly quite uncommon. Most nonindustrial, nonurban, nonliterate populations have primarily exhibited very local or "primordial" attachments to near kin and to the immediately experienced customs and social structures related to them. Broader ties or allegiances among such populations are normally restricted to their immediate political, religious, or cultural elites (local nobility, clergy, and scribes) who *have* had nonlocal experiences which *have* exposed them to the ideas and the structures of ethnocultural unity and the organization of authenticity.[5]

Lest we assume that such localism is limited to dark and distant backwaters it should be pointed out that all European histories are replete with accounts of the separatism and particularism of their rural populations until comparatively recent days. It is, of course, true that the last extensive manifestations of such views and behaviors in Europe are restricted to its least modernized Central, Eastern, and Southeastern areas. These began to seem anomalous in the middle of the last century when Brauner [a participant in the first All Slav Congress, Vienna, 1848] told an anecdote of how peasants in the district of Sacz in West Galicia, when asked whether they were Poles, replied: "We are quiet folk." "Then are you Germans?" "We are decent folk" (Namier 1944, p. 107). However, the continuation of such narrower or smaller scale affiliative beliefs, values, and behaviors even in modern days in somewhat the same area is indicated by Znaniecki's report that a 1934-35 ". . . investigation of the inhabitants of the marshy Pripet area (which between the two World Wars was included within Poland) showed that nearly half of those peasants who were ethnically White Ruthenians did not know that such a nationality existed and considered themselves as merely belonging to local communities" (1952, p. 82). It is out of just such ethnocultural fragmentation that nationalism creates a broader and more conscious unity.

Broader Unity

A basic component, then (at least of early nationalism), is an insistence on the expansion of the scope of perceived commonality of ethnocultural characteristics to a point far beyond their original, directly experienced, primordial, bounds. Nationalism, at least for hitherto traditional or transitional populations, represents an expansion of affiliative beliefs, attitudes, and behaviors so as to include far more distant (indeed, purely figurative) kin, far more distant authorities, and far more inclusive commitments than those that are immediately available to or directly impinge on their daily experiences. This is not to say that premodern societies have been entirely removed from central value systems, for this would be overstating the case (Shils 1961), particularly in the light of the ability of larger religious systems to penetrate into even the most backward and isolated areas and to maintain personal "spokesmen" there. However, in premodern periods the articulation between peripheral and central areas was, at best, fragmentary, both because of functional and structural difficulties. Communication difficulties and differences in beliefs, values, and behaviors reinforced each other[6] to the point that only clearly overwhelming social forces could overcome the overriding cognitive and affiliative isolation of traditional populations for more than brief interludes.

Not infrequently the unifying social forces involved were (and are) not merely multidirectional social and economic changes but the direct force of arms as well. Looking back, scarcely half a century after the Revolution, upon the royal as well as the republican contributions to the unification of France, Michelet had no doubt but that its broader unity, purchased at the cost of countless lives, was a supreme good: "This sacrifice of the diverse interior nationalities to the great nationality which comprises them undoubtedly strengthened the latter . . . . It was at the moment when France suppressed within herself the divergent French countries that she proclaimed her high and original revelations" (1846, p. 286). Thus, even later nationalisms, those which combine smaller regional nationalities into greater nationalities—rather than merely those that transform particularistic ethnic groups into initial nationalities—often include broader unity among their basic drives.

It is via the experience of broader unity that the common man comes to recognize his relationship and his interdependence with a human population most of whose members he has never met and to believe that this relationship and interdependence are and have always been quite naturally rooted in various ethnocultural similarities between him and his far-flung "kin." However, two exaggerations need to be guarded against in this connection. The first is of a *post hoc ergo propter hoc* nature, namely to conclude that perceived broader unity *necessarily* stems from perceived *ethnocultural* similarity (rather than from other integrative bonds along more purely economic, political, religious, or special purpose grounds). Broader ethnocultural similarity is not a "natural" basis of human grouping; certainly it is not the prime basis for *political* integration throughout human history.[7] It is also not a necessary outcome of perceived broader unity of purpose or values. Thus, where it *is* attained and stressed it deserves attention in its own right, rather than as a natural consequence of increased flow of communication or other possible expressions and implementations of broader unity per se.

Second, it would be wrong to imply that either broader unity or any of its possible consequences and concomitants are either fully replacive or neatly stagewise phenomena. Rather, it represents awareness and experiences that wax and wane differentially in various population segments and, therefore, it must be understood as always coexisting with narrower and sometimes more primary awarenesses and experiences.

Stressed Authenticity

"When seen as a movement, nationalism represents a series of stages in the struggle of a given solidarity group to achieve its basic aims of unity and self-direction" (Symmons-Symonolewicz 1965, p. 1965). A second basic component of nationalism is its stress on ethnocultural characterization and on the authenticity, purity, and nobility of the beliefs, values, and behaviors that typify the community of reference. In its most generalized and theoretical form, as expounded by those who could rise above the problems of their own local nationalities in order to seek out more encompassing rationales, nationalism became an ode to the beauty, the morality, and the value of diversity per se. It was claimed that "no individual, no country, no people, no history of a people, no state is like any other. Therefore, the true, the beautiful, and the good are not the same for them. Everything is suffocated if one's own way is not sought and if another nation is blindly taken as a model. Civilization consists primarily in the potentialities of a nation and in making use of them" (Herder, *Sämtliche Werke*, v. 4, p. 472; cited by Kohn 1944, p. 433).[8]

It is part of the specific nature of the nationalist (rather than any more generally reformist) stress on authenticity to find it in the lower classes and in the distant past. "The lower orders are seen as being not simply primitive peasants, but as the source of national creativity . . . . Salvation must come from below" (Minogue 1967, pp. 60-61) if only because the peasantry has hitherto been more isolated from the foreign fads and influences to which others (particularly cosmopolitan intellectuals, estranged upper-class strata and urbanites more generally) are so likely to be exposed or to seek exposure.[9] The peasantry, and, at times, the lower classes more generally, have more fully and faithfully preserved the ethnocultural distinctiveness of the past and it is the past, in all its authenticity and glory, that constitutes the main storehouse from which nationalism derives its dynamism for changing the present and creating the future.

Whereas traditionalisms of various kinds seek a return to or a preservation of the genuine past,[10] nationalism seeks to "render the present a rational continuation of the past" (Bromage 1956, p. 29), indeed, it seeks and creates a usable past. "The very idea that they [specified populations] should be united is founded upon the doctrine that, however much their folk cultures may differ they are essentially similar as compared with those of other collectivities and that this similarity is essentially due to a common historical background" (Znaniecki 1952, p. 30).[11]

While it is true that nationalism both seeks out and cultivates the Little Tradition of an ostensible past—with its folksongs, folktales, proverbs, folk dances, costumes, pastimes, and expressions—it finds not only purity and authenticity in the past but also (and particularly) greatness. It is this greatness, rooted in authenticity, that can (it is hoped) inspire current masses to make new efforts, to overcome new dangers, and to achieve new (and even greater) greatness. Thus, in seeking the collaboration of the Hungarians in his quarrels with the Habsburg Emperor in 1809, Napoleon issued a proclamation saying "You have national customs and a national language; you boast of a distant and illustrious origin; take up then once again your existence as a nation. Have a king of your choice, who will rule only for you, who will live in the midst of you, whom only your citizens and your soldiers will serve . . . . Meet therefore in a National Diet, in the manner of your ancestors" (cited by Kedourie 1961, p. 94).[12]

Similar reconstructions of the past were made by other nationalist spokesmen. Rumanian leaders proclaimed all the contentious polyglot areas that lay before them to be elements of the ancient Roman colony of Dacia (held by Rome from A.D. 107 to 270) and the Rumanians to be the heirs of the Romans in bringing Christianity and civilization to the Balkans (Kolarz 1946, p. 173). At roughly the same time, Irish leaders called upon their fellowmen to recognize that they constituted a " . . . race which at one time held possession of more than half Europe, which established itself in Greece and burned infant Rome . . . after overthrowing and trampling on the primitive peoples of half Europe . . . We alone . . . escaped the claws of . . . the victorious eagles of Rome; we alone developed ourselves naturally upon our own lines outside of and free from all Roman influence; we alone were thus able to produce an early art and literature, and—we are our father's sons" (Hyde 1894; pp. 117-31). All this being true "it behooves us to know the nature and source of that former greatness, that we may be encouraged to restore as far as possible all that was great and beautiful in the past and so make our country—as we fervently hope—a 'Nation once again!' " (Flannery 1896, p. 13). As we read these and similar words today we cannot but recognize their energizing, mobilizing purpose and effect. The past is being mined, ideologized, and symbolically elaborated in order to provide determination, even more than direction, with respect to current and future challenges.

Nationalism is not so much backward-oriented—particularly where, as in most of Europe, it has been free to be eclectic with respect to the past and with respect to a very distant past at that—as much as it seeks to derive unifying and energizing power from widely held images of the past in order to overcome a quite modern kind of fragmentation and loss of identity. In this sense, nationalism may be seen as quite reality-oriented, both in its intuitive recognition of the power of past images of greatness, as well as in its intuitive response to the anonymity and insecurity that are common concomitants of actual or impending change to post-traditional life-styles. Nationalist movements stress authenticity in order to legitimize their demand for goal-oriented unity, a unity that is purportedly also authentic, in that it too existed at an earlier time when small communities and emotionally satisfying interactions between community members were still the rule. The division of labor and the differentiation of experience are not only interrelated with the emergence of unnatural and impersonal societies but also with the loss of broader unity and authenticity. Thus, nationalism claims to reverse the modern affective imbalance between mechanical and organic solidarity,[13] between Gemeinschaft and Gesellschaft, between the sacred and the secular, in order thereby to release for current puposes the ancient but still available (though too often dormant) unity and genius of populations who would otherwise be fractionated and de-ethnicized by modern adversaries, both human and technological.

Nationalism's stress on authenticity-oriented belief, attitude, and behavior may well be crucial in modern and modernizing mass-societies in order to reach, influence, and activate large numbers of individuals who actually lead quite different and separate daily lives and who only interact with a very small proportion of the total community of broader unity throughout their entire lifetimes. Small communities can transmit and implement their narrower unity and authenticity directly through the social structure, i.e., through the face-to-face interactions that are permissible according to local cultural norms. Larger societies must transmit and implement fidelity to large-scale unity by means of the institutions of mass culture: formal organizations, communication media, schools, and goverment per se.[14] Thus, nationalism is likely to utilize the institutions and techniques of massification at the very same time that it seeks to provide an ethnocultural solution for the rootlessness and meaninglessness that technologically based massification itself engenders.[15]

BASIC FORCES: SOCIAL CHANGE

Economic Development

Nationalism provides a redefinition and mobilization of personal and group indentity, purpose, and possibilities. Such redefinition and mobilization becomes attractive when their prior, more traditional counterparts, are rendered inoperative or nonproductive as a result of social change. Throughout human history populations have become more conscious of and more concerned with their ethnicity when it has been impressed upon them that they could expect certain benefits—or that they were denied certain benefits—as a result of it. In more or less modern days such impressions have most frequently spread together with the spread of basic and far-reaching social change. Thus, nationalism in Europe spread most rapidly at a time when, on the one hand, Napoleon was disrupting its political concepts and conventions, and, on the other, when " . . . the industrial revolution, accompanied by a prodigious increase in population, was gradually penetrating everywhere, transforming methods of production, disturbing traditional social relations and creating vast urban conglomerations. New wealth was being created and new social classes were coming to the top who would, sooner or later, claim and obtain their share of political power" (Kedourie 1961, p. 95).

A constantly recurring theme in analyses of modern nationalisms is to point to industrialization in particular (or to economic change somewhat more broadly) as its most basic or important cause.[16] This view is justified on the grounds of the undeniable disruptive impact of industrial and other economic transformations on prior affiliative and integrative bonds and rationales. It is further justified on the basis of the use to which nationalism has more recently been put in connection with planned economic development efforts and in the mobilization of successively poorer strata of the world's population.[17] This argument has then been traced back to historical parallels which imply that it is particularly compelling at a "transitional" stage in economic development, when "the masses are mobilized but not yet assimilated" (Ingelhart and Woodward 1967, p. 40, paralleling similar statements in Deutsch 1953), and when a new awareness dawns with respect to the attainability of personal achievement and the real social mobility consequences of such achievement (McClelland 1961). Some students of nationalism have carefully attended to both the disruptive and the facilitative or motivating aspects of economic change. Thus, Friedland comments perceptively that "the social structures generating prenationalist movements are already transitional in that . . . inroads have been made into the subsistence economy and the society is increasingly involved in the cash nexus; stratification of the indigenous population is beginning, particularly as some autochthones are educated along Western lines" (1968, pp. 17-18).

Several students of nationalism have pointed to the fact that its economic preconditions have successively come into being in different parts of the world. As a result, when its early disintegrative and reintegrative consequences had already spent their force in one part of the world (to be followed by subsequent stages that we will examine below), its impact then began to be felt in yet other, initially neighboring and ultimately quite distant areas, into which industrialization or other basic economic change had subsequently penetrated. "If the whole world could have been industrialized simultaneously and uniformly, national differences might not have been emphasized. As it was, however, no two countries were at any given time in exactly the same stage of industrialization and each sought . . . to insure its own industrial development" (Hayes 1931, p. 236). If we add to the above temporal variation the fact that most countries undergoing industrialization or other profound economic changes were by and large multinationality states, and that economic changes generally tended to favor one region of such states over others, then we obtain a picture not only of *inter*state nationalistic tensions but, even more basically, of *intra*state cleavages as well. "The integration of the plural society is based primarily on a system of relationships between culturally differentiated groups of unequal status and power. This system of relationships not only reflects the power structure of the political order under which it is subsumed, but it also serves to express the maintenance or change of that political order. More precisely, any change capable of altering the structure of intersectional relations will have consequences for the political order of the society" (Depres 1968, p. 7).

Around each newly developing center of major economic ascendency, systems of ethnocultural, social, and political integration were developed which tended to favor those populations that controlled newly necessary human and natural resources and that tended to exploit, submerge, or displace those about them that did not. It became increasingly difficult for the latter "to improve their life chances without changing their sectional membership or, alternatively [if that was felt to be impossible], without seeking to improve the status and power of their respective cultural sections" (Depres 1968, p. 7). Thus, as a concomitant and consequence of widespread and fundamental economic changes influencing both interpolity as well as intrapolity relations, and the impact of which was both disruptive (for masses of common folk) and facilitative (for the favored few), nationalist movements initially spread as newly favored populations (from the point of view of whatever economically based changes were then uppermost) sought to protect themselves from the claims and controls of concurrently less preferred (but previously or coestablished) sociopolitical units e.g., England vis-à-vis France). Subsequently, nationalist movements spread as hitherto backward groups, formerly under the sway or shadow of regions that had already experienced social change and social advantage, began to savor or even only to anticipate their own day in the sun, i.e., their own growing correspondence between newly valuable and localized natural and human resources (e.g., Ireland vs England). Finally, nationalist movements spread even further as counterreactions against the policies of once submerged populations that, having come to possess newfound power based on economic development, wielded it most pointedly against former partners in poverty (e.g., Hungarians vis-à-vis Slovaks in the Habsburg Empire). Economically advantaged groups are always relatively more conscious of and protective of their groupness. Disadvantaged groups become similarly conscious only as a result of partial changes in their circumstances which, more than anything else, merely serve to heighten their sense of relative deprivation and the fact that it is enforced on the basis of group membership. There is thus a strong contrastive element in nationalism, which, like broader unity and stressed authenticity, is likely to have language planning consequences as well.

The sequential economic development argument, predominant though it is among students of nationalism, is frequently felt to lack a final clincher. That is, sequential economic development and all of its ensuing disorganization, reorganization, rivalry, and opportunity may well be facilitative of various kinds of reintegrative and reformist movements. What evidence is there of a *necessary* link between such developments and the massive appeal of broader ethnocultural unity as well as of stressed ethnocultural authenticity? In large part, the argument for such a direct link is based on a presumed need to restore ethnocultural bonds, but of a kind appropriate to the new level of economic massification, once the old primordial bonds have been rendered inoperative. Nationalism thus appears as a natural cure for a natural ailment: the restoration of more meaningful and appropriate ethnocultural loyalties subsequent to the disruption of older ones that are no longer functional, in the light of widespread economic change. The view that distinctive ethnocultural integration is a basic human need, that modern technology is disruptive of this need, and that nationalism represents a natural attempt to *restore* ethnocultural balance (or to *create* it at a higher level) is well over a century old in writings on this matter. [18A]

Nationalism: One of Many Cooccurring Responses to a Variety of Cooccurring Changes

In contrast to those many scholars who have viewed nationalism as following inevitably or, at least primarily, from the dislocations occasioned by rapid and large-scale economic transitions and from the increased integrative capacities, opportunities and needs which these have fostered, are those who have emphasized the equal or greater importance of noneconomic causation. Some, like Hayes, have pointed to the fact that in earlier eras economic change led to multination states or empires rather than to the crystalization of single-nationality states.[18B] Others, like Akzin, have pointed to the importance of long-drawn-out armed conflicts as formative of political centralization and, subsequently of nationality consciousness, as a result of state-sponsored efforts to resist external threat via unified and stressed action.[19] Still others have pointed particularly to the modern decline of religious affiliation as a primary integrative bond of broader sorts and have considered nationalism as nothing more than the "religion of modern man."[20] Others, finally, have stressed the contagious power of the ideals of nationality as such. Presumably these ideals were always waiting for recognition and finally, when first recognized and propagated, due to whatever circumstances in whatever part of the globe, they inevitably spread to others by infection, by example, and by the inexorable workings of the *Zeitgeist*.[21] The latter view is sufficiently vague, that it does not so much propose a particular rival to economic change as it suggests that such change must itself be viewed in a broader framework of ongoing change as well as continuing stability. This last position, then, leads us conveniently to more complex (multifactor) interpretations of the links between nationalism and social change.

Although no other single "basic cause" has received as much attention as the economic, most modern scholarship has shifted to an emphasis on economic change as one of several concurrent kinds of large-scale social change and nationalism as one of several interrelated responses to the problems and opportunities concurrent with or resulting from such change.[22] The most common cited trio of interacting and coocurring causes and effects is that cited by Talmon in connection with the question "Why did nationalism appear and triumph precisely at the time it did?" In his reply he points to "the decline of religious sanctions and the weakening of the religious framework; the doctrine of the rights of man and the democratic sovereignty of the people; and economic and social processes at the onset of the Industrial Revolution" (1965, p. 17). Essentially, Talmon is pointing to the functional demise of a former principle of broader unity, to the rise of an ideology of mass participation and free competition in political processes, and to the dislocation of small-scale ethnicity such that ethnocultural bonds on a wider scale became both necessary and possible.[23]

Since the political consequences of nationalism have been of greatest interest to American social scientists, it is the relationship between nationalism and mass participation in politics that has received the greatest amount of attention.[24] Deutsch has stressed the fact that in the multinationality states it was usually not really desired nor immediately feasible to economically and politically absorb all of those who were dislocated (mobilized) by economic and technological change. On the other hand, even those who were absorbed normally met "serious disappointments and frustrations of many of the new hopes, claims and expectations." As a result, the first steps toward economic and political modernization were normally "followed by the rise of more extremely nationalistic leaders, platforms or parties within each ethnic group, and by a more exclusive stress on ethnic in-group values and interests" (1957, p. 62). These leaders, in turn, courted popular support by stressing the need for greater popular participation in the political processes of the multinationality state and greater popular gain from ultimate political separation from the state. Thus, "nationalism is historically tied to the growth of democracy. Indeed, it has been asserted that nationalism was the essential condition for the democratizing of the modern state. Against such a view, it seems sounder to see democracy and nationalism in a 'dialectic' relation . . . . They were in their origin contemporary movements and therefore many of the conditions for one also served to condition the other" (Friedrich 1963, p. 560).

While nationalism remained primarily concerned with the ethnocultural basis of organized activity and democracy with the processes of free participation and competition, both borrowed adherents and platform planks from the other. Both were strengthened by masses of dislocated humanity that clamored for activization and organization on the basis of wider bonds and behaviors. "Where the disease is various, no particular definite remedy can meet the wants of all. Only the attraction of an abstract idea, or of an ideal state, can unite in common action multitudes who seek a universal cure for many special evils and a common restorative applicable to many different conditions" (Acton [1862] 1907, p. 222). Nationalism was (and is) one of a small number of such "abstract ideas" dealing with an "ideal state" which have competed with each other and increasingly intermingled with each other during the past 200 years of worldwide efforts to cope with the pains and pleasures of basic and rapid social change.

BASIC FORCES: ELITES

Widespread, basic, and long-continuing social dislocation capable of fundamentally changing the opportunity and power relations between groups within multiethnic states must be *perceived* as such, *exploited* as such, and, to some extent, *made* into such. The crucial catalysts in this connection are protoelites who are (or feel) excluded from the power and influence they covet and who possess the personal gifts or material resources to move symbols and masses toward desired sociopolitical regroupings. In the development of nationalism the above general formulation can be further refined by considering the elites who recognized, moved, and represented the broader collectivity before the advent of nationalism and its concurrent social and economic changes. In country after country, we find that only the nobility and those clerics and other intellectuals united with them were conscious of their broader unity and of their national roles. Thus, "the French nobility [in the eighteenth century] had long regarded themselves as racially and morally distinct from the rest of the French population. They alone were the nation[ality]" (Minogue 1967, p. 10). Slowly, at first, those social classes included within and recognizing themselves as part of the nation[ality] began to expand, particularly with the growth of the higher bourgeoisie, which was generally the first class, outside the nobility and the intellectuals, to be incorporated into the ruling or political class. This expansion of power and of national identity occurred first in Western Europe. Thus, notwithstanding Rousseau's identification of the "nation" with the "people," it remained true there, as elsewhere, that by the mid-nineteenth century only the upper classes consistently "identified themselves with the nation and the national interest . . . . The lower classes . . . [were] excluded from both a real stake in the national economy and an active partnership in the determination of the policy of 'their' nation" (Kohn 1968, p. 64). Indeed, when nationalist doctrines and aspirations were first communicated to localistic populations they were often initially rejected, precisely because they were interpreted as self-serving upper-class, intellectual, or urban fabrications,[25] if they were understood at all. The spread of nationalism is, therefore, marked not by its existence in the upper reaches of society, but by its successful communication to and activation of the urban (and ultimately also the rural) lower middle and lower classes. Such spread frequently involved a new intellectual and economic protoelite just as much as it involved a new class of respondents.

Successful nationalist protoelites "form an increasingly coherent intellectual community activated by the ideal of a culturally united and socially solidary national society, which should include all the people whose folk cultures are presumed to be essentially alike, and who are supposed to share the same historical background . . . [and] who should be equally separated from peoples with different cultures" (Znaniecki 1952, pp. 25, 81). These protoelites, then, are the essential synthesizers, separators, popularizers, and organizers on whom the spread of nationalism depends. They not only create or further the broader unity and heightened authenticity that they seek, but they plant an awareness of both of these desiderata in a population that is becoming increasingly receptive to unifying and activating solutions of many kinds;[26] they point to the success of nationalist struggles in distant cultures and in other times with which the ordinary man would hardly be familiar,[27] they spread the views of spokesmen that might otherwise remain unnoticed,[28] and, in general, they heighten awarenesses that are only latent, so that not only will masses come to feel that they constitute a nationality but that they will also be willing to act upon the basis of that feeling.[29]

The role of elites in creating both the awareness and substance of broader unity and authenticity is of particular interest to us in view of the parallels that exist between these efforts and directions and those that pertain to language planning per se. Obviously, intellectuals and other elites begin not only with their own goals and biases but also with some preexisting raw materials which these biases can shape. "A leader is almost bound to utilize those elements in the underlying population and its culture which lend themselves to . . . manipulation and exploitation" (Friedrich 1963, p. 557). History and ethnography are the reservoirs of symbols and myths, heroes and missions which nationalist elites first mine and then refine in their quest for ethnically unifying and energizing themes. Every group has "some heroic forefather who called for national unity or national reassertion in the past" (Deutsch 1964b, p. 51), some gallery of great poets or sayers and some archive of moving poetry and sayings, some aspirations that have remained with it as echoes and memories in folktales and folk songs. These are the building blocks of unity and authenticity that nationalist elites discover, augment, and combine. "We find everywhere a curious searching for historical ancestors . . . to reconstruct . . . [the] past as the most glorious, like a lost paradise . . . in search after what a Magyar poet called 'ancestors, ancestors, you glorious ancestors . . . you tempests shaking the whole world' " (Joszi 1929, pp. 259-260).

The crucial role of scholarship in this entire enterprise is clear, but it is also clear that many nationalist scholars "acted in the dual role of scholars and men of politics, their scholarly work was directly influenced by political demands.

Their efforts in either field were inseparable" (Kohn 1955, p. 158). The origins of broader unity were pushed back further and further.[30] Literatures were discovered and, if necessary, created wherever "what was admirable did not exist and what existed was not admirable."[31] At the same time, boundaries also had to be established. If unity and authenticity within the pale were intensified, then the differences separating insiders from outsiders were magnified. Here, too, the elites worked with preexisting building blocks, as well as with their concepts of the feasible and the desirable, in order to define "who should stand with whom against whom" (Sulzbach 1943, p. 134). By serving in each of these capacities, as unifiers, as cleansers, and as differentiators, nationalist leaders revived and created affiliative symbols, beliefs, attitudes, and behaviors which could, in time, lead toward the objective integration that "had always existed." Just as folklore itself is merely the accumulation in the public domain of items that had their definite individual innovators, so the creation of nationalist unity and authenticity represent an elitist acceleration and organization of the normal and constant interaction between *gehobenes Primitivgut* and *gesunkenes Kulturgut*.

The success of elitist efforts was not always startling. It often came haltingly, in little things, and among the petit bourgeois rather than among the masses.[32] In part, this was due to quite understandable and predictable counterforces existing fully outside of the elite ranks, but in part it was also due to the nature of the early nationalist elites themselves. Large proportions of them stemmed from other backgrounds than the people whom they sought to organize.[33] Others had long lived or been educated abroad, or in exile, and were only marginally ethnic in their personal lives.[34] In one way or in another, they had become so different from those whom they were trying to unify and to energize that part of the emotional and intellectual intensity of their work is interpretable as a search for personal identity and for a usable personal past.[35] In truth, the intellectuals of whom mention has been made are in large part more accurately designated as an "intelligentsia," i.e., as a "phenomenon essentially connected with the transition. An intelligentsia is a class which is alienated from its own society" (Gellner 1964, p. 169).[36] It was this fact of alienation which enabled these elites (whose own life-styles, self-understandings, and power potentials had changed) to envision broader unities and deeper authenticities than those that really existed, and, at the same time, to experience additional hardships and rebuffs in initially communicating their vision to others. Nationalist elites frequently went through an agonizing process of remaking themselves before they succeeded in remaking "their" peoples. Such individuals could also envision the remaking of language itself![37]

BASIC FORCES: THE URBAN CONDITION

If widespread and basic social disorganization and reorganization constituted the major need- and opportunity-systems to which nationalism was a possible response, and if elites were the major formulators, synthesizers, and emphasizers of this response, then urban centers were the primary arenas in which these needs, opportunities and responses encountered and magnified each other. The city has long been pointed to as the vortex of social change in general and of the kinds of change related to the entire gamut of modernization-and-development processes in particular.[38] Dislocation from the social structure of the traditional countryside was there maximized, as were the cumulative impact of occupational and educational change, the growth of voluntary organizations and associations, the influence of mass media, and the constant interaction of insecurity, competition, and conflict. The eighteenth and nineteenth century fathers of modern sociology, Durkheim, Mannheim, Simmel, and Weber, all reflected at length upon the impact of the city on social life, upon its uprooting tendencies, as well as upon its consequences in terms of the expansion and reformation of linkages between individual, group, community, and national functioning. Twentieth-century sociology has been filling out this picture on an increasingly empirical, quantitative, and international scale ever since.

While most investigators have been at work detailing the contribution of urbanization and urban centers to the appeal of (and need for) new and massive solutions for the ills of mankind, students of nationalism have been similarly attentive to the links between urbanization and urban centers on the one hand, and broader ethnocultural unity and authenticity on the other. These links include the reestablishment of collective or supraindividual identification and the creation of broader kinship ties,[39] which nationalist movements have provided and stressed for those who have not only lost their former individual statuses and group identifications, but, who, additionally, have often found themselves blocked from attaining new status and security subsequent to urban relocation, precisely on ethnocultural grounds.

From the point of view of social history, it is convincingly evident that the city not only grew as a result of the very same changes that disrupted primordial localism, but that it also (a) attracted those whom it had uprooted and (b) put them in touch with the elites who had congregated in urban areas even earlier, and (c) as a result, finally put the uprooted in touch with each other and converted them into a new force in social, political, and cultural affairs.[40] The city was thus a factor not only in creating and fostering nationalism, but also in providing nationalism with the power that it attained, i.e., nationalism captured urban elites and proletarians at the very time that urban centers definitively displaced the countryside as the loci of national power, national culture, and, therefore, national identity.

The growth of nationalism is, to a large extent, marked by the *occupation (or reoccupation)* of the city by hitherto largely rural ethnocultural groups and by their *utilization of the city* as a device for their own greater ethnocultural unity, authenticity, and modernity. The city has everywhere been a gathering point for foreign residents.[41] However, in multiethnic states before the growth of nationalism the foregoing was further complicated by the fact that the cities were dominated by economically more advanced culturally "foreign" groups who blocked the economic and cultural advancement of the few indigenous rural folk who were attracted to it.

"In the early 19th century Bucharest was still a Greek town, in 1848 Prague, Plzeň [Pilsen] and Ljubljana had German majorities, and as late as the second half of the nineteenth century, the most important towns in Finland were mainly Swedish, Riga and Tartu (Worpat) were German, the towns of Bulgaria mostly Greek and those of the Dalmatian coast, Italian" (Kolarz 1946, p. 14). As long as these "foreign" islands were largely commercial in nature they neither absorbed nor attracted major numbers from their respective rural hinterlands. Whenever such movement did occur on a minor scale, it resulted in a change from rural-peasant to urban-commercial nationality and language. "Thus, the Ukrainian migrating to town became Russian, the Slovak leaving his village became Magyarised, the Czech moving to the German town enclaves of inner Bohemia and Moravia became Germanized" (Kolarz 1946, p. 15). Even if some of them were of the populist persuasion and halfheartedly glorified the "pastoral harmony" of the countryside, they tended to view this same culture as an integral part of the peasant way of life, and, as such, as unbecoming for men of refinement and education" (Nahirny and Fishman 1965, p. 322). From the point of view of the peasant "the contrast between the city and the village was . . . regarded in a painful way. For them the city was not Ukrainian and the city was not peasant. The city was alien and hostile" (Skoreventanski 1919, cited by Sullivant 1967, p. 47). However, growing industrialization of the towns and other attendant and concurrent social changes[42] finally made it impossible for these centers to remain "foreign," either numerically or culturally. "Great masses of population, which the feudal agricultural system could not employ, gathered in the manufacturing towns and often altered . . . their former ethnic composition" (Jaszi 1929, p. 256). The conflict that ensued on behalf of social amelioration, political participation, and cultural recognition was, therefore, an urban conflict. The growth of nationalism is the spread of this conflict, from the intellectuals to the middle classes to the proletariat *within* the towns, from the primary industrial centers to those of secondary importance, and from a purely conflictual or reactive to an increasingly creative and more encompassing level.[43] Thus it was with considerable justification that Michelet referred to the towns as the points "in which the nationalities [he meant, of course, the sub-French nationalities] have condensed their self-expression (ont résumé leur génie" [1846] 1946, p. 27), while Kolarz, writing 100 years later about a very different part of Europe, observed that nationalism "centers on the town and regards it as the very symbol of national existence" (1946, p. 16).[44] This was the case notwithstanding the fact that some cities, like Vienna, served several different nationalist causes at one and the same time (see Trevor-Roper 1962, p. 15).

The importance of the city in enabling elites to "interact with each other and to concentrate upon the tasks of communicating" (Doob 1964, p. 245) has been stressed by several investigators.[45] Indeed, Deutsch makes the complex cooccurrence of elites-masses-communication channels-economic interaction and city part of his basic definition of nationality in the modern age. Far fewer are those who have pointed out that the national cultures created by nationalist elites were essentially urban cultures even when they included strongly antiurban ideological components. It was from Geneva that Rousseau pointed out that the distant provinces were the ones most closely related to "the genius and customs of a nation,"[46] but it was the Genevans themselves and other urbanites that he hoped to influence. Similarly, the German nationalists who believed that "urban growth was something positively evil—an alienation from the countryside and from the rural virtue which was specifically German" (Minogue 1967, p. 75) were all members of the urban elite who wanted nothing more strongly than to influence other city folk and to shape the content of their urban lives. The ideology of nationalism is antiurban only in that it locates the origin of broader unity and authenticity in the preurban past. However, having identified the source of all that is good (whether in language or in other respects) it then seeks to make the values, beliefs, and behaviors stemming from this source available to, acceptable to, and incumbent upon those living in modern urban settings. The first "urban revolution," that of the Ancient Near East, "produced one invention, the invention of writing, which changed the whole structure of the cultural tradition" (Goody and Watt 1963, p. 344). The urban revolution during the growth of nationalism produced another invention (or innovation) of similarly great significance: urban national culture. Both of these urban by-products have had very definite consequences for language change and language planning.

DIALECTIC

It is quite apparent, from the foregoing, that there is a built-in dialectic within nationalism, a quite inevitable tension between its major components. Most obvious is the tension between the requirements of modernization and those of authentification. The one emphasizes the instrumental uniformities required by modern politico-operational integration and is constantly straining toward newer, more rational, more efficient solutions to the problems of today and tomorrow. The other emphasizes the sentimental uniformities required by continuity-based sociocultural integration and is constantly straining toward purer, more genuine expressions of the heritage of yesterday and of long ago.

A potential conflict also exists between the goal of authentification and that of unification since, in reality, prenationalist authenticity is highly localized. As a result, the supralocal authenticity sought by nationalism must, to a large extent, be elaborated and interpreted rather than merely returned to or discovered ready made. The more stress on real authenticity, therefore, the more danger of regionalism and ultimate secessionism. The more stress on unification/ uniformation, the less genuine authentification.

Even unification/uniformation and modernization are frequently at odds with each other. Some modern goals might well be more fully or easily attained via the encouragement of diversity (e.g., relations with important neighboring sources of supply might well be improved if ethnic minorities speaking the same languages as those used in the sources of supply were encouraged to maintain their distinctiveness), while some preexisting uniformities are actually weakened rather than strengthened by industrialization, urbanization, and other modernity tendencies (e.g., the weakening of religious bonds).

It is part and parcel of the essence of nationalism to incorporate these potentially conflicting themes in its basic ideology. Similarly, it is part and parcel of the essence of nationalism to engage the dialectic that is caused by the tension between these themes and to derive from this dialectic a constant procession of solutions to the problems engendered by its own ideological commitments. It is this dialectic between potentially conflicting elements which constantly recharges the dynamism of nationalist causes. Their business is always unfinished because none of the goals of nationalist ideology is ever fully attained or even substantially assured, not only because of possible outside opposition, but also because of the internal instability of any resolution between its own contending components. "Nationalism is a device for reconciling the universal with the particular. The adaptation of a universal theory or ism to a special circumstance is the creation of an ideology in the truest sense of the term" (Binder 1966, pp. 197-198). Universal gods have always had their special people; universal ideals, their special champions. Social intellect and social emotion seem to require both.

NATIONALIST INTEGRATION AND DIFFERENTIATION: REALITY AND LIMITS

There has been considerable difference of opinion during the past century as to whether the basic ideological premises of nationalism were (or are), in fact, true or false. The brunt of recent writing, on this topic, particularly those that emanate from Western centers of scholarship, tends to stress the mythical nature of the unity and authenticity that nationalist movements need to create and then seek to implement.[47] It is obviously true that folk custom and ethnicity frequently shade off into one another via endless minor variations and that the inclusive and exclusive lines that have been drawn in relatively modern times are frequently marked by arbitrariness, opportunism, and irrelevant appeals to long vanished and dubious geographic, cultural, or political entities. However, it would seem equally irrational, if not more so, to refuse to see that the *validity* of these appeals has been of lesser significance, by far, than their efficacy.[48] Their efficacy is indicative of far more (and more pervasive) flexibility and malleability of self-definition in relatively recent times than most scholars seem to have thought possible. Indeed, if it is also true that even the seemingly homogeneous populations of the distant past were themselves products of integration processes operating upon diverse ethnic components (see below), then we are faced by a remarkable as well as reoccurring human capacity to bring about and to accept changes in ethnocultural group membership.

However, an understanding of the rise of nationalism does more than indicate that unmobilized populations can be ethnoculturally integrated via recourse to a large number of different but equally dim and artifically colored or manipulated "memories." It does more than indicate that the outer limits of the "includable" are often flexible and can be stretched to the most distant reaches manageable in terms of the available means of influencing, coordinating, and controlling mass behavior. Indeed, it shows that populations frequently cannot tolerate such integrative attempts and that there are integrative "times and tides" which set limits that seem to be every bit as real as the technological and economic factors on which the control of human behavior is based.

Thus, if broader ethnocultural integration often appears to be far more acceptable than anticipated, so does ethnocultural differentiation. Indeed, once the limits of further integration have been contested, ideologized, and imple-mented in certain ways and to certain degrees, it seems very difficult for those affected thereby to surrender one set of elaborated ethnocultural self-definitions on behalf of others (see, e.g., Clark 1938).

Several investigators have pointed to conflict or confrontation with other groups that are *already* at the nationality level of awareness as a limiting factor upon the further integration of two indigenous or contiguous populations. Thus, whereas isolated "foreign" islands may undergo repeated reethnizations if their hosts are economically and culturally receptive, it is posited that neighboring indigenous groups cannot continue to do so once intergroup conflict has contributed to mutual nationality consciousness and to Great Traditions incorporating the experience of intergroup conflict.[49] At this point further integration seems to be possible only as a result of the realization of long-term superordinate threat[50] or the defeat and systematic denationalization of one of the two parties. Even these latter circumstances seem to leave traces that last for centuries, even at a purely oral and secretive level, and that protect the seeds of differentiation until some subsequent opportune time arrives.

Thus, exactly because the "natural distributions" of ethnocultural integration and differentiation are either too gradual, too inconsistent, or too nonsalient for the purposes of effective mass organization of human and physical resources, nationalism intensifies and restructures both. In this respect nationalism, like much other goal-directed behavior, constitutes a self-fulfilling prophecy.

However, in addition, while so doing, it also sets into motion self-perpetuating and self-intensifying processes (processes that are aided and abetted by other concurrent social change) that render the centers of nationality conscious societies extremely resistant to either other-integrative or disintegrative efforts.

THE TRANSFORMATIONS OF ETHNOCULTURAL INTEGRATION

Most of our observations thus far have concentrated upon the early stirrings or the *appearance* of nationalism among hitherto traditional populations within multiethnic states. It is well known, however, that nationalism often continues to function well beyond the period of initial mobilization, although there would seem to be nothing inevitable about its subsequent stages or their sequencing. One of the most common features of nationalist development is that which focuses nationalism upon the attainment of the political-operational integration attainable via the machinery of the state. The possible relationships between these two types of integration, ethnocultural and politico-operational, have been frequently (and varyingly) commented upon. These relationships between nationality and polity present us with further useful perspective on the transformations of ethnocultural integration,[51] particularly since it is the machinery of the state that is so frequently paramount in language planning.

The relationship between nationalism and the monoethnic state has appeared to be so natural and so inevitable wherever it *has* come into being, that it is not surprising that the particular relationships and sequences obtaining in given parts of the world at given times in history have seemed to contemporary commentators to be the only (or the only "natural" and "normal") relationships that could (or should) obtain.[52] Thus, while it seems clear that the Fichtean-Herderian ideal of the monoethnic state is, today, quite closely approximated in several Western European (as well as other) nations, it is also clear that in each of these, if one looks back far enough and deep enough, one finds the process of successively broader unification of once ethnically different groups. " . . . Like the worlds of which the astronomers tell us that some are in the nebulous stage, some supporting life, and others growing cold, [so] all Nationalities not simple are combinations of Simple Nationality and into a Secondary Simple Nationality fused from all the primary they all tend to pass" (Zangwill 1917, p. 43). Where the consolidation of the state preceded the age of mass nationalism, "where the framework of the state was strong enough and persistent enough, it . . . *created a common nationality* out of very different linguistic and cultural groups. *Languedoc* was very like Catalonia and very unlike north France, yet it finally became thoroughly French" (Strayer 1966, p. 23).

The wonder of what had happened is apparent in the sensitive observations of contemporaries: "Today all the inhabitants of France who were born within the Kingdom are reputed to be of the same nation . . . They are all French-men . . . Now birth rules nationality: In those times [during the great wars with

England] it was filiation through the male line . . . 'People' and 'nation' then meant very different things. A nation consisted of persons living according to the same laws or customs. A people was a collection of nations. Now these two words have the same signification" (Dubos 1735, pp. 260-262; cited by Barzun 1932).[53] Obviously, the stable centralized state had not only brought those under its rule "into closer and closer association with each other" while cutting them off from those outside of its control, but it had, in the selfsame process and over centuries, forced them "to work together and to adapt to each other, to gain a clear sense of identity, to smooth out some of their regional differences, and to become attached to their ruler and the institutions through which he ruled" (Strayer 1966, p. 23).[54]

The State-Nation[ality]

Because of the firm establishment of the state in Western Europe before the appearance of modern mass nationalism,[55] and because of the substantial ethnocultural integration ensuing from the long stability of politico-operational institutions there, a very definite view of the *nature of nationality* had developed in the West and a very definite impression of the primacy of *polity over nationality* had come to be widely accepted by the time mass nationalism appeared as a predominantly Central, Eastern, and Southern European "aberration." As for the nature of nationality, it was in the West primarily a territorial attribute. " . . . A child of whatever parentage, if born under the British flag, can claim British nationality. Indeed, the [popular] English language lacks a word to describe 'nationality' distinct from or contrasted with the citizenship derived from territory and State" (Namier 1952, p. 21). As for the sequential relationship between the formation of nationality (in the ethnocultural sense in which we have been using the term in this essay) and the attainment of statehood, it was obvious that "it is the state which has come first and created nationality and not vice versa." This was as obvious to dignified churchmen and bourgeois political leaders who sought to *preserve the state* against the onslaught of foreign concepts of nationalism, as it was to Western socialists, anarchists, and communists who were committed to the *demise of the state* and, thereby, to the demise of nationality as a force which fragmented the proletariat.[56] It is this view of the nationality-polity relationship and this stage of ethnocultural and politico-operational integration which Pflanze and others have recently designated as the "State-Nation" and which may be contrasted with the "Nation-State," the latter being a view and a stage of more recent and noticeably turbulent origin.

Because nationalism in Western Europe was already a creature of well-established states by the opening of the nineteenth century it was subjected to the controlling influences which nineteenth century Western European political doctrines imposed upon the state itself. As a result, Western nationalism—a nationalism that flowed from common institutions and their evolved safeguards—seemed to Western observers to be respectful of and based upon individual liberties, a loyal opposition, the balance of powers, etc. Even today, there are those whose view of European nationalism is so strongly colored by the Western experience alone that they can claim that "in Europe the strong independent state with a fairly effective government and a common pattern of law enforcement and observance preceded nationalism and both preceded democracy" (Myrdal 1968, p. 119). However, the majority of Western intellectuals around the middle of the nineteenth century clearly recognized the difference between their presumably open and rational nationalism and the closed, tribal, vindictive, disruptive, and altogether wicked nationalisms then brewing among the Central, Southern, and Eastern Europeans upon which they heaped scorn and invective. "The State may in course of time produce a nationality," they claimed, "but that a nationality should constitute a State is contrary to the nature of modern civilization . . . . [Such a creature] is an ideal unit, founded on the race, in defiance of the modifying action of external causes, of tradition and of existing rights. It overrules the rights and wishes of the inhabitants, obsorbing their divergent interests in a fictitious unity, sacrifices their several inclinations and duties to the higher claim of nationality and crushes all natural rights and all established liberties for the purpose of vindicating itself" (Acton [1862] 1907, p. 288).[57] Two and three generations later enlightened Westerners were still convinced that theirs was the only legitimate link between state and nationality. "The facts of the situation are, that the nation born of the emancipation of the peasantry effected, for reasons which were primarily military, the unity of the language, then of the culture, and thus left the impression of a common race. But by a singular inversion of perspective, education has contrived to spread exactly the opposite view to be the initial factor which, by means of the mother tongue has imposed upon all its sons traditions, aptitudes and a genius which is their own and made them brothers united into one nation" (Delaise 1927, p. 219).

   This inclination to deride ethnocultural nationalism has, by and large, been continued in the West for over a century, with little scholarly and even less general recognition that such derision itself reflects a stage in the evolution of ethnocultural and politico-operational integration. While others were just beginning to dig into and reconstruct their ethnic pasts, Western intellectuals were already beginning to extoll nonethnic and supraethnic rationality. Instead of still seeking unsullied rural models of broader unity and authenticity they could already extol the classically evolved, regionally neutralized and centrally reinforced or validated nature of their institutions, processes, and symbols.

The Nation[ality]-State

The Western European model of state-nationality could, with some little effort, be slightly amended to apply beyond the primary confines and experiences of England, France, Spain, Portugal, Holland, and Scandinavia from which it was derived. As nationalist pressures built up in other parts of Europe it became impossible to deny them *all* any legitimacy whatsoever. A distinction came to be drawn, therefore, between the somewhat legitimate claims of Italian, German, Hungarian, Polish, and Greek nationalists, and the patently illegitimate ones of the primarily Eastern and Southern smaller Slavic nationalities. The former at least represented the aspirations of "historic peoples," that is, of peoples who had once been formed by states of their own and who had, due to the misfortunes of history, lost their political independence. Their agitation for political unification, recognition, or liberation could, at least, be understood, particularly since it left the major premise of the primacy of the state untouched. The same could certainly *not* be said for the atomized nonhistoric peoples that also clamored and intrigued for attention. Friedrich Engels' views in this connection coincided exactly with those of bourgeois commentators and demonstrated how terrified the left and the right *both* were of the "chimera" of nationality which obsessed the ethnic rabble of South-East Europe and which could "never be satisfied or exhausted and always continued to assert itself" (Acton [1862] 1907, p. 298). Engels, like Acton, felt that it was absolutely necessary to distinguish between "the right of the great European nations to separate and independent national existence... and those of numerous small relics of peoples which, after having figured for longer or shorter periods on the stage of history were finally absorbed as integral portions into one or another of these more powerful nations" (cited by Namier 1944, p. 51; for the full original see Engels 1866 or Rjasanoff 1916).[58]

It is not possible to reconstruct here the complete interaction between the Western view that the Eastern and Southern European nationalities were "peoples without history" and the feverish efforts of the latter, intensified as the nineteenth century progressed, to discover, formulate, and create their respective (as well as their joint) histories. It should be clear, however, that the so-called peoples without history also initially lacked two of the major forces which are essential for the creation of history in modern days: their own upper classes[59] and their own centers of ethnic culture and communication.[60] As these came into being (with the increased penetration of industrialization into their areas) so did their nationalisms and their histories; the process of *nationalities seeking to create their corresponding monoethnic states*—a process that had already vanished from the memory of Western European historiography—was fully launched. So intense were their efforts and so widely shared were their ideals in the universe with which they were concerned that the nationality-state and the objective primacy of ethnocultural nationality became as self-evident in the intellectual and mass movements of suppressed Eastern and Southern European nationalities as were the state-nation and the primacy of political nationality in the intellectual and mass movements of Western Europe. "Nationality in the West (west of Germany) means your passport. In Central and Eastern Europe, with their mixed population, it means ultimately your race" (Talmon 1965, p. 21).

The model of nationality accepted by the "peoples without history" was both a reaction *against* Western European views as well as a wholehearted *adoption of* Western European attainments. The ideal model was that of "a single people, traditionally fixed on a well-defined territory, possessing a distinctive culture and shaped to a common mould by many generations of shared historical experiences" (Emerson 1962, p. 103). The philosophical and ideological underpinnings of this model were primarily Herderian in the most immediate sense, both in its deprecation of the multiethnic polity as well as in its deification of the unique and pure nationality.[61] However, whereas Herder was concerned only with safeguarding the beauty and originality of each and every culture—and particularly with cleansing German culture of its fascination and inferiority in the face of all things French—his ideas quickly had political consequences as well.[62] The nation came to be defined and pursued as a cultural rather than as a political entity, as a unit that could remain healthy only if it grew "within the chrysalis of the individual [i.e., of the autochthonous] culture" (Snyder 1968, p. 58) and only if it served the unity and authenticity of the culture that had given birth to it.[63] More so even than the historic nations, the so-called ahistoric nations required governmental protection and encouragement of their cultural uniqueness. It was not enough to "discover their ancient history, find the continuity of their ancient traditions, recreate their half-forgotten languages, remember their old literatures, and, with the aid of ingenious statistics retrace on the map the generous . . . frontiers of the past" (Trevor-Roper 1962, pp. 18-19). It was also necessary to shield and to further these desiderata, via the machinery of the state, so that they would never again become or be viewed as peoples without history.[64]

Historical perspective reveals that questioning the legitimacy of an opponent's nationality is undoubtedly an ancient ploy. Similarly old is the tack of seeking recognition for one's self by joining in the nonrecognition of less fortunate claimants.

"At the Council of Constance (1414) . . . the English being the least numerous, posed as champions of the right of each nation[ality] to be counted as the equal of every other. Yet, to 'appease' the Germans, they joined with them in ignoring the rights of Hungarians, Czechs, Poles and Scandinavians to separate identity and separate vote" (Hayes, 1942, p. 8; also see Loomis 1939).

Even within the ranks of the nineteenth century latecomers themselves, invidious distinctions of this kind were common.

"Croat leaders demonstrated little interest in the project (a Congress of Nationalities planned for 1895). . . . reluctant to place themselves on the same level as the so-called 'non-nations'— the Rumanians, the Slovaks and particularly the Serbs — for fear that they would jeopardise the constitutional status of Croatia" (Hitchens 1970, p. 394).

Similarly, those nationalities recently (re)admitted to the ranks of the politically recognized quickly championed the primacy of state-nationality over nationality-state processes to their own advantage. Thus, quite obviously, both processes have long been in operation, have frequently been purposefully misconstrued, and have often been cyclically related to each other.

Other Transformations

While state-nation and nation-state processes may thus fruitfully be viewed as contrasted transformations of each other (without at all being viewed as necessary or exhaustive processes re the accommodation of their components in the annals of history), they have both revealed instances of further expansions as a possible subsequent stage of their development. Even broader cultural unities and more abstract authenticities are recognizable, which indirectly confirm the arbitrariness of the boundaries set at previous stages of nationalism. These broader aspirations may claim *irridentas* not previously liberated or united during earlier integrative efforts, or they may point to *similarities* with neighbors that come to be viewed as more basic and as stemming from a still earlier and even more authentic cultural era than that responsible for dissimilarities formerly noted. Such broader nationalisms are frequently referred to as "pan movements."[65] However, even with respect to their pan movements, the state-nations and the nation-states show differences which are consistent with their developmental stages and their resulting needs and aspirations. The pan movements of state-nations smack of thinly disguised imperialism (economic, territorial, or cultural) since they involve expansion beyond well-defined and traditionally established cultural borders and political controls.[66] The pan movements of nationalities-seeking-states involve an exploration of delimitation and integration possibilities, a search for reliable strength, for the power of numbers as a substitute for weaknesses of various kinds.[67]

Finally, unsuccessful nationalism too must be recognized as a possible outcome of attempts at sociopolitical mobilization and integration. This outcome obtains where potential changes in the allocation of roles and resources do not materialize or are reversed, when protoelites do not succeed in mobilizing populations toward a certain definition of unity and authenticity, or when a competing elite (and the particular underlying socioeconomic changes and over-arching symbolism with which it is associated) succeeds in attracting support or marshaling forces to a greater extent than do its rivals. Various examples of nationalisms that vanished but "might have succeeded" will be mentioned in the following sections and notes. Suffice it to say at this point that nationalism exists as an "alternative instrumentality which is exploitable on behalf of culturally differentiated groups in any plural society" (Depres 1967, 1968) as well as on behalf of any segment of the social pluralism that remains strong long after ethnic pluralism per se has weakened (Mazrui 1969b). Nationalism is a phoenix that is repeatedly capable of arising not only out of its own ashes but out of whatever other injustices modern societies perpetrate.

NATIONALISM IN THE "NEW" OR "DEVELOPING" NATIONS

The appearance of several score "new" polities since the conclusion of World War II has stimulated a somewhat strengthened interest in nationalism among American social scientists, much as did the redrawn map of post-Versailles Central, Eastern, and Southern Europe. Much of this interest is contrastive, i.e., it is sensitive to differences and similarities between developments in parts of Africa-Asia, on the one hand, and parts of Europe-America, on the other. However, far more attention has been lavished upon such comparisons in the sphere of political-operational integration than upon sociocultural integration, and the concepts of modernization and development which dominate recent inquiries into the "new" polities have relatively seldom been focused upon the transformations of nationalism per se. Thus, our concluding effort in this essay will be to review the literature on the "new" polities from this very point of view, particularly since it is in the same "new" polities that the lion's share of language planning ventures are currently underway and will continue in the foreseeable future.

Broader Ethnic Unity and Greater Authenticity

We may conveniently begin with Friedrich's reminder that ethnic diversity is far from sufficient "cause" for the development of nationalism or the growth of nations. With very few exceptions, nationality-states and state-nationalities "did not happen in [pre-World War II]China, India or Africa, though in all these continent-wide human societies, various kinds of political orders—states—were erected" (1966, p. 22). Nevertheless, the rumblings of modern nationalism in these areas can be traced back quite far and seem, in many respects, to be quite similar in emphases to those that we have already reviewed in connection with various stages and regions in European social history. Certainly, purposive emphases on the broader ethnocultural unity of traditional and particularistic-ally oriented populations living in isolation from each other are much in evidence 50 and even 100 years ago, particularly in areas throughout which indigenous Great Traditions had been long established. Thus it was claimed that "the Hindus of every part of India resembled each other in all essential matters, in their traits of character, in their modes of thinking, in their social institutions and even in their dress and amusements . . . Socially, religiously and ethno-logically they all belonged to the same race. All showed descent from common ancestors, worshiped the same gods and goddesses, employed the same scriptural language (Sanskrit), and, in ordinary intercourse used one of the dialects derived from the same mother tongue" (McCully 1940, p. 244; paraphrasing an editorial in the Calcutta *Tribune* of September 19, 1885).[68] As in Europe in an earlier period, age-old struggles are remembered, indeed heightened, as indicators of ancient nationality. For the Vietnamese their Great Tradition includes "the winning of independence from China in the tenth century and their own later expansion into Chan and Khmer territories" (Kennedy 1968, p. 80). Similarly, Htin Aung "has cited evidence for Burmese nationalism from the eleventh century and has claimed that throughout their long history the Burmese have always been conscious of their nationality, bordered as they have been by great neighbors in China and India" (Kennedy 1968, pp. 81-82).

Whether of early vintage or not, there is also a widespread and recurring emphasis on indigenous authenticity as the basis of internal sociocultural integration and simultaneous divergence from foreign (normally European) ways.[69] Observers mention not only such mundane matters as the readoption (or invention) of indigenous dress,[70] footwear, or hair styles,[71] and not only protests against European models in connection with each of these and other aspects of everyday life,[72] but also the rapid ideologization of authenticity. Authenticity was proclaimed to be valuable because it was an autochthonous creation,[73] handed down from periods of past greatness,[74] and incorporated within itself the promise of future glories yet to come.[75] Indeed, the very names adopted by several new nations upon their (re-)birth were such as to recall the glories of a culturally indigenous broader unity which had existed in the past (e.g., Ghana, Mali) and which could serve as guiding (or, at least, as motivating and stimulating) examples with respect to the future. Nevertheless fuller authenticity and broader unity were, in and of themselves, not enough.

From Indonesia we hear that what is wanted is "both Western science and Eastern philosophy, the Eastern 'spirit' in the culture" (Sjahrir 1947, pp. 67-68; written 1935, while a political prisoner). From Japan: "What is merely modern —as science and methods of organization—can be transplanted, but what is vitally human has fibres so delicate and roots so numerous and far-reaching that it dies when moved from its soil. Japan . . . cannot be turned into a mere borrowed machine. She has her own soul which must assert itself overall." (Tiedemann 1955, pp. 55 and 81). From the Arab world: "The Arab wants modernization, but has no desire to lose his own identity in the process. To be an evolué is too heavy a price to pay. In brief, the problem for the Arab is to westernize without becoming westernized" (Pfaff 1970, p. 165). Is this possible? Is it possible most particularly, where it is firmly believed that "Our Imperial Ancestors have founded our Empire on a basis broad and everlasting, and have deeply and firmly implanted virtue. Our subjects, ever united in loyalty and filial piety, have from generation to generation illustrated the beauty thereof. This is the glory of the fundamental character of our Empire . . . guard and maintain the prosperity of our Imperial throne, coeval with heaven and earth. So shall ye not only be our good and faithful subjects, but render illustrious the best traditions of your forefathers. The way here set forth is indeed the teaching bequeathed by Our Imperial Ancestors, to be observed alike by their Descendants and Subjects, infallible for all ages and true in all places" (from the Japanese Imperial Rescript on Education, 1890; cited by Tiedemann 1955, pp. 113-114). Almost miraculously, a reconciliation of the old and the new *is* possible, indeed all the more possible, if "the new regime, so alien to all the traditions of the past, is [viewed as] only a return to [even more] ancient institutions. The new era is called Maiji, which means *restoration* [of enlightened rule]" (Delaise 1927, p. 231). All in all, however, "periods of extensive Westernization" are likely to be followed by "periods of retreat during which 'excesses' and 'incongruities' are violently attacked and the quest for 'the true Japanese way' undertaken. One can discern at least four great swings of the pendulum in the hundred years that followed 1860" (Scalapino 1964, p. 126).

Indeed, if there is any difference between earlier European and later Asian-African nationalisms it would seem to be not so much in the nature of the sentimental and instrumental components utilized, or in the compromises between them, as in the earlier primacy of state-formation over sociocultural integration in the new polities of Africa and Asia. Perhaps this is because continuity with the real and immediate past is too great to permit the sheer *amount* of purposive selection and reformulation practiced in Europe. Perhaps it is because state-formation came everywhere before major industrialization and dislocation had destroyed the ethnic identity of major population segments. For whatever reasons, it seems that African and Asian nationalisms have thus far experienced little that parallels the fragmentation of the Austro-Hungarian, Czarist, and Turkish Empires as a result of the awakening reunification and self-authentification of submerged nationalities. In most cases the colonial administrative boundaries have been maintained and (almost everywhere but in postindependence India) the thrust of mass-mobilization has clearly focused much more upon political-operational integration within those boundaries than upon their abandonment on behalf of the self-actualization of submerged nationalities. The retention, by and large, of ethnically irrelevant international boundaries has probably resulted in greater prominence being given more quickly to supraethnic ideologies and programs[76] than was the case in Central,

Eastern, and Southern Europe where the nationality and its own mononation state was so commonly the initial rationale for mass mobilization. It may be, therefore, that language planning too, in these nations, is likely to be proportionately less influenced by ideologies of ethnocultural unity and authenticity and, to the extent that it is centrally sponsored, that it will be under relatively greater pressure to further supraethnic political-operational integration than was the case in early stages of language planning among awakening and newly awakened European nationalities. This is, at least, a reasonable hypothesis for investigation, although it requires basically historical reconstruction, on the one hand, and that plus the empirical evaluation of still current efforts, on the other.

Pervasive Social and Economic Change

Several investigators and commentators, indigenous, European, and American, have observed that nationalism in Africa and Asia is a concomitant of the severe dislocation and fargoing disruption of traditional life that both colonialism and anticolonialism bring into being (see e.g., Ranger 1968). Some have pointed to nationalism as appealing to those whose lives have become dislocated by the introduction of modern cash economy. Others have pointed to the annihilation of tribal, ethnic, and linguistic barriers which the rapid modernization of either commerce or industry of necessity brings to pass.[77] Several have also pointed to the improvements which the new economy permits, to the problems that follow in their wake, to the opportunities available to a selected few,[78] and how these few subsequently utilize the rhetoric of nationalism in order to distribute and exploit these opportunities more fully.[79] Nationalism is, therefore, not merely a by-product or a response to the evils or the disorganization of unplanned change. It is also an instrument on behalf of further directed changes.[80] Even the agony of military defeat by Western powers has such consequences in that it helps bring to the fore new indigenous elites that are more selective with respect to the uses of the past in directing the future.[81]

To some extent the eclectic and imaginative use of the past that we reviewed in conjunction with more recent European nationalisms seems to be more evident in many parts of Negro Africa than in most parts of Asia (Abu-Lughod 1967). The great indigenous ethnoreligious traditions of Buddhism, Confucianism, Shintoism, and Islam seem, thus far, to have been too omnipotent and omnipresent to be innovatively reformulated for new nationalist purposes. Rather, they seem to have been put to most active use by early nationalists primarily for the sake of their large-scale integrative potentials. "By means of this [Hinduism] all Hindus would be bound by the tie of brotherhood. By means of it, the Bengali, the Hindustani, the Rajput, the Maratha, the Madrasi, in short, all Hindus, would be of one heart. The aspirations of all would be the same . . . for the Hindu nation, by retaining its ancient religious and moral civilization . . . would stand as the best and foremost of all nations on the face of the earth" (McCulley 1940, p. 262; paraphrasing an article by Raj Narain Bose, 1881-82). Only at much later stages, after the preindependence boundaries of new states have been successfully maintained, are there also movements to break or decrease the traditional influences of the ethnoreligions by means of state regulation, much as there had been, earlier, in Europe.[82] Nevertheless, since language planning is also quite often engaged in, from the very outset, as a *means* of first attaining or approximating much needed stability, it may be reasonable to expect that it too will initially be greatly influenced by religious considerations in those new nations that correspond to indigenized ethnoreligious Great Traditions. In all of these cases this might be viewed not merely as religious intrusion but as the necessarily greater influence of the old (including religion) on the emergence of a new view of nationality, where the old is still part and parcel of daily ethnicity itself, even among elites, and is, therefore, an integral part of nationalism throughout its formative years. In the West, religion and nationalism were institutionally separable forces that utilized each other (or opposed each other), whenever they could for their own purposes. In the East, no such alternation is possible as long as these forces are still to such a large extent intertwined and viewed as being one and the same.

Elites

Nationalism in Asia and Africa began, as an ideological and organized movement, much as it had in Europe, i.e., as an elitist-intellectual phenomenon (if we can include students, young officers, and bureaucrats among the elites).

"An outstanding common feature of Asian nationalism has been the remarkable role of its student communities. Both in Burma and in Indonesia the major strength of the nationalist forces was provided by their student populations. In Burma even the principal leadership came straight from the University" (Singhal 1967, p. 281).

However, the same picture is reported from Africa as well.

"It is generally true that students while abroad were emphatic and radical in their nationalism. Complete physical separation from Nigeria . . . aroused a desire, particularly among the more sensitive and impressionable, to glorify their traditional culture, usually by surpressing its unattractive features and exaggerating the qualities that they believed superior or unique . . . Most of the efforts to awaken respect for and appreciation of African culture started among African students abroad" (Coleman 1963, p. 63).

It is no accident, therefore, that so many of the nationalist and indigenized socialist movements of the third world were, as they had been earlier in Eastern

Europe, movements of the educated young. They were truly young in more than name. But these movements frequently continue to be primarily an elitist concern, largely because of the absence of a substantial bourgeoisie and the seeming failure of most national economies to materially and irrevocably alter the daily lives of the bulk of their populations. In Asia and Africa alike nationalism is not yet a self-priming mass phenomenon. Rather, it is primarily "an attempt of intellectuals to arouse the masses," first for the attainment of independence, and then for attaining modernization goals.

"Nationalism . . . is commonly seen as a force for good by all those in the intellectual elite who are bent on planning policies aimed at development. To them fostering nationalism will provide the means of breaking down inhibitions and obstacles" (Myrdal 1968, pp. 111 and 118).

At a less consciously utilitarian level nationalism in both Africa and Asia is an attempt on the part of intellectuals to identify with the masses. However, as was the case, previously, in Europe, many Asian and African intellectuals are also alienated from the masses.

"Am I perhaps estranged from my people? Why am I vexed by the things that fill their lives and to which they are so attached? Why are the things that contain beauty for them and arouse their gentler emotions only senseless and displeasing for me?" (Sjahrir 1947, p. 66).

Consequently,
". . . conscious of the wide gap between their modes and levels of living. . . and those of the villagers and urban slum dwellers, the intellectual elite compensate for their alienation by romanticizing the masses. . . The peasants are [viewed as being] rational, intelligent, hard-working and zealous" (Myrdal 1968, p. 62).

Similar also to earlier European nationalisms is the built-in dilemma between modernization goals for the future and the glorification of the virtues of the traditional past. Throughout much of Africa this is resolved at a very abstract level since "the African nationalist still has before him almost the entire task of creating the nation[alities] in whose name he professes to speak" (Emerson 1962, p. 94). Thus, "in arguing the basis of *ujamaa* or African socialism, Julius Nyerere of Tanganyika contended that its roots lay in the traditional communitarianism of the indigenous society that had broken down with contact with the West" (Friedland 1968, p. 22).[83]
However, no such total breakdown occurred in Turkey, Egypt, India, Pakistan, Burma, Japan, or pre-Communist China. Thus, when many of their intellectuals rejected the West as a model for national regeneration they were not

merely following in the footsteps of earlier English, German, and Italian rejections of French culture, or of Slavophilic rejection of mechanistic Western European enlightenment. On the one hand, their romanticized indigenous Great Traditions were much more alive and pervasive than the eclectic and frequently mythological reconstructions referred to in Europe. On the other hand, both the help and the ways of the West were far more necessary for immediate modernization purposes than were either French culture (to Germany) or Western enlightenment (to Russia) a century or a century and a half ago. Thus, while both African and Asian nationalism must quickly aim at modernization (rather than go through a prolonged emphasis on ethnic authenticity)[84] and, therefore, cannot afford to really bite the Western hands that feed them, much Asian modernization, in particular, is also encumbered by the proximity and vitality of the wider ethnoreligious traditional unity on which it leans in its efforts to attain mass mobilization and reintegration.

The Urban Condition

If, as is likely, the city had earlier contributed to, intensified, and finally exploited the " . . . pervasive uncertainty arising from the breakdown of immemorial rural routines" throughout Europe, and, therefore, "lent special emotional intensity to late 19th century nationalism" (McNeill 1963, p. 819, it seems to play a similarly crucial role in forming whatever mass base there is for African and Asian nationalism. Once again we find the city (and its economic opportunities) mentioned as a prime factor in bringing together dislocated and ethnically divergent populations,[85] in intensifying their miseries by highlighting both relative and actual deprivation,[86] and in providing the organizational structures whereby these dissatisfactions could be channeled into nationalist movements.[87] As a result, nationalist movements throughout Africa and Asia were able to develop substantial degrees of urban support,[88] particularly for short-term and concrete goals, even though the towns have long remained primarily commercial rather than industrial in nature.[89]

"Often the major urban centres provided the setting for 'middle class nationalism,' while the surrounding countryside was virtually untouched by the movement. In the story of Arab nationalism, Damascus, Baghdad, Cairo and Ankara all loom large, and this pattern is paralleled elsewhere, from Bombay to Rangoon and from Bangkok to Tokyo. . . Large urban communities tended to develop a character of their own and to concentrate some of the tensions which were elsewhere dispersed. . . The towns provided the natural centers for political demonstrations, attacks on the property of alien governments or groups and internal revolutionary plotting and activity" (Kennedy 1968, p. 91.

However, it is Asian nationalism, particularly, which has also made the more concerted effort to reach into the rural areas, in part as a result of its specific ability to rely upon a large number of local religious functionaries to carry its message, and in part because of its greater utilization of the ethnoreligious tradition in general. The impact of radio on bringing nationalist views into rural areas and, generally, to nonliterate populations, has, thus far, been little discussed (but note Kennedy 1968, p. 93, and several indexed references in Fishman et al. 1968a) and even less studied in any systematic fashion. It is undoubtedly of major importance, both for language planning as well as for modern nationalism as a whole.

Integration and Differentiation

To some extent traditional intra-Asian and intra-African divergences have been utilized for the purposes of modern national differentiation. Long-standing anti-Japanese memories have played just such a role in China and in Korea, the record of ancient anti-Chinese struggles are part of Vietnamese national awareness, anti-Islamic consciousness is a common aspect of popular Hinduism,[90] etc. However, more prevalent by far, and more differentiating, is the anti-Western sentiment that is reported in the literature dealing with country after country, particularly so in the cases of countries with ancient and indigenous ethnoreligious traditions. The West as such has been attacked not only for colonialism but for "mental colonialism,"[91] not only for debasing indigenous cultures with foreign values but for having no values to offer at all other than material gain and technical mastery. This alone would not be too different from earlier intra-European rejections (most of which contrasted indigenous moral and cultural beauty with shameless and exploitative foreign avarice) were it not that an early functional compromise with the avowed enemy is required in order to attain the very goals that are most immediate for all postindependence Asian and African nationalisms. "The nationalist movement, especially in those underdeveloped countries which have older traditions, must willy-nilly make a new synthesis. The real problem is that of finding the terms on which they can coexist honourably with the technology and civilization of the West. . . [since] it is not possible for these societies to accept the West completely" (Gadgil 1955, p. 150). Thus, nationalist movement after nationalist movement in Asia that has started out as primarily anti-Western in nature has been forced by the course of events to pursue Westernization,[92] in a way that Germans never had to turn to France, nor Czechs to Germans, nor Slovaks to Hungarians, nor Ukrainians to Poles, nor even Russians to the West.

The process of differentiation in Africa (and in those countries of Asia that do not correspond to indigenous Great Traditions) is only partially the same as that just sketched. The discovered fragments of lost civilizations permit the more unambiguous retention or adoption of Western ways and their easier combination with those indigenous fragments that have been interpreted as nationally unifying and authentic. Subsequently, a "new generation bursts forth with a 'discovery' of their national essence, amazed that its novelty has never been recognized before" (Hartz 1964, p. 12). Between this national essence and modernization no great dilemma exists and no painful compromise is required, since both are essentially new and unencumbered by established or ideologized large scale animosities. It may, therefore, be that westernisms or internationalisms will be less fully barred from Tanzanian or Indonesian language planning, at least in its early stages, than from that in India or in Egypt.

The Transformation of Ethno-Cultural Integration

While it is true that "the term 'nationalism' [has been] . . . applied indiscriminately throughout the vast [African and Asian] continents to every show of resistance against the old colonial rule" (Snyder 1968, p. 66), as it has to most anti-Western or even anti-White reactions since the termination of colonial rule, it nevertheless seems true that ethnocultural nationalism is very much a growing part of the Afro-Asian scenes. "Nation building in the contemporary world. . . is a matter of building group cohesion and group loyalty for purposes of international representation and domestic planning" (Friedrich 1966, p. 32) and this is the very purpose to which nationalism is most frequently put in the new nations. Precisely because it is so necessary to "divert Afro-Asian peoples away from parochial concerns toward the larger issues of modernization" (Minogue 1967, p. 89) it is revealing to find country after country utilizing (and struggling with) the most unifying and authenticating contours of the indigenous pasts available to them for this very purpose. "Not the least interesting aspect of the modernization of [these] profoundly diverse societies is the recurrent theme of nationalism. The nation-state remains both fulcrum and goal: increasing modernization stays within the framework of nationalism rather than . . . internationalism" (Snyder 1968, p. 10).

Superficially the nationalisms of most "new nations" show similarities to those of the recent nation-states of Europe as well as to those of that continent's older state-nations: Like the "unhistoric" submerged nationalities many of the peoples of sub-Saharan Africa had lost contact with their past unity or greatness. They needed new elites (even if they had never lost their old ones) in order to attain statehood. However, here the similarity ends, since statehood did not come as a result of nationality (re)formation and intensification, nor did it follow nationality lines. The peoples of several Asian countries on the other hand had not lost contact with either their immediate or their larger ethnoreligious histories and elites. Nevertheless, once again differential ethnicity was not usually the basis of their political-organizational independence. Thus among all the new polities the number of nationality-states (i.e., states whose borders correspond reasonably closely to the territory inhabited by a single newly self-conscious nationality) are rather few.[93] "The exceptions apart, it is striking that existing boundaries have remained intact as colony after colony has become independent. . . . Countries including many languages and culture groups, like most African and Asian ones, have not split up, and those taking in only part of a single language group . . . have [usually] . . . not united" (Kautsky 1962, p. 35). In the large, therefore, we are dealing primarily with the development of state-nationalities,[94] whether or not substantial great traditions are available to them. If no such integrating traditions corresponding roughly to the national frontiers are available, then obviously they must be created by the state for the purposes of its own preservation and modernization. If such *are* already available, then their *supraethnic* realizations are utilized by the state in order to avoid the fragmentation-potential inherent in their more local or regional deviations. However, in almost all cases we are dealing with state-nationalities that lack the centuries of previous consolidation around supraregional symbols and institutions of statehood which marked nineteenth-century England, France, Scandinavia, Iberia, or even Russia and the Austro-Hungarian Empire.[95] We are dealing with state-nations whose lack of experience in statehood is like that of the more recent European nation-states some forty years ago, but who generally lacked the internal cohesiveness that those had and who are infinitely less developed vis-à-vis their former masters than was true either in Eastern Europe or in the Americas. Finally, we are dealing with state-nations who utilize nationalism in order more quickly to become like nation-states on the assumption that greater group cohesion and group loyalty will bring the attainment of modernization more quickly into reach.

There can be little doubt that the relative absence of ethnic correspondence in connection with the political borders of most new polities is related to the interest in pan movements revealed by some of their elites. In Africa, pan-Negro movements or, at least, pan ideologies and philosophies, began prior to independence, just as they had in the Balkans and among the Tartars prior to World War I[96] and in the Near East and other parts of Asia prior to World War II.[97] The more remarkable thing about pan-Islamism and pan-Africanism, however, is their continuation as ideologies even after the creation of separate states. In some pan movements, this may be ascribed primarily to personal vision or ambitions,[98] in some it may be due to the apparent danger of superordinate threat,[99] but in all cases their success or failure would also seem to be related to the absence or presence of overriding ethnocultural differentiation between the populations or regions involved.[100] Certainly, however, the attainments of pan movements have thus far been too limited (even if the European Common Market and the Scandinavian efforts at cooperation are added to pan-Arabism and pan-Africanism) to lend much support to Hans Kohn's prediction that the twentieth century might yet become known as "the age of pan-nationalism" (1968, p. 64).

Part II

The Impact of Nationalism on Language and Language Planning

"... when the minde is fraught with matter to deliuer, it is still in pain vntill it haue deliuered, and therefor to haue the deliuerie such, as maie discharge the thing well, and content all parties, both by whom and to whom the matter is deliuered, it seeketh both home helps, where theie be sufficient, and significant, and where the own home yeildeth nothing at all, or not pithie enough, it craueth help of that tung, from whence it receiued the matter of deliuerie. Hence commeth it that we haue our tung commonlie both stored and enlarged with our neighbours speches, and the old learned tungs."

Richard Mulcaster, *The First Part of the Elementarie*, 1582.

"... Charlemagne enriched his native tongue, which was Teutonic, by reducing it to rules, composing its grammar, and naming all the months and winds in that language."

François Eudes de Mézeray, in his *Abrégé chronologique, ou Extraits de l'Histoire de France*, 1676.

"... As literature and politeness gain ground in a nation, and according to the duration of their reign, they extend their influence in the language, the commonality in such times acquiring the knowledge of several expressions invented by the learned ... "

Johann David Michaelis, in his *Commentationes*, 1774.

"... By what Hands, and what way Improvements in Language are capable of being effected or promoted: Individual and simple Practice, individual Instruction, free Association, governmental Authority."

Jeremy Bentham, in his "Essay on Language," 1820.

"... If Welsh had been developed as German had been developed during the past 100 years by some of the greatest men who had ever lived ... Welsh today would have been looked upon as one of the most perfect languages on the face of the earth."

Father Hayde of Cardiff, 1837.

"... The want of modern scientific words in Irish is undeniable ...[but] once Irish were recognized as a language to be learned as much as French or Italian our dictionaries would fill up and our vocabularies ramify, to suit all the wants of life and conversation."

Thomas Davies, 1845.

The Impact of Nationalism
on
Language and Language Planning

THE VERNACULAR AS THE MEDIUM OF NATIONALISM

The lingering hostility of American social science scholarship (as well as of much of Western social science scholarship more generally) toward nationalism has also been transferred to the role of the vernacular in nationalist movements. Although this scholarship has produced numerous observations to the effect that a common vernacular is, in itself, insufficient *cause* for sociocultural or political-operational integration, and, although there are similarly many observations that both kinds of integration *have* come to pass without the presence of a common vernacular, both of these observations tend to miss a major point that needs to be examined. Such observations are more concerned with proving or disproving the validity of nationalist ideology (or of a particular nationalist ideology) concerning the crucial role and the superior quality of the vernacular (or of a particular vernacular) than they are with clarifying *why such views have so frequently come to be held and to be held so fiercely and by so many.*

It is not at all necessary to take a position with respect to the absolute necessity of a common vernacular for the formation of broader integrative or affiliative bonds to recognize that nationalist movements have very commonly utilized and championed vernaculars in order to attain their particular broader integrating and authenticating goals. Indeed, it is not even necessary to claim that nationalism was particularly unique among modernization movements in this respect. Humanism, the Renaissance, and the Reformation—all of them being European intellectual movements whose populist and nonuniversalist facets became apparent far before the advent of mass nationalism—all utilized and prized the vernaculars for reasons somewhat similar to one large cluster of reasons that also obtained in the subsequent case of nationalism itself.[1] Thus, vernacular emphases, purely as a *functional* matter, began in the West "with the decline of supranational and theoretically universal cultural elements such as the founding of all Western education on a thorough and often exclusive training in the classical languages, the role of French as the language of diplomacy and international relations," and, in the East, with the decline of "erudition [solely] in [classical] Arabic in all Islamic countries, [and] the exclusive use of classical Chinese as the literary language until Hu Shih's language revolution in 1917" (Kohn 1968, p. 65). Even the classical Western European empires recognized and utilized the local vernaculars for communication and control on a mass basis. Thus Barrow indicates that "native languages flourished in the Roman Empire" and that "St. Augustine, as Bishop of Hippo, found it necessary to engage priests who knew Punic, and this though Africa had been a province for centuries" (Barrow 1949, 115-116). Therefore, as in many other respects, nationalism's *utilization* of the vernacular is not so much a clear break or departure relative to earlier periods as much as is the intensity with which it pursued this utilization and, in particular, its rationalization thereof.

The functional dependence of new protoelites on the vernaculars was a reflection of the need of these elites to communicate with, organize, and activate recently urbanized but still predominantly illiterate populations. Less obvious is the fact that these populations often had neither a single vernacular (but, rather, a socially, regionally, and experientially differentiated *continuum of vernaculars*), nor a vernacular that could readily be put to the modern ideologizing and organizing purposes that new protoelites had in mind. Even less obvious is the fact that many would-be elites themselves did not know the vernacular that had to be utilized if their goals were to be attained. The sociocultural alienation of the aristocratic and bourgeois leadership of the prenationalist period had produced an imposing array of discontinuities between the masses and those normally expected (and expecting) to be their leaders. The early and mid-17th century Irish chronicler Conell MaGeoghagan laments that "because they cannot enjoy that respect and gaine by their said profession as heretofore they and their ancestors receaved, they set naught by said knowledge . . . and choose rather to put their children to learne English than their native language" (cited by Ó Cuív 1969, p. 2). Two hundred years later we encounter the same lament not only in nationalist writing of awakened protoelites of Western European minorities (e.g., "We have no Royal, princely nor aristocratic families among us to influence our customs. The few rich ones who live in the country are strangers to the people as regards language, and foreigners in respect to religion" [Southall 1893, p. 250]) but in similar writings throughout Central, Eastern and Southern Europe as well. By the end of that century the linguistic reethnification of new protoelites was far advanced throughout formerly "nonhistoric" Europe.[2] A rather similar process has more recently been evident in African and Asian nationalist movements (e.g., "Just how powerful this feeling is may be seen in the number of English-educated Chinese [in South East Asia] who are now furtively and hurriedly learning the Chinese language" [Purcell 1953, p. 243]), although South Asian elites in particular had commonly combined their earlier personal modernization with continual allegiance to intact or restructured , regional great traditions. The protoelitist conversion comes prior to mass nationalist mobilization. The former also has more than a tinge of *mea culpa* to it.

The reethnification of protoelites is no less an authentification experience for the fact that it served personal and class interests.

"Had the mineral wealth of the principality been discovered by the natives, and could it have been properly put to use before they ·were subdued to English rule, they might have preserved their language and been the foremost among British subjects in wealth, manufacture and arts" (H.L. Spring, *Lady Cambria*, 1867; cited by D. G. Jones 1950, pp. 113-114).

How much more appropriate then that this wealth be returned to the nationality to which it rightfully belonged by self-proclaimed guardians who not only appreciated this wealth but the language as well. The control of the one legitimized the control of the other. Indigenization of the language, at the very least, was "a great stirring up [that] portended no one knew exactly what; meanwhile it was a useful lever for doing many desirable things" (a paraphrase of the views of the Irish nationalist leader Moran; McCartney 1969, p. 48), including, of course, "excluding from their jobs the old bourgeoisie and substituting for them new men" (Meillet 1928, p. 52), men who identified with the people, who were increasingly of the people, and, therefore, genuinely deserving of their stewardship. For all of these reasons nationalist protoelites have been much more than "theoretically" interested in the vernacular, as well as in language learning *per se*. For prospective protoelites the vernacular was (and is) very much an instrument of power—for themselves and for the people.[3]

Whereas vernacular literacy and vernacular education had begun to gain ground slowly in Europe prior to the appearance of mass nationalism, the latter was crucially dependent on both, particularly in an age when the mass media included neither radio nor television but only the popular lecture or the printed word in one form or another. The coming of vernacular education (often by means of illegal schools[4]) and the introduction of vernacular literacy often brought very dramatic consequences in their wake.[5] As one who lived through such a period recounted: " . . . the older peasants called themselves Masurians their speech Masurian. They lived their own life forming a wholly separate group, and caring nothing for the nation. I myself did not know that I was a Pole till I began to read books and papers, and I fancy that other villagers came to be aware of their national attachment in much the same way" (Slomka 1941, cited by Kedourie 1961, p. 120). Obviously, the reading of books and papers referred to was possible on a mass basis only in the vernacular. Such reading among the previously illiterate not only forged a new bond with language, an awareness of language as part of a rebirth of self and of assertive self consciousness, but it also put protoelites into touch with masses whom they would otherwise hardly have reached and never have influenced. The crucial functional role of vernacular education for the arousal and maintenance of nationalism leads Gellner to conclude that "modern loyalties are centered on political units whose boundaries are defined by the language . . . of an educational system" (1964, p. 163).[6]

The vernaculars were functionally favored not merely by elites seeking to unify and to activate the masses, but by the very processes of urbanization and modernization of which nationalism in developing nations is so often a part and which new elites sought and seek to harness for specific substantive purposes. Industrial urban life is dependent upon widespread literacy (which normally means vernacular literacy) and/or on vernacular mass media in order to train and coordinate its skilled labor force. However, modernization involves not only literacy-dependent economic changes and the coordination of intricate literacy-dependent economic roles, but also secure political-operational consolidation which, as several recent observers have pointed out, is based upon the attainment and maintenance of mass consensus.[7] Even those nations following the state-nation pattern toward nationality formation are often dependent upon vernacular literacy, if not upon vernacular education, in order to secure the modern political-operational stability and participation without which ultimate socio-cultural integration cannot come to pass. Thus, nationalist theoreticians need not be suspected of either conscious or unconscious self-aggrandizement when they stressed the need to recognize, utilize, standardize, and modernize the vernaculars. Some saw it simply as a military necessity ("How were recruits to be instructed if they did not understand the language of their leaders? How were orders to be rapidly transmitted to these immense moving bodies of men? Above all, how was moral cohesion between them to be attained?" [Delaise 1927, p. 172]). Others saw it as an invaluable tool for the spread of nationalist ideologies in the light of which nationalism itself was merely a first stage (Dadrian 1967, p. 32). Most recognized that it not only had "identitive integrating power" (Etzioni 1965), but that such power was *useful*, all the more so because its broad boundaries were vague and manipulable.

The instrumental dependence of unificatory nationalism on the vernacular is, therefore, not greatly different from that of other modern mass movements, whatever their political or economic coloration. Thus, it is particularly in connection with the authenticity emphases of nationalism that its more unique interrelationship with the vernacular becomes manifest. Modern mass nationalism goes beyond the objective, instrumental identification of community with language (i.e., with communication)[8] to the identification of authenticity with a *particular* language which is experientially unique and, therefore, functional in a way that other languages cannot match, namely, in safeguarding the sentimental and behavioral links between the speech community of today and its (real or imaginary) counterparts yesterday and in antiquity. *This* function of language tends to be overlooked by other mass modernization movements and *its* utility tends to be ignored by them. Nationalism stresses this function, a deeply subjective function, as a *summun bonum*, and demonstrates decisively that "the rational and the romantic are not wholly alternative or antagonistic but are at least in some measure, complementary . . . The romantic form is essential to the solution of the problem of identity, for *its* content can only be categorical" (Binder 1964, p. 136).

LANGUAGE AS [PART OF] THE MESSAGE OF NATIONALISM

Although there are pitifully few studies that focus on a vernacular as a substantive (rather than as a functional) hub of nationalism, the view that a people's individuality resides in its language is very old. One ingredient of the holy trinity (holy people, holy land, holy language), language has been regarded as a defining characteristic of a nationality, within the sphere of the Judeo-Christian tradition, since Biblical days. It is this context of *potential* sanctity that so long preserved vernaculars in the West (as well as in the East) as *potential* symbols, until more recent times when they actually became overwhelmingly powerful symbols and causes[9] (e.g., "An Arab is a person whose mother tongue is Arabic, who has lived or who looks forward to living on Arab soil, and who believes in being a member of the Arab nation." Article 10 of the Constitution of the Socialist Arab Resurrection Party [Ba'th] cited by Sharabi 1966, p. 96).

For our purposes it is necessary to differentiate between the question of whether language is *indeed* a necessary and sufficient criterion of nationality and the question of whether such has been the view of modern nationalist movements. While both questions have received very little social science attention (notwithstanding Snyder's claim that "All major works on nationalism stress in detail the significance of language" [1954, p. 20]) the first has generally been answered in the negative and the latter in the affirmative.[10] It is to the latter question alone that we will direct our attention in the hope that an attempt to illuminate it will also help us understand *why* "the criterion of nationality" has so frequently been found "in the shibboleth of language" (Toynbee, *A Study of History*, VII, p. 536) and *why* nationalism so often "generates a new kind of political community occupied with a common cultural heritage, especially in terms of language" (Friedrich 1963, p. 559).

Language as the Link with the Glorious Past

One of the major motivational emphases of modern nationalism has been that the ethnic past must not be lost for within it could be found both the link to greatness as well as the substance of greatness itself. It was on both of these accounts that "the mother tongue became almost sacred, the mysterious vehicle of all the national endeavors" (Jaszi 1929, p. 262), particularly for those whose current greatness was far from obvious. For the "peoples without history," history and language were two sides of the same coin. The vernacular was not merely the highroad *to* history, it was *itself* "the voice of years that are gone; they roll before me with all their deeds" (from Macpherson 1760, cited by Hayes 1937, p. 16). It was felt that "in its mother tongue every people honors itself; in the treasury of its speech is contained the charter of its cultural history" (Ludwig Jahn, cited by Rocker 1937, p. 295). As a result "a language [and] a history" were viewed as twins since together they constituted "the two first needs of a people .... There is not a new nation in Europe which has not been preceded by from fifty to eighty years of philology and archeological studies" (Etienne Fournol, *Les Nations Romantiques*, Paris, 1931, p. 206; cited by Sulzbach 1943, p. 24). Little wonder then that linguists were, on occasion, "compared to surgeons who restore to its natural function a limb which had been almost paralyzed but not severed from the national body" (Kahn 1950, p. 157).

Lest it seem that only the "upstart" nationalities of Central, Eastern, and Southern Europe viewed their vernaculars as direct bonds with historical glory (and, therefore, with either the reality or the potentiality for current glory), it should be pointed out that the historic nations too were not averse to such views. Michelet, in mid-nineteenth century, held that "in this [French] is continued the grand human movement [so clearly marked out by the languages] from India to Greece and to Rome, and from Rome to us" [1846] 1946, p. 240 while the first stirrings of Pan-Indian nationalism produced claims that "Sanscrit was the most enduring monument of the past greatness of the country and was destined to act as one of the most powerful agents in India's future regeneration" (McCully 1940, p. 255). As for Arab thinkers in the latter part of the nineteenth century, "the 'great days of their past' were not just, as in the West, the flowering of a vaguely related culture—the way that Greece and Rome were vaguely related to Britain and France—but were directly related to the men of this period linguistically, religiously, and, as the Arabs loved to emphasize, by ties of kinship" (Polk 1970, p. xiii). The heirs of past greatness deserve to be great again. The heirs of triumphant unity in the past must themselves be united in the present and future. The heirs of past independence cannot but be independent again. The purported continuity of the language was the authenticating device for finding, claiming, and utilizing one's inheritance.

Language as the Link with Authenticity

i. Directly, via the language per se.

History consists of names and dates and places but the essence of a nationality is something which is merely implied or adumbrated by such details. This essence exists over and above dynasties and centuries and boundaries; this essence is that which constitutes the *heart* of the nationality and which leads to its greatness; the essence of a nationality is its spirit, its individuality, its soul. This soul is not only reflected and protected by the mother tongue but, in a sense, *the mother tongue is itself an aspect of the soul*, a part of the soul, if not the soul made manifest.[11] The major figure in placing language squarely at the emotional and intellectual center of modern nationalism's concern for authenticity was doubtlessly Johann Gottfried Herder (1744-1803). Although he was himself influenced by others (particularly by the works of Vico, e.g., *The New Science*, 1725) in developing his views, as well as associated with others in propagating them (e.g., Fichte), the phrases, concepts and emphases that have cropped up again and again during the past two centuries, throughout the world, wherever vernaculars are defended or admired, tend to be his. His writing was seminal in developing the complementary views that the mother tongue expressed a nationality's soul or spirit, that since it was a collective achievement par excellence, language was also the surest way for individuals to safeguard (or recover) the authenticity they had inherited from their ancestors as well as to hand it on to generations yet unborn, and, finally, that worldwide diversity in language and in culture was a good and beautiful thing in and of itself, whereas imitation led to corruption and stagnation.[12] The Slavs openly recognized him as the fountainhead of Slavic nationalist thought. Consciously or unconsciously his words have been repeated by those who claimed that "without Finnish we are not Finns" (Wuorinen 1931, p. 62) or that "the role of Arabic in the life history of the Arabs. . . is [to be] the register of their creativeness, a symbol of their unity, and an expression of their mental and artistic aptitudes" (Nuseibeh 1956, p. 69) or that "Our language, the expression of our people, which can never be given up . . . is the spiritual foundation of our existence" (Catalonian Cultural Committee 1924, p. 13). [13]

The contrastive position of "Germany" vis-à-vis its insultingly proud Romance neighbors to the west and its hopelessly crude Slavic neighbors to the east may have contributed to the Herderian view that languages were huge natural divides. Perhaps personal preoccupation with the literary, standard language was also contributory to the view that the boundaries between languages were more fundamental, lasting, clearer, and implicational than political boundaries, religious boundaries, or other behavioral systems. Politically, religiously, and behaviorally Germany was even more fractionated than the Slavic east! Only language implied an ideal genotypic unity that could counteract the phenotypic horrors of the day. From the very first a distinction of the langue-parole type permitted Herder and other language nationalists both to have their cake and to eat it too: to champion an ideal norm and to create it at the same time.

Both the exact nature of the nationality-and-language link, and the strength of this link, have been argued by seemingly dispassionate social commentators and social scientists on the one hand and by proudly passionate nationalist writers and activists on the other. The views of these two types of participant observers are typically and predictably different. In the first case we find doubt if not derision. The "requiredness," of the link, i.e., the view that it is unquestionable and given-in-nature, is obviously questioned by those who consider that social conventions have social rather than supernatural or species-wide bases. Thus, Pfaff states that "considerations of language, history or geography are valuable, to justify what one already believes, but they do not necessarily lead to that belief" (1970, p. 159). Sapir is more charitable. He admits that "a particular language tends to become the fitting expression of a self-conscious nationality" but adds that "such a group will construct for itself . . . a race to which is to be attributed the mystic power of creating a language and a culture as twin expressions of its psychic peculiarities" (1942 [1930], p. 660, i.e., the link is ultimately man-made but ascribed to supernatural forces in order to hallow it. Such a thorough student of nationalism as Lemberg is more critical however. He considers the imputed link to have been put to uses which reverse the natural order of things. In discussing the early fifteenth-century Hussite revolt he observes "Hier war das Umgekehrte dessen eingetreten . . . Nicht ein Staat hatte seine Bewohner zur Nation gebildet, sondern ein durch Sprache abgegrenztes Volk hatte sich an einer sozialen und *religiosen* Revolution die es als seine Sendung auffasste, zur Nation geformt und hatte den über seine Grenzen hinausreichenden Staat erobert" (Lemberg 1964, vol. I, pp. 108-109).

Between the foregoing views (essentially that nationalisms tend to find or inflate the symbols that they require in language as in other respects) and those of most involved nationalists there is a huge chasm. Between the two major positions only few adopt the view that language has *become* symbolic and as such *should* be preserved, cultivated, protected, and advanced. Such moderate views were more common in premodern dettings (e.g., "Methinks the nations should make their language triumphant also, and the rather because there are Laws against it. For why should a free people retain any marks of slavery?" Robert Huntington, Provost of Trinity College [Dublin], 1686; cited by Ó Cuív 1969, p. 2), but are still sometimes encountered (e.g. "Are we not able to rise above our sectional interest and local patriotism and adopt as our national language the mother tongue of Dr. José Rizal, our greatest hero and martyr, who ardently wished that some day we should speak one language," Rojo 1937, p. 60; or "Remember, you have a national language of your own. Use it [Malay] when you are together," Abdul Rahman cited by Miller 1959, p. 47). What is striking about such views is, on the one hand, their awareness of language as a prime and fitting group symbol, and, on the other hand, of the need for organized human intercessation on its behalf.

The view that language and nationality are inextricably and naturally linked also begins in a low key. When St. Stephen's crown was offered to Ferdinand of Austria (1527), in order to strengthen Hungary's resistance aginst the Turks, the new ruler pledged "Nationem et linguam vestrum servare non perdere intendimus" (cited by Dominian 1917, p. 154). Spenser, in his *View of Ireland,* indicates the naturalness of the link by a single phrase: "So that the speech being Irish the heart must needs be Irish" (cited by Flannery 1896, title page), as does a Welsh writer of the same period ("Our tongue cannot be learned by a stranger; its fire burns only in a native breast," cited by Southall 1893, p. 212).

With the coming of modern mass nationalism the entire relationship is not only more urgent but more demanding as well. What was hitherto often enough viewed as a natural link is now also a cause, a goal, and obligation. "Without its own language," Herder wrote, "a Volk is an absurdity (*Unding*), a contradiction in terms" (vol. I, p. 147; cited by Barnard 1965, p. 57). As a result "Die Sprache ist nicht des Menschen wegen da, sondern dieser hat die Pflicht die als nationales Idol zu ehren . . . Die Sprache hat Rechte; der Mensch hat keine" (Koppelman 1956, p. 93). From modern Germany this emphasis spreads its way throughout Europe. In Ireland Davies writes (in English) precisely what Herder might have written: "To impose another language on . . . a people is to send their history adrift . . . to tear their identity from all places . . . To lose your native tongue, and learn that of an alien, is the worst badge of conquest—it is the chain on the soul. To have lost entirely the national language is death; the fetter has worn through . . . Nothing can make us believe that it is natural . . . for the Irish to speak the speech of the alien, the invader, the Sasanoch tyrant, and to abandon the language of our kings and Heroes . . . No! oh, no! the 'brighter day shall surely come' and the green flag shall wave on our towers and the sweet old language be heard once more in college, mart and senate" (Davies 1945 [1845], p. 73). How natural then that the slogan of the times became "Ireland, not free only but Gaelic as well; not Gaelic only but free as well!" (Beckett 1966, p. 417). Language equals nationality and nationality equals language; the slogan finally reverberates far beyond its initially European boundaries. "A land qualifies as part of the Arab patrimony if the daily speech of its inhabitants is the Arabic language" (Izzeddin 1953, p. 1) is essentially a modern European view of the matter (indeed Chejne claims that "It was at the insistence of Christians and Westernized Muslims that the language took on a new dimension and became a secular symbol of a national creed as embodied in the concept of 'urūbah (Arabism);" 1969, p. 172), as is the view that "it is because of our language that the Senhalese race has existed for 2400 years" (from a debate in the Ceylonese State Council 1944, cited by Kearney 1967, p. 748).

However, the inseparability of the God-given link between language and nationality is not the most that can be claimed. Such a claim might well be advanced for other desiderata as well. The ideological pinnacle of language nationalism is not reached until language is clearly pictured as *more* crucial than the other symbols and expressions of nationality. This pinnacle too has been scaled time and again in the annals of modern nationalism and in very characteristic contrastive contexts at that. In prenationalist days the primacy of the language-nationality link, on the rare occasions that such primacy was claimed, was in terms of its greater collective significance than the symbols with which elites alone (or primarily) were involved. "A language is mightier far than any number of books which may have been written in it, for such productions, great though they be, at best embody what was in the hearts and minds of individual men; but language, on the other hand, is the impress and life of a nation" (cited by Southhall 1893, p. 236). When viewed from the perspective of nationalist ideology, however, language primacy is claimed precisely in comparison with other collective symbols, in comparison with other referents of mass participation, mass involvement, and mass sanctification. Language is worthier than territory. "A people without a language of its own is only half a nation. A nation should guard its language more than its territories—'tis a surer barrier, a more important frontier than fortress or river" (Davies 1945 [1845], p. 71), Language is worthier than the institutions of government. "Even if a Volk's state perishes the nation remains intact, provided it maintains its distinctive linguistic traditions" (Herder 1877/1913, vol. XIV, p. 87; cited by Barnard 1965, p. 58) and, therefore, "Although the Arabs find themselves politically divided, their language betrays a unity more basic than any single institution" (Chejne 1969, pp. 174-175). "Language is not an art form, it is *the* art form of the Arabs" (Polk 1970, p. xvii). Indeed, language is even worthier than religion, for "There is no doubt that the unity of language is more durable for survival and permanence in this world than the unity of religion" (Rendessi 1958, p. 125). Little wonder then that "the theorists of Arab nationalism have assigned to the language the first place as a factor constituting the Arab nation" (Nuseibeh 1956, p. 77). The same conclusion has been reached by the theorists of other modern nationalisms as well. Political fortunes wax and wane. Religions are often shared with other peoples and, at any rate, have a too firmly established elite of their own, tradition of their own, and task orientation of their own to be easily captured and manipulated by newly aspiring protoelites. Religion is often viewed as an embarrassment by modern man. In language, on the other hand, one has a secular symbol (if such is desired) that can simultaneously draw upon and lean upon all of the sanctity that religion has given to texts, to writing systems, and to word imagery per se (see below), at the same time that it is manipulated by and that it serves a basically new elite and a new set of problems, goals, and methods. Modern societies have an endless need to define themselves as eternally unique and language is one of the few remaining mass symbols that answers this need without automatically implying one or another short-lived and non-distinctive institutional base. Institutions may come or go, but none of them get to the heart of that which is eternally unique. Institutions must routinize in order to maximize and therein lies their failure, emotionally, and ultimately, practically as well. Language, on the other hand, is viewed as contraroutine. It is for its readers a universe which is simultaneously constantly expanding and, yet, very much their own. "Y se extiende como si no tuviera término ni orillas el mar inmenso del castellano. Y no pone el sol" (Capdevila 1940, p. 164).

ii. Indirectly, via widespread oral and written imagery

Nationalism glorifies the vernacular not only directly but indirectly as well, by honoring and experiencing as symbols of collective greatness and authenticity the most pervasive products of verbal versatility. "The sagas of the Norsemen, the vedas of the Hindus, the Pentateuch . . . of the Hebrews, the Homeric poems, the Virgilian hexameters, all the famed deeds of the brave men before Agamemnon . . . have served to inspire linguistic groups with corporate consciousness and to render them true nationalities" (Hayes 1937, p. 17). The mother tongue was the vehicle whereby history reached the lower mass and whereby folklore reached the upper class. Poetry, songs, proverbs, mottos, and tales—these all involve basically language behaviors and language products and both history and authenticity are manifestly made and safeguarded by their recitation. Over and over again one finds that both the context and the form of vernacular oral and written literature are pointed to, by elites and laymen alike, as inspiring, unifying, and activating nationalist stimuli. It was even so in the case of Latin literature. "Rome is the heroine inspiring Romans to heroic deeds to fulfull her destiny" (Barrow 1949, p. 117). In the case of nationalist literature, however, the target population was no longer elitist but, rather, the largest audience attainable.

The interaction between the mother tongue and experiences of beauty, devotion, altruism, and righteousness—in short, the tie between the mother tongue and collective "peak" experiences—does not depend on abstract ideologies concerning the "ethnic soul" or the "national spirit." Such experiences are more directly and formatively provided via the oral and written literatures in the vernacular that both anticipate and accompany mass nationalism. Herder's view that national character was an impossibility in the absence of a folk-song tradition has since been echoed by others, both laymen and literati, in the East as in the West. "Literature has always consolidated the nation-forming power of language . . . For men of feeling, destiny will ever be hailed in the word that stirs. The harvest reaped by Cavour was of Dante's sowing" (Dominian 1917, pp. 318-319). Whereas Macpherson merely claimed that his forged fragments had been collected "among a people so strongly attached to the memory of their ancestors" "as to have preserved" "in a great measure uncorrupted to this day" the poetry of their ancestors, nationalist spokesmen also recognized a crucial causal nexus in the opposite direction, i.e., the literature (oral or written) preserves the nationality, rather than vice versa. Thus "[Grimms' fairy tales] have enabled us to understand that we, the German people, bear the power and the conditions in our selves to take up and carry on the civilization of old times, that we are a folk with a high historical mission" (Franke 1918, p. 176) and "In his [Runeberg's] poems we recognized ourselves and felt that we were one people, that we had a fatherland and were Finns" (cited by Wuorinen 1931, p. 79). Similarly, the *Marseillaise* is sung "so solemnly, so ceremoniously" that it and the language of which it is a part must be viewed as "outpourings of an eternal French soul" (Hayes 1930, p. 235). The Kalevala (self-styled as "Songs of ancient wit and wisdom/Legends they that once were taken/from the pastures of the Northland/from the meads of Kalevala") is hailed as a "Homeric poem which the people had brought forth in times imme-morial . . . handed down from generation to generation in the course of centuries . . . A mighty monument to the genius of the Finnish people . . . no foreign influences had ever marred it" (Wuorinen 1939, p. 75). Similarly, "the guzlar's ballad is the symbol of national solidarity. His tunes live within the hearts and upon the lips of every Serbian. The pjesme may, therefore, be fittingly considered the measure and index of the nationality whose fibre it has stirred" (Dominian 1917, p. 322). We find the link between language, language product and nation expressed even more directly in Arndt's patriotic hymn:

Was ist das deutsche Vaterland?
So nenne endlich mir das Land!
So weit die deutsche Zunge klingt
Und Gott im Himmel Lieder singt.
Das soll es sein, das soll es sein
Das ganze Deutschland soll es sein.[14]

However, even Tagore's more gentle and lyrical images often served a definite nationalist purpose. "Thus lyricism was the second note in the emotion we felt at the coming of nationalist agitation and its poignancy lay in the continuous evocation of the beauties of nature: the waters, the green grass, the golden cornfields of Bengal, the fragrance of mango blossoms in the Spring" (Chaudhuri 1951, p. 221). Similarly, religious verse helped many to find "a new definition of Maharashtra: The land whose people go to Pandharpur for pilgrim-age . . . Marathi speaking people, coming from different castes but singing the same songs, the same verses of the Varkari cult" (Karve 1962, p. 22). The use of established genres for collective peak experiences ("Men shouted, women wept, youths went into near-hypnotic trances. The effect was electric" [Hanna 1964, p. 15]) sealed the bond between the vernacular and goal directed collective emotion.

Such examples can be multiplied endlessly. One point that these examples serve has already been made, namely, that vernacular literature (oral and written) provides the masses with the emotionalized link between language and nationalism that exists for elites at the level of ideological and intellectual program. The beauty of the vernacular, the greatness of the nationality, the purity of the common cause are grasped by many for the first time—and thus associated with their personal emotional and intellectual "rebirth"—via the popular literature of nationalism. The Finnish writer Estlander (early nineteenth century) realized this link when he wrote "No fatherland can exist without folk poetry. Poetry is nothing more than the crystal in which nationality can mirror itself; it is the spring which brings to the surface the truly original in the folk-soul" (Wuorinen 1931, p. 69). Half a century later a Hindu nationalist expressed the same thought, namely, that "a nation[ality] could rise in its greatness only when the literature of its motherland was well studied. It would certainly lead to the love of national greatness and to the adoption of national habits and manners" (from a letter to the editor, *Indian Mirror*, July 17, 1885; cited by McCully 1940, p. 255).

However, a second and related point still remains to be mentioned: that the link between vernacular literature and nationalism provides yet another avenue for the influence of nationalist sentiments and principles upon language planning. The lexical, phonological, and grammatical forms which become popularized and emotionalized via the moving literature that is prompted by or contributory to the mass awakening of nationality sentiments and nationalist activity have a subsequent directional grip upon language planning which it may well be impossible to displace. Just as Lönnrot's reconstruction of the Kalevala "revealed the startling resources of the Finnish language and came to play a decisive part in the development of modern Finnish both as a spoken tongue and as a literary vehicle" (Wuorinen 1931, p. 75) so other inspirational literatures in periods of developing nationalism have influenced the subsequent development of languages all over the globe.[15]

Contrastive Self-identification via Language

The frequency with which vernaculars have become part and parcel of the authenticity message of nationalism (both directly and, again, indirectly, through their oral and written products) is certainly, in no small measure, due to the ease with which elites and masses alike could extrapolate from linguistic *differentiation* and literary *uniqueness* to sociocultural and political inde-pendence.[16] However, the latter extrapolation was not always made, to begin with, and was even explicitly rejected on some of the occasions on which it *was* made. Smaller and weaker nationalist movements were particularly likely to consider political independence as a surface phenomenon that might be here today and gone tomorrow. On the other hand, the uniqueness of folk spirit and life-style that was represented by the vernacular was considered to be a truer and more lasting independence.. "If he had to choose between language and freedom," De Valera told his friends of the early Gaelic League, "he would choose language" (Bromage p. 226); and so did, and do, the leaders of several other smaller nationalities, both then and now.

Nationalist leaders and masses frequently viewed the vernacular not only as the most undeniable indicator of uniqueness, but, precisely because it was so viewed, also as an indubitable nationality-contrastive or continuative device, depending on which view was felt to be in need of reinforcement. Obviously language had not always been so viewed among ordinary prenationalist ethnics. Nor was it always to be so among postnationalist cosmopolitans. "Language may invite us to unite, but it does not compel us to do so" (Renan, cited by Singhal 1967, p. 278). In the heat of nationalist awakenings, however, language is as basic a division as is the continental divide. It is the shibboleth that differentiates friend from foe. The anti-French tone of German nationalist thought ever since the middle of the nineteenth century[17] was repeatedly reflected in German views of the French language per se and of how German differed from it. Since the French (Franks) were originally a Teutonic people, one of their sins was that they forsook their native speech for a neo-Latin language. As a result they not only were guilty of treason to themselves, but also justifiably punished by inheriting all of the faults which led to the downfall of the Romans, namely, "lack of seriousness about social relations, the idea of self-abandonment, and the idea of heartless laxity. Had they retained their original speech they would never have allowed such degradation to befall them" (Fichte, cited by Kedourie 1961, p. 65). Although Herder was less invidious in his views, he was equally deterministic ("a so-called education in French must by necessity deform and misguide German minds. In my opinion this sentence is as clear as the sun at noon." Sämmtliche Werke, Vol 17, p. 157) and, if anything, more striking in his rejection of French ("And you German, returning from abroad/Wouldst greet your mother in French?/Oh, spew it out before your door/Spew out the ugly slime of the Seine/Speak German, Oh you German!"; cited by Kedourie 1961, p. 59). Jahn, a somewhat later German nationalist spokesman and activist, finally took the position that "He who teaches his children to learn the French language, or permits them to learn it, is delirious; he who persists in doing this sins against the Holy Ghost; he who allows his daughter to study French is about as good as he who teaches his daughter the virtues of prostitution" (cited by Snyder 1952, p. 28). The impact of such views on German language planning is not hard to find, e.g., in preferences such as the rejection of internationalisms from Graeco-Latin roots. Purification of the

German language (through the substitution of German derivatives for "borrowed words," e.g., *Landshauptmann* for Gouverneur, *Befehlshaber* for Kommandant) was supported by many who did not necessarily support "purification of the German race."

Contrastive self-identification on the basis of language is a very ancient human proclivity.[18] However it is also a proclivity which in prenationalist days is unideologized and, therefore, conveniently bridgeable or forgettable. "Even the linguistic distinction between Turks and Iranians was of little importance [in early twentieth century Central Asia]. The best proof of this is the existence of an ethnic group known as 'Chagatay' consisting of both Iranian and Turkic language speakers who regarded themselves as very close to each other but different from other 'Uzbeks' " (Quelquejay and Bennigsen 1961, p. 14). Language-and-nationality cooccurrences exist as widespread latent images of no activating or predictable significance. In the period of mass nationalism this cooccurrence becomes much more than a widespread image; it becomes a manipulable image, not merely with respect to the kinds of integration to which we have been referring, but with respect to the future of the vernacular itself. By rejection of English, the Irish and Indian nationalists, e.g., could not only establish their uniqueness[19] and not only conclude from "philological evidence" that their masters had really copied from *them*,[20] but could also operate directly upon a corpus of ethnic behavior and symbolism, a corpus that was (actually or potentially) at their very tongue and fingertips, that they were (actually or potentially) especially skilled to manipulate, and that was the (actual or potential) medium of the influence that they sought to exert. Thus the links between nationalism and the vernacular are many and mutually reinforcing. While they ultimately derive from the human dependence upon language to communicate and to channel experience, they derive more directly from the human tendency to "seek for the 'essence' or reality in the words used to designate this reality as experience" (Friedrich 1963, p. 45). Nationalist beliefs, like all societally patterned beliefs, are language dependent. That nationalists recognize and exploit this dependence is, for our purposes, more noteworthy than the fact that, at times, it also comes into being without nationalism. As a result of such recognition, masses are tied into nationalist integration "through their emotional investment in system symbols" (Katz 1965, p. 361).

That the vernacular so commonly becomes such a symbol is (to review its sentimental component alone) partially a reflection of the fact that it is the *carrier* of all of the other notions and symbols advanced by nationalism (" ... the people need the word to find a new way;"[Pye 1961, p. 219], "If a man is robbed of his earthly home he finds a spiritual home in his mother tongue, which is everywhere and always present to his senses, and can, therefore, at some time again become concrete and have an earthly home;"] Vossler 1932, p. 123]), partially a result of the fact that it is made into a prime symbol by "intellectuals" and other influentials who more than any others are adept at its use and manipulation, and partially a result of its infinite interpretability as a symbol that stands for the entire nationality. Hence its surprising acceptability to the most varied interaction networks who might easily differ as to other acceptable symbols of nationality. Nationalism is fundamentally a step toward modernization. As such it basically needs group symbols that are more *evocative* of the past than unyieldingly *anchored* (or anchoring) to it; more *indicative* of uniqueness than disablingly mesmerized by it. As other symbols of unity and authenticity become problematic because of their delimited and evaluatable nature the vernacular remains to be reinterpreted in accord with one's own most favored memories and longings, as well as in accord with what is considered most dear and most laudable about the ethnic collectivity. ("In days of doubt, in days of gloom and anxiety about the fate of my motherland, thou alone art my support and my stay, oh great mighty, true and free Russian tongue . . . It is unthinkable that such a language has not also been given to a great people" [Turgenieff, *Poems in Prose;* cited by Vossler 1932, p. 129]). Through nationalism masses of people attain and maintain a new and a constantly renewed sense of identity and purpose. Their new (or old-new) songs, poems, slogans, and proverbs, the moving phrases of their leaders and teachers, their national epics, and their national literatures, are all part and parcel of a sense of (re)birth, awakening, and mastery. ("Irish Irelandism helped to create something of the excitement of an intellectual discovery and an awareness among Irishmen that as a nation they were reborn . . . it fostered self-confidence and self-reliance and cultivated a pride in national distinctiveness" [McCartney 1967, p. 52]). But a (re)birth requires a bountiful mother and in the case of nationalism it is not surprising that this is so commonly the mother tongue (Daube [1940] records the earliest reference to "Mueterlich deutsch" as occurring in 1349). Without the mother tongue, which too is viewed as reborn (see, e.g., Blach 1883), it is clear that neither songs nor poems, nor slogans, nor proverbs, nor speeches, nor epics, nor books, nor schools, nor nationality, nor nation would have come into being, nor be what they are, nor what they could be; and, in a very real sense, this is so, both as a result of the "accidents of history" and as a result of conscious planning.

NATIONALISM'S NEED FOR LANGUAGE PLANNING

The term *language planning* refers to the organized pursuit of solutions to language problems, typically at the national level (Jernudd and Das Gupta 1971). Several investigators have enumerated rather similar types or kinds of language planning (see, e.g., Al-Toma 1971, Gastil 1959, Guitare and Quintero 1968, Hamzaoui 1965, Kirk-Greene 1964, Heyd 1954, Kurman 1968, Minn

Latt 1966, Whiteley 1969). Thus Neustupny (1970) has suggested (see Table I) that when the *problem* to be faced is that of *code selection, planning* is concerned with *official policy formation* by authorities in control of power. When the *problem* is that of *stabilizing the selected code* (in view of its variability over space, time, and experiential networks), *planning* is concerned with *codification* via dictionaries, grammars, spellers, punctuation, and pronunciation guides, etc. When the *problem* is that of rapidly *expanding* the number of available options (as a result of the addition of new functions for the selected code), *planning* is concerned with *elaboration* via nomenclatures, thesauruses, etc. When the *problem* is that of *differentiation* of one variety from another within any particular code, *planning* is concerned with *cultivation* via the preparation of style manuals, the subsidization of literary creativity in a variety of genres for various purposes and audiences. Neustupny clearly sees the above four *problem-planning correspondences* as normally standing at least in a rough sequential relationship to each other such that the least developed or least advanced speech-and-writing communities may need to be disproportionately concerned with *policy formation planning*, whereas the most developed or most advanced communities are able to devote proportionately more attention to *cultivation planning*. Haugen's well known list of types or kinds of language planning (1966) includes norm selection, codification, elaboration, and implementation. The crucial difference between Haugen and Neustupny is easily reconciled since the one type of planning each uniquely includes might be regarded merely as an iterative procedure from the point of view of the other.

Table 1

Problem/Process Correspondences in
Language Planning
(per Neustupny 1970)

	1	2	3	4
Problem→	Selection	Stability	Expansion	Differentiation
Process →	Policy Decisions	Codification	Elaboration	Cultivation

Neustupny's emphasis on cultivation (which he considers to be a concern that American students of language planning have tended to overlook—in comparison to Czech and Japanese students) might be from Haugen's point of view merely the reiteration of his four basic types in connection with successive varieties of any given code. On the other hand, Haugen's emphasis on implementation (an important emphasis indeed from the point of view of students of planned change in other-than-language) might be for Neustupny merely the reiteration or modification of decisions with respect to selection, codification, elaboration, etc.

If we accept Haugen's slightly simpler fourfold subdivision of language planning—at least for the purpose of giving initial organization to our review— it is interesting to note the extent to which nationalist movements have encouraged efforts in each of these divisions with respect to the actual or hoped for vernaculars of the population whom they sought to mobilize. Even where no unifying vernacular has immediately been available, nationalist movements have commonly set out to either find or create one, "not only as a symbol but also as an agent in the diffusion of national sentiment among a wider segment of the population and in the growth of centralization" (Elsbree 1953, p. 121).[21]

Code Selection

The initial decision as to the "proper vernacular" for the population under consideration is often far more complicated than either the concurrent or the subsequent picture presented by the nationalist leaders to their followers. To begin with, the ethnic identity of the population itself is often sufficiently amorphic, sufficiently continuous rather than discontinuous, that the drawing of a linguistic line is every bit as judgmental as is the act of drawing the ethnic line itself. Although there are often many "talented and enthusiastic investigators" eager to "demonstrate the unity and solidarity of the national language in spite of the variegated diversity of dialects" (Jaszi 1929, pp. 263-264), they frequently differ with one another in their definition of the outerlimits of the nationality as well as in their preferences for the precise linguistic basis of its unification. Thus, some of the pioneers of the Slavic renaissance of the mid-nineteenth century dreamt of "uniting all Slavonic peoples in one great Slav nation which would be the most numerous and powerful in the world. Some saw the best road to this aim in an amalgamation of all Slavonic languages in a common tongue" (Kahn, 1950, p. 88).[22] Where a variety of contending broader and narrower modernizing-authenticity movements compete for control over the same hitherto unideologized masses (see e.g., Zarevand [1930] 1971) the link between language and nationalism cannot itself be closed until both limits of "the language" and of "the nationality" in question are themselves pragmatically determined. Little wonder then that "prodigious philological research (repeatedly) accompanied nationalist agitation" (Barnard 1965, p. 62).

However, even where the vernaculars and nationalities to be linked are essentially agreed upon the utility of these vernaculars for the purpose of nationalism cannot immediately be taken for granted. Such utility depends upon an accepted orthography, a reasonably uniform grammar, a sufficiently ample lexicon, a generally recognized phonology, not to mention the variety of "styles" needed for technical and nontechnical, serious and humorous, formal and intimate communication. None of these are "naturally" available to the "natural" vernaculars of immobilized peasants and artisans and must be created before such vernaculars can serve the unifying, authenticating, and activating purposes of nationalism or of other mass movements. Obviously, most of the vernaculars utilized by mass nationalist movements during the past two centuries required substantial planning in order to *make* them simultaneously the unifying, authenticating, and modernizing tools that they were expected to be. However, the view that the perfection of vernaculars might, in some way, be created, planned, or produced by mere men rather than be entirely *god-given* was also to some extent *anti*nationalist in its assumptions. This may account, in part, for the resistance which such planning has encountered to this very day. It strikes some as presumptuous and others as impossible, as presumptuous and as impossible as it would be to artificially create the breath of life. As a result, language planning normally *merely* admits a resuscitating and invigorating role rather than any intention—let alone any attainment—along the lines of creation *de novo.*

Obviously, language planning had to be tried; for, not to do so would have meant to accept defeat on many even more crucial grounds. Not to standardize and enrich the vernacular would not only have meant that nationalist movements could not parsimoniously become mass movements (particularly so since most of them were so dependent on the inexpensively printed page and the itinerant lecturer for their more lasting and more massive impact), but it also would have meant that their vernaculars would forever remain in the intellectual and pragmatic shadows of others that had been fortunate enough to undergo slow but sure enrichment and standardization, both consciously and unconsciously, in prior generations. Obviously, neither of these alternatives has ever been acceptable to nationalist movements, no matter how much circumstances may have forced some to compromise with them.

When newly awakening English commercial and social elites began to throw off their dependence upon French and Latin, Roger Mulcaster (end of the sixteenth century) ventured a relativistic hypothesis: "I do not think that anie language, be it whatsoever, is better able to utter all arguments, either with more pith or greater planesse, than our *English* tung is, if the English utterer be as skillful in the matter, which he is to utter, as the foren utterer is . . . It is our accident which restrains our tung and not the tung itself, which will strain with the strongest and stretch to the furthest, for either government if we were conquerers, or for cunning if we were treasurers, not anie whit behind either the subtile Greeke for couching close, or the statelie Latin for spreding fair. Our tung is capable, if our people would be painful" (cited in Whiteley, 1969, p. 95). Two centuries later (1790) the great Leibnitz pointed to the unenviable condition of his mother tongue, full of foreign expressions and constructions when used by the educated, and used arguments quite similar to those of Mulcaster in rejecting the then common "assertion that the German language was unfitted to express higher thoughts" (Blackall 1959, p. 4). However, unlike Mulcaster (but in accord with modern nationalist thought) he also urged that *an institution be established* so that the necessary terms and forms be made readily available and in *accord with the spirit of the language.* "Sein besonderer Zweck aber und das Vornehmen (order Objekt) dieser Anstalt wäre auf die Teutsche Sprach zu richten, wie nehmlichen solche zu verbessern, auszuzieren und zu untersuchen" (Blackall 1959, p. 6).

At that time the French Academy was already 160 years old (Robertson 1910) and French was already firmly established as the only "fully civilized" vernacular of Europe. "Ennobling the language, defining the usage of spoken and written language, classifying its vocabulary, and giving uniformity to French phonetic and written forms . . . [were] regarded . . . as a state and political concern" (Vossler 1932, p. 126). No wonder then that several German writers considered their mother tongue to be in a sad state, and were eager to point out that "it is mere prejudice which leads us to consider languages that have been neglected or that are unknown to ourselves, as incapable of being brought to a higher perfection" (Friedrich Schlegel, approximately 1812; cited by Hayes 1937, p. 54). This point has required constant reiteration from that day to this, because although new protoelites were often willing and eager to use, and even to promote the vernacular for guidance of the masses, they and older elites were often far from enthusiastic in their own utilization of the vernacular, particularly for a number of their own higher intellectual and cultural purposes. At stake in the upper reaches of society were those long-established diglossia patterns which in themselves simultaneously defined culture as well as its custodians. In the absence of mass nationalist movements that could bring in their wake a revolutionary redefinition of the basis of sociocultural integration, traditional diglossias continued in full sway, particularly in the upper reaches of society. At the same time that Janssaeus boasted that "the French language has succeeded . . . the Latin and the Greek languages . . . It has become so general that it is spoken today throughout almost the whole of Europe, and those who frequent society feel a kind of shame if they do not know it" (in his *La Véritable Clef de langue française,* 1697; cited by Brunot 1927, vol. V, p. 137), others had to plead for the creation of a "literature en françcois" (Claude de Seyssel, historian to Louis XII; cited by Kohn 1944, p. 130) and for instruction in French within France itself.[23, 24]

If such was the fate of the vernacular in the older state nations in which formerly diverse ethnic groups has already been fairly well integrated along sociocultural and political-operational lines, then the grip of traditional diglossia upon the intellectual life of the submerged nationalities on which modern mass nationalist movements focussed their attention was stronger yet. In the latter context the earlier trials and tribulations of languages now great but once also without honor among their own native elites are pointed to as an indication of how the worm can turn. It is now a Pilipino advocate who reminds us, via appropriate quotations, that "Even English was barren of scientific terms as late as the 16th century . . . As late as 1532 Olivetan speaks of the French language as a barbarous jargon compared with Greek and Hebrew . . . Queen Elizabeth talked Latin with foreign ambassadors; Cromwell had Milton for his Latin secretary" (Rojo 1937, pp. 51-52) and that "Tagalog or any other dialect can be expanded and modernized for scientific purposes within a generation or two, or sooner, given the proper determination and provided the additions are made on the advice of linguistic specialists" (Rojo 1937, p. 55). As had been true in early periods so also in the cases of the latecomers: advocacy, use of development of the vernacular was regarded as (and was intended to be) rejective of traditionally ascribed statuses, of traditionally limited access to the languages of power and prestige, and of traditionally limited access to the roles of power and prestige. In many cases the rejected superposed languages were those of recognizably foreign conquerors and colonizers. However, in many instances the subjugation that was rejected had occurred in centuries past and had appeared to have become perfectly indigenized. When the Fennomen of 1963 raised the battle cry "we must win Helsinki for the Finnish language" (Wuorinen 1931, p. 130) and when Ziya Gökalp demanded that "religious worship should be conducted in the language of the people, that is in Turkish instead of in Arabic. . . the whole liturgy with the exception of the fixed Qur'an recitation should be recited in the national tongue. . . the Qur'an should be taught in schools in the Turkish translation" (Heyd 1950, pp. 102-103) the sociocultural implications were easily as extreme (if not more so) as when Czechs rejected German; Slovaks, Hungarian; or Ukrainians, Russian. In each case, however, the language decision was inevitably linked to further language planning, precisely because nationalism was not only a movement of the masses and for the masses but, rather, also a movement to replace one elite with another, one sociocultural philosophy with another and one political-operational system with another. These replacements often required far more (and more prolonged) language planning than did the more obvious phase of nationalist massification alone.[25] Thus, we may well look to instances of traditional traditionalized diglossia today (instances in which an intrenched elite utilizes a language of wider communication that does not really reach through to the masses) when we attempt to predict the settings from which future nationalistically guided pressures for language planning may come.[26]

Codification

Subsequent to language selection the variety of language planning tasks still to be faced are, nevertheless, legion. Even within the selected language the variety of spoken variants is likely to be great, whether because of the number of regional and historical variants, like those which complicated the growth of the nationalist movement in Greece,[27] or because of the number of social class variants, like those which complicated the nationalist movement in Hungary.[28] Even within the same social class a vernacular which serves primarily as a lingua franca for multitudes who know it only as a second language reveals irregularities which create bars to efficient communication.[29] Furthermore, where a written variety exists, the inevitable gap between the written and the spoken language must be coped with, else it may grow to such proportions that literacy is difficult to acquire even for native speakers.[30] All in all, an initial major task of nationalist inspired language planning is "that of linguistic organization, popularization and standardization" (Kahn 1950, p. 243).[31] Each of these tasks is potentially fraught with great national danger or great national gain. Before language is highly ideologized minor differences are easily introduced which can later have major consequences (see, e.g., Omar 1971). "The Austrians got the Slovaks in the 1840's to standardize their spelling of a dialect which was remote from that of the Czechs and, therefore, made for two separate languages" (Deutsch 1964b, pp. 52-3). Similarly, initially minor similarities can later be put to great service. Thus, M. A. Castren, the first major grammarian of Finnish to appear during the period of early nineteenth century anti-Swedish-pro-Finnish nationalism wrote: "I have decided to prove to the people of Finland that we are not a . . . nation isolated from the world and world history, but that we are related to at least one-seventh of the people of the globe. If the cause of this nation in thereby served, all will be well . . . Grammars are not objective, but without them I cannot attain my goal" (Wuorinen 1931, p. 99).

Elaboration

So much for codification. But lexical expansion too is conscientiously pursued as a nationalist task of potentially monumental consequences. The users of developing languages are particularly aware of their lexical shortcomings. Leibnitz considered German "rich in words denoting real objects, especially in words connected with occupations like mining, hunting and seafaring, but . . . lacking vocabulary to express those things not experienced by the senses, so that the scholar has been driven to Latin to describe such matters" (cited by Blackall 1959, p. 5).[32] The developing language is always relatively impoverished when it comes to the more abstract subtleties of imported or recently innovated higher learning and fashionable society. One sign of the development of a language is its growth in exactly these respects. "In his 'Neology,' published in 1801, [Sébastien] Mercier mentions over two thousand words unknown in the age of Louis XIV . . . 'New words and expressions assailed the language in such numbers that newspapers and periodicals of that time could have been understood by Louis XIV only by means of a translation' " (Rocker 1937, p. 291). However, modern nationalism is concerned not only with increasing the number of such new terms (including, of course, the fields of modern technology) but also with delimiting the source (and, therefore the model) of their formulation, since "the preservation of the language and the enthusiasm for serving it by reinvigorating its life through new styles and idioms" are not in themselves sufficient. These tasks must be accomplished in a manner that also provides "proof that a nation[ality] has personality and self-respect." (Ahmad 1960, p. 103).

Thus, nationalist movements must not only fashion an apparently unified, authenticated, and modern-problem-oriented nationality out of the countless manifest interaction networks engaged in daily ethnic routines and beliefs, but they must fashion an equally apparently unified, authenticated, and modern-problem-oriented language out of the manifest diversity of phonological, lexical, grammatical, and semantic systems inherited from prenationalist speech networks. Nationalisms consciously undertake to produce self-consciously modern, authentic, and unifying standard languages, which are to be consciously employed and conscientiously espoused, where previously there existed only regional and social varieties, unconsciously employed and unemotionally abandoned. Language planning is, therefore, a definite service to and by-product of the nationalist cause, and like that cause it may retire to the sidelines — at least temporarily, when its major goals *seem* to have been attained or are no longer at issue.

The dependence of nationalist-inspired language planning on elitist leadership is apparent at every step. Whether it be at the point of initial selection,[33] subsequent codification and elaboration [34] or final implementation,[35] the major forces at work seem to have been (and to be) elitist. They alternately *appealed* to each other to overtly take a hand at language planning[36] and *disguised* their efforts as being merely those of organizers of natural riches.[37] In all cases, however, as with most other nationalist activity, elites and their needs were instrumental in *bringing about* (rediscovering, disinterring, reassembling) the "natural" uniqueness, and the unified pure language which nationalist theory and nationalist practice simultaneously assumed and required. Although we cannot today decisively pinpoint the factors responsible for either language planning successes or failures (see, however, Rubin and Jernudd 1971), it is quite clear that new protoelites also need(ed) language planning for the explicit purposes of elitist role behavior and power aspirations, and that the language planning in which they engaged was as much a *necessity* in the realization of their more purely instrumental goals, as it was a captive of *their unity and authenticity ideology.* If the one need provided the lion's share of the urgency, the other provided the lion's share of the direction.

NATIONALIST PRESSURES ON LANGUAGE PLANNING

Language planning implies directed change toward a desired goal. The goal constrains and explains the activities engaged in on its behalf. Nationalist ideologies frequently provide such constraints and rationales for language planning. In so doing they provide a definition of the good or desirable language which language planning intends to bring into being, or, at least, to further and to strengthen. If we consider the linguistic self-perceptions and goal perceptions of various nationalist movements, it is not difficult to discern the differences separating them from linguistic self-perceptions of prenationalist (or post-nationalist) speech communities. Like all self-perceptions nationalist language planning too tends to be, in part, a reflection of rationalizations after the fact and, in part, an indirect definition of a more desirable state of affairs yet to be attained in the future.

Language as an Active Agent

A major parameter of prenationalist (and postnationalist) evaluation of vernaculars is undoubtedly the esthetic. In 1599 Daniel's fond dream for the English language, namely that it might spread throughout the world, was justified merely on the basis of its supposed delicate beauty ("What worlds in th'yet unformed Occident/May come refind with th'accents that are ours?" cited by Whiteley 1969, p. 95).

Subsequently

"Ronsard and the 'Plèîde" ... discovered in Italy the 'canons' of ancient beauty ... [and] viewed the French language only as a musical instrument to which new strings must be added if the new songs are to conform to the aesthetic principles of Greek and Roman beauty.

Tous ceux qui ces vers liront
S'ils ne sont Grecs et Romains,
Au lieu d'un livre ils n'auront
Qu'un pesant faix dans les mains.

... All were of the opinion that beauty and thought are subject to universal laws, and for this reason never hesitated to seek their inspiration beyond national frontiers" (Delaise 1927, pp. 188-190).

Coupled with this view, however, is frequently another which is purportedly related to it, namely correspondence to *natural* beauty, to the natural order of thought, to the natural state of events, objects, or ideas. Thus Bonald praised French for being "a language which is simple without baseness, noble without bombast, harmonious without fatigue, precise without obscurity, elegant without affectation, metaphorical without conscious effort; a language which is the veritable expression of a perfected nature" (written between 1796 and 1819, published 1864, p. 329). His explanation for the widespread use of French was that it was "the most perfect of modern languages and perhaps of all languages, . . . it follows most closely the natural order of things and their relationships, the objects of our thoughts, and it is the most faithful expression of the truest ideas" (p. 393).[38] This prenationalist view remained the dominant lay linguistic self-perception in France almost to this very day. When the French Academy, "with all its authority and force . . . explains to the French people . . . how superior the French language is to any other" it does so in terms of "the tradition that the French language is the clearest, most precise language in the world [and, therefore] the natural language of international diplomacy" (Hayes 1930, pp. 9 and 207). Obviously this view was not only initially a rationalization after the fact but it was also a reflection of France's long continental primacy as a state-nation.

"The beauty of modern French, as well as the attraction it exerts on cultivated minds is due to its well-balanced blend of northern and southern elements. French of our day is the shrine in which the treasured remains of earlier centuries are still preserved. In it the sunshine of the south pierces with its warm rays the severity of northern earnestness. No other European language can boast of an equally happy composition" (Dominian 1917, p. 11).

This view contains no clearly nationalist flavor or fervor, as is the case with many languages of more recent nationality-states and of nationalities still seeking cultural or political security. There is no indication that some typically or uniquely French behavior is fostered or facilitated by means of the French language. French is viewed as a gift to all of mankind, as an instrument of pure reason and as a creation of sublime and natural beauty, rather than as something parochially and primarily French. Not to use good French words in France, even given the antifranglais feeling of recent years, is merely to be gross and to show one's lack of good taste. Not to do so today in French Canada, however, is to reveal feelings of national inferiority (Bégouin 1970).

In the case of German we can see both of these views in historical contrast. Schottelius's apologia for German (1663; 1466 pages plus introduction and index) is entitled (in part) "Ausführliche arbeit von der teutschen haubt sprache worin enthalten gemelter dieser haubt sprache uhrankunft/uhraltertuhm/ reinlichkeit/eigenschaft/vermögen/invergleichlichkeit/grundrichtigkeit . . . ". Lest it appear that ethnic specificity is being stressed above, it should be pointed out that the author's intention was merely to claim for German the same desiderata as applied to the very few other "haubt sprache" of the world (in whose company he dearly wanted German to be included). This becomes clearer, a century later, from Klopstock's "Die deutsche Gelehrtenrepublik" (1774) in

which he still characterizes German as "eine reichhaltige, vollblühende, frucht-
schwere, tönende, gemesne, freye, bildsame, männliche, edel und vortrefliche
Sprache." However, the relative lack of recognition of German also leads him to
conclude on a note of invidious comparison with other languages, on the ground
that German "Kaum die griechische und Keine der andern Europäersprachen
bieten darf" (p. 109; cited by Blackall 1959, p. 326).

The need to justify German vis-à-vis French, and finally, the need to claim
German superiority and particularity (i.e., "Germanness") vis-à-vis French,
becomes increasingly apparent as German nationalism continues to gather
momentum. In 1794 Klopstock defends "unsere männliche Sprache" against
objections to its guttural sound. "Töne, welche zu tief aus dem Halse
heraufkommen, verrathen im [i.e., the Frenchman] Barbarey; und Tone, die
man mit Selbstgefallen in die Nase hinauftreibt, überfeine Kultur" (in his *Gram-
matische Gesprache;* cited by Blackall 1959, p. 327). By this time the view had
already been expressed that German was superior to French (and to English and
Italian as well) "because it does not proceed from the mingling of the language
of several peoples" (Gottsched; cited by Blackall 1959, p. 119). It was therefore
only a minor advance along the same front for Fichte to claim that the Germans
were "honest, serious, sober and speak a language which is shaped to express the
truth" (cited by Reiss 1955, p. 105).[39] Within a century this view had
developed further to claim that the "Nordics' superiority of physique fitted
them to be vehicles of the superior language" (Childe 1926, pp. 211-212).
Obviously within the framework of nationalism the vernacular not only makes its
speakers authentic in thought and action, but it itself strains toward the
authenticity which is inherent in it. The vernacular "comes to be personified.
The language, it is said, accepts or rejects foreign words" (Doob 1964, p. 231).

The typically prenationalist and nationalist views of what was laudable about
particular vernaculars are nicely contrasted if we compare Ribinyi's observations
concerning Hungarian with Korais' concerning Greek. Writing in Latin, Ribinyi,
a teacher at the Lutheran school at Sopron, admitted in 1751 that "Italian is
pleasant, French beautiful, German earnest; but all these qualities are so united
in Magyar that it is difficult to say wherein its superiority consists" (in his *Oratio
de Cultura Linguae Hungaricae* 1751; cited by Marczali 1910, p. 236).
However, for the nationalist spokesman, a century later, Greek was not merely
endowed with "exceptional charm," it not merely influenced its speakers to
become "more eloquent and wise" but it influenced them to pursue political and
cultural freedom. "It is a rare thing for one to submit to. . . .slavery if one has
once managed to drink to the full the charm of the Hellenic language" (cited by
Sherrard 1959, p. 183). In the annals of nationalism the vernacular is not
merely unanalyzably lovely. It is quite specifically powerful. Thus, with respect
to Swahili "Let us use it as a right, clerks and farmers, and though you may not

believe it, English will move out. We don't want foreign languages. We feel they are a reproach. Swahili is a good language, our original language" (translated from Swahili by Whiteley 1969, p. 161). With respect to Arabic it is necessary to "comprehend its superior qualities over other languages and the special endowments which enabled it to achieve complete mastery over . . . . vast regions" and it is desirable "to discover the secret of this vitality and to lay our hands on the unique powers which our language represent *in order to utilize these powers in organizing our present and building our future*" (Costi Zurayq, "Al-Wayi al Qawmi" [Nationality Consciousness], Beirut 1938, p. 38; cited by Nuseibeh 1956, p. 70). Such unique vitality is more than just a metaphor of hyperbolic literati or an unreasoned stereotype of demagogic politicians. It is a view which frequently comes to be legitimized by whatever are the most responsible sources of legitimization available to a speech community. Given the total constellation of circumstances outlined above, few indeed will hesitate to remind all who will listen that "the Anglo-Saxon language is the simplest, the most perfectly and simply symbolic that the world has ever seen; and that by means of it the Anglo-Saxon saves his vitality for conquest instead of wasting it under the Juggernaut of a cumbersome mechanism for conveyance of thought" (McGee 1895, p. 280).

Nationalist language planning aims not at esthetics or euphonics (or parsimony or clarity) per se but at a definite cluster of overt, behavioral goals. Its image of language is an overt behavioral one as well. Nationalism intends that language use and language planning both should encourage and facilitate behaviors of broader unity, deeper authenticity, and various modern implementations of sociocultural and political-organizational integration. Nationalisms hold that it is part of the very nature of their vernaculars to advance their respective causes. It is this active, overt spirit of the language that language planning must, somehow, both observe and enhance. As ethnic fidelity alone is merely an incidental and superficial consideration vis-à-vis language in pre-nationalist periods—although it is an intermittently present consideration in such periods as well—so estheticism or parsimony alone are considered unworthy of socialized man in the age of nationalism. Beauty is only skin deep. It is what is below the surface that really counts and with respect to which language must be used and shaped.

Fostering Unity and Authenticity via Differentiation from Undesirable External Linguistic Influences

Nationalist language planning reveals a pervasive abhorrence of foreign influences. Whether this is viewed as merely an expression of a "natural" abhorrence on the part of the language itself or whether it is acknowledged as a human evaluation aimed at human goals, it is encountered again and again in the directive pronouncements which serve as guides to official and unofficial guardians of the vernacular. Of course, an antipathy toward foreign elements and a preference for indigenous ones is certainly also found in prenationalist sources as well. Leibnitz, e.g., expressed this view ("Besser ist ein original von einem teutschen als eine copey von einem Franzosen seyn" [Blackall 1959, p. 4]) but with little if any ideological or behavioral follow-up for this preference. However, such is no longer the case for those German writers who subsequently warned against foreign borrowings on the grounds that they ultimately denied a people its original and autochthonous character. Thus Fichte goes significantly beyond Leibnitz when he argues that "Original, primitive languages are superior to composite, derived languages. German is an original language, its speech must be cleansed of foreign accretions and borrowings, since the purer the language, the more natural it is and the easier it becomes for the nation to realize itself and to increase its freedom" (Kedourie 1961, pp. 66-67).

Similarly, Bentham's views concerning English authenticity were merely based upon general principles of learning and understanding.[40] Noah Webster, however, in arguing for the development of an authentically American spelling of English a decade after the American Revolution admitted that "a capital advantage would be that it would make a difference between the English orthography and the American . . . . I am confident that such an event is an object of vast political consequence . . . A national language is a bond of national union" (cited by Mencken [1919] 1939, p. 10). "As an independent nation," he wrote, "our honor requires us to have a system of our own, in language as well as in Government. Great Britain, whose children we are, and whose language we speak, should no longer be our standard; for the taste of her writers is already corrupted and her language on the decline" (cited by Bram 1955, p. 56). Irish nationalists paraded the purity of Irish as further evidence of the wickedness of English. "Of 100,000 English words not more than 33 percent are pure English or Teutonic, the rest being of classical or otherwise foreign origin; whilst of 100,000 Irish words, it is certain that 80 percent would prove to be pure Celtic" (Flannery 1896, p. 97). Similarly focused "antiforeign" emphases have characterized nationalist language planning of Finnish vis-à-vis Swedish (Wuorinen 1931, 1954), of Estonian vis-à-vis Finnish (Kurman 1968), of Turkish vis-à-vis Persian and Arabic (Heyd 1950), of Urdu vis-à-vis Sanskrit, and of Hindi vis-à-vis Persian (Chatterji 1943), etc., etc. Of course, parallel to cleansing the vernaculars of foreignisms in general (but of foreignisms derived from certain languages in particular), there goes the process of enriching these vernaculars from one's own most authentic sources. This process serves the same purposes of external separation and internal consolidation as does the cleansing process which it accompanies. " . . . With the ugly development of Hindu-Muslim communalism, High Hindi and Urdu became symbols of this conflict. Each is going its own way, intense Persianization [of Urdu] on the one hand and almost equally intense Sanscritization [of High Hindi] on the other, so that in their more elegant forms one would be unintelligible to the speakers of the other" (Chatterji 1943, p. 19).[41] While St. Stefan of Perm [fourteenth century] could consciously choose to utilize not that form of Komi which was considered " 'purest' or 'best' but one that [was] . . . spreading rapidly by the process of migration and urbanization" (Ferguson 1968, p. 258), a modern nationalist language planner would also have found that the latter form was also the more authentic. At the very least nationalist language planning claims to press in the same direction as that which represents the genius of the language itself. "The genius or language spirit of a nation is no mythological being; [rather] it is a force, a talent, a temperament. It is . . . the nature of genius to . . . be true and genuine, to remain true to itself . . . The true life of a national language is centripetal and inward, not centrifugal" (Vossler 1932, pp. 138-139). However, in crisis situations the genius of the language must not merely be followed but actively protected and abetted by language planning. "Es verrät eine geringe Meinung von der Muttersprache, wenn man ihr nicht die Kraft zutrut, mut eigenem Mittein alles zu sagen . . . Und die heiligsten Rechte hat die Sprache in ihrer Eigenschaft als besondere nationale Sprache. Eine besonders schwere Sunde ist es darum, wenn man das echte, eigene Sprachgut mit fremden Wörtern durchsetzt" (Koppelman 1956, 97-99).

A view such as the latter is common enough in nationalistically inspired language planning. However, it is often a correlate of a difficult struggle, not only against newly discovered linguistic "strangers," but also against those indigenous populations that have been particularly exposed to various "foreign influences" (foreign names, foreign foods, foreign dress, foreign beliefs, and even "such foreign and fantastic field sports as lawn tennis, polo, croquet, cricket and the like" [Beckett, p. 417]). Some of the linguistic by-products of such exposure may have become so completely indigenized as not to be foreign marked in the eyes of most speakers and, indeed, as not to have indigenous synonyms. The protection of purity requires an attack against habits of speaking and against specified speech networks. It is not always a popular or a simple pursuit.

Fostering Unity and Authenticity via Differentiation
from Internal Linguistic Alternatives

For nationalism, the enemy is not only without the gate; he has already, to some extent, crept inside as well and must now be expelled. In large measure, the enemy within is simply the same as the enemy without. Those varieties of the vernacular that have been most influenced by foreign models are, obviously, less preferred that those that have escaped such influences.[42] However, another enemy exists, namely the multiplicity of vernacular varieties per se, each pulling toward a different norm of pronunciation and spelling and, on occasion, of vocabulary and grammar as well. "Citizens," cried Bertrand Barère, a leading Jacobin, in 1794, "the language of a free people ought to be one and the same for all" (cited by Hayes 1931, p. 63). Internal diversity of usage is not only inefficient and potentially dangerous (for it fosters and protects behavioral and ideological disunity more generally), but it also invites invidious comparisons with more favored and better established rivals. Thus, "it was through the initiative of these [nationalist] congresses that the compilation of a great dictionary was undertaken in order to establish once and for all a standard for the Netherlandish language" (Clough 1930, p. 79).

However, the selection or determination of a standard from among many available and competing varieties presupposes some model of the desirable. For nationalism ultimate desirability is coextensive with greater authenticity, even while the goals of unity and modern problem solving are being pursued. As for authenticity, where is it to be found? In the annals of nationalism, again and again, it is to be found in the past or in those regions or populations that have been least exposed to the contaminating influences of modern foreign forces (and, therefore, in those that remained most faithful to the purity of the past).

Fichte's view, that it was "incumbent on a nation[ality] worthy of the name to revive, develop and extend what is taken to be its original speech, even though it might be found only in remote villages, or had not been used for centuries, even though its resources are inadequate and its literature poor – for only such an original language will allow a nation to realize itself and attain freedom" (Kedourie 1961, p. 67), was widely shared and extremely influential among nationalist movements. A particularly frequent directive source of nationalist language planning, therefore, was the image of the noble and uncontaminated peasant who kept his language pure and intact, precisely as it had been in the golden past. It was the language of the inaccessible peasant (or of some other but equally sheltered population) that provided the linguistic *model* (the basic langue) upon which the elaboration, codification, and cultivation of the modern standard vernacular was to be performed and by which these processes were to be guided. In Ireland, De Valera, whose Irish was originally marginal, was urged by Pearse "to do as Pearse himself had done, to seek out the people of the West [i.e., those furthest from English influences in particular and from modern, urban influences in general] as the fountainhead of Gaelic Ireland" (Bromage 1956, p. 30)."[43] In Finland, the "unspoiled peasant" not only "came to be considered as the embodiment of 'national' traits and characteristics" but, even more strikingly, the model for "vocabulary and idiom for the upbuilding of the new and 'purer' national language" (Wuorinen 1950, p. 47). In Estonia, the great linguistic reformer "Aavik acknowledged a preference for 'those linguistic forms in which the national characteristics of the language were best realized"

(Kurman 1968, p. 58) and, therefore, rural and historical forms rather than literary and more modern ones.

In the Slavic world this tendency to emphasize the rural and the distant past was particularly strong, because the recent urban past was so overwhelmingly colored by foreign influences. From the first, when "Herder insisted on the rights of nationalities. . . at a time when the Bohemians, Rumanians, Croatians and others had hardly any consciousness themselves of their nationality. . . [and] at a time when their languages were no more than vernaculars spoken by illiterate peasants and deemed to be without future or dignity" (Kohn 1944, p. 432) the richness of peasant speech has continued to be glorified. Thus, when Ljudevit Gaj sought to produce a common written language for the new southern Slav ideology of Illyrism "he did not propose Croatian, his own language and that of the most numerous, historically most significant of the Austro-Slav peoples, as the basis of 'Illyrian' but favored the primitive southern Dalmatian 'Schto'" (Kahn 1950, p. 246).[44]

In the Islamic world the quest for purity and authenticity led Gökalp to prefer the Turkish "used by the women, who had more than others preserved its native harmony and sweetness" (Heyd 1950, p. 116). In the Arabic world, Lutfi, who "did not believe. . . that the spoken language should be adopted as a medium for literature," nevertheless believed that "languages lose their vitality when no longer rooted in the daily life of the people" (Ahmad 1960, p. 104) and, therefore, urged that the classical language be simplified and vitalized in the direction of common speech which alone would be "the natural source of its growth (p. 104)."[45] Thus, all in all, the quest for internal authenticity led repeatedly to the common folk, and, among them, to those who were assumed to have been in the most favored position to *maintain* the vernacular as it had been in the past, before foreign influences, foreign domination, foreign fads, and foreign models had begun to spoil the authentic and authenticating linguistic heritage bequeathed by generations of ancestors.[46] In its language planning theory, as in other matters, nationalism pursues modernization by beginning with the authenticity of long ago; it seeks the inspiration or drive required to meet urban needs by first returning to the preurban (if not the antiurban) heritage. The return to origins, to purity, in language, is part of a more general yearning for Gemeinschaft, part of a hope or pretense that in the simplicity of Gemeinschaft may be found the solutions to the complex problems of Gesellschaft. The long ago is a desirable point of departure for several reasons. It is relatable to religious[47] and temporal glories. ("Steket also in Teutschen Altertum und sonderlich . . .der Ursprung . . .des uralten Gottesdienstes, der Sitten und Rechte des Adels," Leibnitz, as cited by Blackall 1959, p. 460). It is uncontaminated by the currently stigmatized anti-models. Finally for the man in the street, any claims made for it are less confirmable and therefore, as a langue model, it is infinitely more manipulable than those closer at hand.

Several basically conflicted tasks are obviously on the agenda of nationalist inspired language planning vis-à-vis the internal linguistic scene. To begin with there is the same revolutionary (or antiestablishment) turning of the tables, as is evident in connection with the two previously discussed types of decision making: native language rather than foreign language and vernacular of the people rather than classical of the old elite. The foreign masters and the subservient old elites both derided the language of the rural population as uncouth, impoverished, and lawless. "It was looked down upon as a vulgar dialect not deserving the distinction of being called a language. For the most part only the lower classes in the . . . provinces spoke it and their accents varied from village to village" (Clough 1930, p. 56). However, it was (and is) precisely such a variety that nationalist ideology most commonly purports to select (on the basis of its avowedly greater purity, honesty, dignity and authenticity) as a reflection and as a part of the national soul. However, unlike most modern linguistic views which also consider the spoken language as "the only linguistic reality," nationalist language planning proceeds to utilize the preferred spoken variety in fashioning and deriving the basic language model for a standard written language. This then is another conflicted task for modern nationalist language planning. The spoken language (in all of its regional and situational variability) is proclaimed as model but the standard written language (for industry, education and government) is definitely a major goal.

All of these internally contradictory tendencies of nationalist language planning have elicited their share of derision among those who can afford to be aloof. The pursuit of the "genuinely authentic" has been characterized as "ein immer wiederkehrendes Irrtum des Nationalismus, und speziell des kulturellen Nationalismus . . . Nichts ist unnatürlicher als das bewusste Streben natürlich zu sein" (Koppelman 1956, p. 102). The imposition of writing norms before the evolution of a written tradition was viewed as a reversal of the natural order of things. "English poets . . . invested their language with eloquence before orthographic or grammatical standardization took place. In Swahili the reverse occurred, the standardization being effected on a non-literary dialect" (Whiteley 1969, p. 95). The dislocating impact of manufactured and standardized authenticity upon any remaining truly authentic populations has been pointed to. "Only those members of the folk society who repudiate their own origin are admitted . . . In this way the [newly] dominated group detaches people from their original groups and at the same time rejects them from itself" (Ponsionen, 1962, p. 105). However, as with all contradictions seemingly implicit in systems or between ideology and reality, the contradictions seemingly implicit in nationalist language planning are such only when viewed from without. From within they are viewed as an inevitable dialectic that serves merely to test the ingenuity, the strength, and the faith of the faithful.

PLANNING FOR MODERNITY WITH AUTHENTICITY

Nationalist language planning must face two extreme positions in its attempts to reconcile modernization and authenticity. At one extreme is the view that such a reconciliation is *impossible;* at the other, that it is *unnecessary.* One camp holds that the national language *cannot* (or should not) be employed for modern purposes. "A quiver of steel arrows, a cable with strong coils, a trumpet of brass crashing through the air with two or three sharp notes, such is Hebrew. A language of this kind is not adapted to the expression of scientific results" (Renan 1888; cited by Spiegel 1930, p. 4). The other camp holds that the delays and the trials of nationalist language planning (which optimally aims at expressing everything modern via indigenous roots) are simply so much *wasted time and effort.* "I would personally like to encourage Hindustani to adapt and assimilate many words from English. . . This is necessary, as we lack modern terms, and it is better to have well-known words rather than to evolve new and difficult words from Sanskrit or Persian or Arabic. Purists object to the use of foreign words, but I think they make a great mistake" (Nehru 1953, p. 456). But neither of the quoted opposing views is nationalist in inspiration. The one is traditionalist; the other modernist. The nationalist *tour de force* is to combine authenticity *and* modernism; indeed, to find that there is no clash between them at all.

Both opposition to and trust in language planning, as an example of conscious and organized intervention in language change and development, predate modern nationalism. However, both reveal a typical lack of central concern for the ethnic, the authentic, the indigenously unique spirit and form. When Robert Gruffydd (1697) has the language of Cambria address the "fond reader" with respect to the author's (that is his own) labors on her behalf she merely claims that "he hath endeavoured to bestow upon me the privilege of Art. . . without even a moment of time to adorn me as he would have wished" (W. R. Jones 1966, p. 4). Even Salisbury (1547?), recognizing that a Welsh capable of handling only rustic experiences was doubly exposed to the danger of extinction, made no ethnic claims and provided no ethnic guidelines for the conscious language modernization that he favored. ("Do you suppose that ye need no better words and no greater variety of expression to set out learning and to treat of philosophy and the arts than you have in common use in daily conversation, when you buy and sell and eat and drink. . . ? And take this as a warning from me — unless you bestir yourself to cherish and mend the language, before the present generation is no more it will be too late" (cited by W.R. Jones 1966, p. 43). On the other hand, early opponents of language planning are also predominantly nonnationalist in their views. A common view is that of de la Ramée, predating the Academy itself and anticipating a recurring reaction to professors who meddle with the language: "The people is the sovereign lord of its language and holds it as a fief free of all obligations, and is obligated to no lord for it. The school for this knowledge is not at all in the auditoriums of the

Hebrew, Latin, and Greek Professors in the University of Paris, as some of our fine etymologizers think; it is in the Louvre, in the Palais de Justice, in the Halles, on the Place de Greve, on the Place Maubert" (1572, cited by Guryceva, 1960, p. 30). Before he himself became a member thereof, Montesquieu admitted (1690) that he had "heard of a kind of tribunal called the French Academy. There is none in the world less respected; for no sooner has it decided than the people annul its decrees and impose laws which *it* is obliged to follow. Some time ago, to fix its authority, it gave a code of its judgements. That child of so many fathers was almost old when it was born" (cited by Robertson 1910, p. 209). A little over half a century later Samuel Johnson was similarly sarcastic, but again without a trace of the nationalist concern for authenticity. "Academies have been instituted, to guard the avenues of their languages, to retain fugitives and repulse invaders; but their vigilance and activity have hitherto been vain: sounds are too volatile and subtile for legal restraints; to enchain syllables and to lash the wind are equally undertaking of pride" (1755, p. v). Thus, we find here repeated vis-à-vis language planning the same predominantly different approaches that we previously encountered with respect to language per se. The prenationalist view (whether positive or negative) is primarily related to dimensions such as beauty, parsimony, efficiency, feasibility, rather than to an ethnically authentic approach to any or all of the foregoing. The latter is typically a nationalist argument, if not always a consistent nationalist approach.

Writing during the period of intense nationalist efforts in Southern, Eastern, and Central Europe, Mauthner observed that nationalist movements might be reluctant to admit foreign *words* into their vernacular but they were not at all reluctant to admit modern (and, therefore, to a large extent foreign) *concepts* into their goals and methods. "Before the intrusion of national consciousness, before the beginning of purist movements, the mass of the people borrowed freely from the treasure of foreign speech. Afterwards, such loans were avoided, but all the more numerously foreign concepts were brought into the language by translation. There are modern people of such touchy national feeling that they have driven purism to the utmost extreme (Neo-Greeks and Czechs). But they can isolate only their language, not their world concepts, their whole intellectual situation" (Mauthner 1906, p. 55; cited by Rocker 1937, p. 238).[48] Such is the view of an outsider. Seen from the inside the quest is for modernity ("Europeanization") *and* authenticity, simultaneously, for seeing the *world* but "through *our own eyes*," for going to the *world* but "*in our own way*." Nationalist language planning seeks and provides a rationale for the simultaneous attainment of what might seem (to uninvolved and unconcerned outsiders) to be disparate aims. In so doing, however, it is in the company of all modern ideologically guided social systems. Like them nationalist language planning is an organized self-fulfilling prophecy.

The favorite motto of Young Estonia (a group of early twentieth-century nationalist writers, intellectuals, and poets) was "Let us be Estonians, but let us also be Europeans" (Kurman 1968, p. 54). However, they were immediately faced with the "regrettable fact that they could not create a national culture of high [i.e., European] quality with the underdeveloped literary language that they had inherited" (Kurman, ibid.). Language planning was an obvious necessity since "the natural evolution of the language was, of course, unable to keep pace with the rapid progress of [European] ideas" (Raun 1965, p. 9). A group of language enthusiasts, Aavik being the foremost among them, set about "to remedy this shortcoming and guide Literary Estonian toward achieving parity with the 'cultural languages' of Europe" (Kurman, 1968, p. 54). They followed three principles: "aestheticism, phonological historicity and enlightened purism" (Kurman, ibid., p. 57), although maintaining, in general, that "all of the sources, programs and rules necessary for the further development of Estonian can be found in the language itself" (Kurman, ibid., p. 65). Thus, authenticity itself still permits and requires enlightened choice between contemporary alternatives, between contemporary and historical alternatives, between more aesthetic and less aesthetic alternatives, and between more indigenized and less indigenized alternatives. Nationalist language planning involves a constant interpretation and reinterpretation of authenticity such that sufficient flexibility is usually provided to accomplish what appears to be necessary and desirable. The vernacular, as a whole, is a means of symbolically indigenizing that which is materially and conceptually foreign and, as such, it can provide the means for indigenizing those aspects of itself which originate abroad.

Gökalp in particular, and the Turkish case in general, provide many illustrations of the rationales whereby nationalist-inspired language planning remains both authentic and enlightened. Gökalp's general position – in poetry and in other matters—was that it was "the duty of Turkish poets to turn their backs on. . . foreign influences. They should learn only 'technique' from the West, but poetical inspiration and aesthetic taste should come to them from heritage of Turkish people—proverbs, legends and folk songs" (Heyd 1950, p. 122). Thus, one opportunity for enlightening purism is to differentiate between that which is merely objective, physical, technical (and, therefore, ethnically inconsequential) and that which is subjective, spiritual and substantive (and, therefore, ethnically crucial). Furthermore, "every word familiar to the people is a national asset." Thus, "there is no sense in rejecting [Persian and Arabic] words. . . which have become part and parcel of the vernacular, merely because they have been borrowed from foreign languages. To change these words for old Turkish words or for new words formed from Turkish roots would be equivalent to banishing from the language living elements and introducing into it words more strange and unintelligible to the common people" (Heyd 1950, pp. 116-117). The usage of the common people, therefore, on behalf of whose authenticity nationalism arises, also serves as a possible court of appeal when purism threatens to become nonfunctional.[49]

Gökalp summed up his goals "in the matter of linguistic reform in the triple formula: modernization and Europeanization of the language in respect of scientific terms, and Turkification in respect of all other words and of grammar, syntax and orthography" (Heyd 1950, p. 119). Obviously the indigenous heartland (ordinary words, syntax, and orthography) are to remain untouched. To the extent that lexical borrowings are needed for technical nomenclature, a preferred nonindigenous source is indicated. However, the realm of concepts is entirely unrestrained. There, the modern, the European may reign supreme without harming the authentic core.[50] Further, the definition of "scientific terms" is also left open so that future interpretation and amplification of this realm remains possible. Indeed, the very establishment of a differentiation between the heartland and the periphery permits further differentiations and interpretations all of which claim to leave the heartland intact. Thus, during the less puristic days of Ataturk "an ingenious cover and stimulant for linguistic adaptation was found in the theory of the Sun Language which, bolstering national pride, eased the pains of making Turkish a more useful modern instrument. Turkish, according to this theory. . . [was] the mother of all existing tongues and 'therefore any foreign term may be' re-adopted 'provided it be given a Turkish assonance.' Alien loan words and international technical terms could thus be incorporated in the language without jarring anyone's sensibilities" (Emerson 1962, p. 138; citing, in part, Szabe 1952).

Escape Hatches

The enlightenment of nationalist purism in language planning thus proceeds along many well-trodden paths: the differentiation between ethnic core and nonethnic periphery, between technical and nontechnical, the differentiation between preferred and nonpreferred sources of borrowing, and, finally, the appeal to common usage among the masses. Thus, in India it is argued that "native Hindi elements failing we should not go to a foreign country for words which can be supplied by Sanskrit; names of new *objects* and *processes* may be European and international; for *ideas* we should have our own words" (Chatterji 1943, p. 29). Similarly in the Philippines it was foreseen that "The [National Language] Institute shall use as a source primarily the Philippine tongues and then, if necessary, the Spanish and English, adopting from these languages such terms as are already familiar to the Philippine tongues, having been [in] general use in the same. Whenever it shall be indispensable to form new words these shall be taken principally from the classical languages such as Greek and Latin, especially for scientific literary and technical use. Foreign words thus newly formed shall be assimilated to Philippine phonetics and orthography" (Commonwealth Act no. 184: An Act to Establish A National Language Institute and

Define its Powers and Duties, in Rojo 1937, p. 64)." Later when Pilipino was more firmly intrenched it was argued that "names are arbitrary words and [so are] expressions used to denote... things that can be felt and seen. In any language names are usually arbitrary... [therefore], whenever it [is] necessary to borrow a foreign word... this [should]...be taken in, assimilated, and then regarded as a single morpheme... [On the other hand] terms expressing complex scientific concepts and relationships, and such abstractions, are best conveyed by words having a consistent and rational [i.e., Austronesian] morphology" (del Rosario 1968, pp. 10-11). It is in this fashion that nationalist language planning is able to go about its task of incorporating and of digesting the foreign in an enlightened (i.e., in an acceptable) way. When successfully accomplished the vernacular is not only expanded and strengthened but it has also retained the appearance of authenticity and the role of authenticator of experience. It is then still felt that a dictionary of the modernized language "so far from being a mere list of unconnected words, reflects to a great extent the character of the people whose speech it is;...This is the kind of dictionary we want to see for our language and for our nation" (Flannery 1896, p. 100).

Obviously, nationalist directed language planning does not proceed along a set, unidirectional path that is universally accepted and admired by the target populations for whom it is intended. While it may be admired for "preserving the purity and cohesion of the language... deliver[ing it] from the fate that befell ancient Latin, which passed out of use and was replaced by off-shoot languages such as French and kindred tongues, [by] devising new terms which our language needs, to denote new things and new ideas" (Jabri 1953, pp. 20-1), it is also criticized for the initial artificiality and unfamilarity of its products. "Not too long ago, when patriotic students in Bandung urged the teaching of certain courses in Indonesian, only two professors were able to comply; then, at the end of a fortnight the students had to reverse their petition because they could not understand the lectures" (Bro 1954, p. 112). Even the planners themselves sometimes look askance at what they have done.

"Most of the Swahili contained in these books is correct grammatically, and may be defended on that ground. Grammatical accuracy, however, does not itself constitute a language, and it is perhaps this very exaggerated application of grammatical rules that has led us away from the real Swahili language and made us substitute something which is, at its best, lifeless though intelligible, at its worst, lifeless and unintelligible"(from the *Bulletin of the Inter-territorial Language Committee*; cited by Whiteley 1969, p. 87).

Nevertheless, given the new functions that the language must fulfill it must, perforce, acquire new units and structures. That being the case, it is a self-proclaimed and increasingly accepted responsibility of nationalist inspired language planning to guide the growth of the language and its involvement in new functions in such a way as "to rid the language of bad influences and guide it along the proper road" (Government of Tanzania report 1965, cited by Whiteley 1969, p. 104).

Nationalist-inspired language planning, like nationalist-inspired activity on all other fronts, escapes from the dilemma and inconsistencies that always obtain between theory and practice, between ideology and implementation. Its royal roads are many. At times one or the other will be stressed; at times all will remain temporarily becalmed tension systems, waiting to spring in the direction of their dominant orientations. Ultimately, it not only works out a functional compromise between the new and the old, the regional and the national, the rural and the urban, the peripheral and the central, the foreign and the indigenous, the efficient and the authentic, but it does much more. Just as the state-into-nationality process requires time and stability to create the unified and natural entity of which it is so proud, so nationalist language planning pushes forward slowly, inexorably, when more rapid roads to its targets are not open. With the passage of time, and with the control over media and institutions of society, it converts the new *into* the old, the regional *into* the national, the rural *into* the urban, the foreign *into* the indigenous, the peripheral *into* the central and the merely efficient *into* the authentic.

In the realm of language planning, nationalism "requires that new words be consciously created to refer to operationally defined referents discovered or created [or borrowed] in the process of specialization . . . [Language planning is possible when men can] de-reify words, treating them as symbols, not as things in themselves; as secular not as sacred. . . [It] is not only a functional necessity for diffracted [i.e., modern, urbanized] systems, but is made possible only by a concurrent transformation in attitudes toward language" (Riggs 1964, p. 141). However the foregoing applies equally well to modernization-inspired language planning of any kind, rather than particularly to its nationalist variety. The latter goes beyond the former in that it constantly keeps an eye on the mirror of unifying authenticity. Indeed, it *must* do so since among the many inborn contradictions of nationalism is yet another which claims that authenticity is spontaneous and unrehearsed. In unabashedly proceeding to produce the spontaneous, nationalism keeps before itself a substantive image (flexible and alterable though it may be) of that which makes its vernacular "richer, more limpid, warmer . . . abounding in metaphor, imagery, idiom, proverb," that which makes it then "truly unique," that which provides it with "the distinctive flavor of genius and authentic experience" (Talmon 1965, p. 105; citing the views of Herder): the spirit of the nationality whose guardian and reflection it is. Nationalism brings new words into contact with this spirit of the nationality. It creates them in accord with the model of this spirit. Nationalism views itself as the guardian of the spirit rather than its creator. In the beginning there is the spirit and all else naturally follows therefrom, even if it must be planned.

RECAPITULATION: EARLY TWENTIETH CENTURY EUROPEAN AND MORE RECENT SOUTHEAST ASIAN LANGUAGE PLANNING

In France

The classical example of language planning in the context of state-into-nationality processes is that of the French Academy. Founded in 1635, i.e., at a time well in advance of the major impact of industrialization and urbanization, the Academy nevertheless came after the political frontiers of France had long since approximated their current limits. However, complete sociocultural integration was still far from attained at the time, as witnessed by the fact that in 1644 the ladies of the Marseille(s) Society were unable to communicate with Mlle. de Scudéry in French, in 1660 Racine had to use Spanish and Italian to make himself understood in Uzès, and even as late as 1789 half of the population of the South did not understand French. The unparalleled literary creativity in French under the patronage of Louis XIV could aim, at most, at a maximal audience of 2,000,000 literates (out of a total estimated population of 20,000,000). However, in actuality, no more than 200,000 participated in the intellectual life of the country and many of these considered Italian, Spanish and Occitan far more fitting vehicles for cultured conversation, whereas for publications Latin too was a common rival. All in all, the French Academy assumed an unenviable task — and one rather consistently ridiculed throughout several centuries — when it presumed to codify French vocabulary, grammar, and spelling for the purpose of perfecting refined conversation and written usage.

Several aspects of the Academy's approach reveal its premodernization goals and views. Far from seeking to provide technical nomenclatures for industrial, commercial, and other applied pursuits the Academy steadfastly refused to be concerned with such "uncultured" and "unrefined" concerns. Instead of attempting to reach the masses with its products the Adademy studiously aimed its publication (at least for three centuries, if not longer) at those already learned in the French language. Finally, instead of appealing to anything essentially French in "spirit," in "genius," in "essence," or in "tradition" it defended its recommendations via appeals to such purportedly objective criteria as euphonia, clarity, and necessity (redundancy). More than 200 years after its founding, when the Academy's continued lack of concern for the technical vocabulary of modernization had come to be accompanied by attacks on *anglomanie* and the tendency to *angliciser,* the worst that was said about overly frequent English borrowings was that they were unnecessary rather than that they were un-French:

"On n'entend que des mots à déchirer le fer,
Le railway, le tunnel, le ballast, le fender,
Express, trucks, wagons; une bouche française
Semble broyer du verre ou mâcher de la braise . . .
Certes, de nos voisins, l'alliance m'enchante,
Mais leur langue, à vrai dire, est trop envahissante!
Faut-il pour cimenter un merveilleux accord
Changer l'arène en turf et le plaisir en sport,
Demander à des clubs l'aimable causerie,
Flétrir du nom de grooms nos valets d'écurie,
Traiter nos cavaliers de gentlemen-riders?
Je maudis ces auteurs dont le vocabulaire
Nous encombre de mots dont nous n'avons que faire."

/Viennet 1853/

In the nationality-into-state context the links between the authenticity component of nationalism and language planning, on one hand, and between the modernization-unification components of nationalism and language planning, on the other hand, are much more prominent and much more conscious. As a result, institutions and guidelines for language planning come into being very early in the mobilization process and remain in the foreground at least until authenticity, modernization, and unification seem reasonably assured. Here we are dealing with more highly pressured situations in which language planning is of top priority, not only because of ideological considerations but also because without it the new elites can neither communicate with each other about specialized elitist concerns while remaining within the limits of authenticity, nor can they move the masses toward greater unification, authentification, and modernization.

In Turkey

The Turkish language planning case is justifiably well known for the speed and the thoroughness with which it pursued modernization. As part of its overall post-World War I program of seeking a *new* Turkish identity (in contrast with the old Ottoman-Islamic identity) governmentally sponsored language planning conscientiously and vigorously moved to attain script reform (Roman in place of Arabic script), Europeanization of specialized nomenclatures (rather than the Arabic and Persian loan words hitherto used for learned or cultured purposes), and vernacularization or simplification of vocabulary, grammar, and phraseology for everyday conversational use (discarding the little understood and ornate flourishes patterned on Arabic or Persian).

Obviously Turkish language planning was a part of Ataturk's overall program of modernization. However, no nationalist movement can continue to push modernization without regard for authenticity. Thus the break with the holy Arabic script soon came to be defended on the ground that it was unsuited for the requirements of authentic Turkish phonology. Since even the prophet had clearly been an Arab before he was a Mohammedan he could hardly dispute the desire of Turks to put the needs of their Turkish authenticity first. The vast Europeanization of Turkish technical vocabulary had to be rationalized on the basis of the Great Sun Language Theory. On the basis of this authenticity-stressing theory it was claimed that all European languages were initially derived from Turkish. In that case all recent borrowings could be regarded as no more than reincorporations into the Turkish language of words or morphs that it had originally possessed but lost under the foreign impact of Arabic and Persian. Thus, the process of borrowing from European sources was ultimately not defended in public as a modernizing step, but, rather as an authenticating step! So too, and even more clearly, was the vernacularization and simplification of nontechnical Turkish. Here the language of the Anatolian peasant was held up as a model of purity and authenticity on the ground that it had been least contaminated by foreign influences and least corrupted by foreign fads.

Thus, on every front, language modernization decisions in Turkey were finally rationalized and legitimatized via authenticity sentiments and a way was found for these two components of nationalist ideology to reinforce common nationalist goals rather than to conflict with them or with each other. Such dialectic skill is by no means rare in the annals of language planning within highly nationalist contexts. On occasion modernization may appear to have the upper hand and, on occasion, authentification is stressed. In the longer run, however, what needs to be grasped is not so much the seesawing back and forth as the need to retain both components (actually all three components since uniformation too must not be lost) and to find a modus vivendi between them. Many examples of arriving at resolutions to the contradictory pressures built into nationalist language planning are to be found in the Estonian, Czech, Ukrainian, Greek, Turkish, and other relatively recent European language planning experiences. These examples deserve at least as much attention as do those drawn from more uncompromising periods in which one or another of three major components of nationalism was stressed.

Language Planning in South and Southeast Asia

The lesser stress on ethnic authenticity in South and Southeast Asian nationalism thus far is reflected in the correspondingly greater roles of both indigenous and imported Languages of Wider Communication (rather than of vernaculars alone) as languages of central government and higher education. The well-nigh complete and rapid displacement of Latin, French, German, Russian, and Arabic which marked the end of Austro-Hungarian, Czarist, and Ottoman hegemony in Central, Eastern, and Southern Europe has had no parallel in South and Southeast Asia. Even the displacement of Dutch in Indonesia was conducted with a regional Language of Wider Communication in mind (a variety of Malay rather than on behalf of a vernacular. Although some vernaculars have gained a level of recognition since independence that they never had in colonial days, the positions of English and French, on one hand, and of Hindi, Urdu, Malay, Indonesian, and Pilipino, on the other hand, are definite signs of the continued supraethnic stress of South and Southeast Asian language planning.

Indeed, the most central symbols and institutions of nationhood, the very processes of modernization and unification per se, are generally not related to vernaculars at all. Thus, as the nations of South and Southeast Asia progress along the path toward politico-operational integration we may expect that the new sociocultural integration that they must seek to develop and the authenticity that they must seek to stress will also be supraethnic. In the language planning field this has taken the direction of protecting and increasing the authenticity of the non-Western Languages of Wider Communication that have come to be adopted for national unificatory purposes. In this sense the views of the language planning agencies of South and Southeast Asia are constantly becoming more and more similar to those of early twentieth-century Central, Eastern, and Southern Europe (even though they are not dealing as exclusively with vernaculars), and less and less like those of state-into-nationality contexts that originally provided them with models.

Romanization of Script
Wherever classical literary traditions existed in preindependence South and Southeast Asia, romanization of script has been rejected (Fishman in press d). Although a modicum of romanization is practiced in conjunction with highly technical and advanced scientific work conducted in India, Pakistan, and Ceylon, e.g., the proposals to introduce romanization of script on a wider front—as an aid to literacy, modernization, or interregional communication—has been resisted as vigorously in those countries as it has been in China, Japan, or Israel outside of the area under consideration. The mass ideologization of this resistance is consistently in terms of indigenous authenticity vs foreign artificiality.

Purification
The tendency to reject European or, more generally, "international" lexical or morphological items, even for rather technical scientific or governmental work, is increasing through South and Southeast Asia. So is the tendency to limit the various vernacular influences on the national languages, even though such influences would tend to make these languages more widely understood. With respect to Hindi these tendencies take the direction of successively more

extreme Sanskritization, ignoring the pleas of educators and statesmen alike that such treatment severely restricts the functional utility of the language. A similar process of Arabo-Persianization (and Islamization) is transforming High Urdu. In Malaysia, Indonesia, and the Philippines it leads to a growing emphasis on Austronesian derivatives, rather than on Graeco-Latin roots, in developing and in orthographically "naturalizing" the specialized nomenclatures that Malay, Indonesian, and Pilipino increasingly require. In most of the earlier twentieth-century European cases of language planning the purification efforts were directed at one or another neighboring vernacular rather than at inter-nationalisms as such. In South and Southeast Asia, given the general identification of internationalisms with Euro-American colonialism, purification shows tendencies of combating "cultural colonialism" much more than neighboring vernaculars, all the more so since the latter have little if any competitive significance. The interest in indigenizing the national languages of South and Southeast Asia is a definite sign of the new and broader sociocultural integration that they must succeed in developing, to the end that a new supralocal ethnic authenticity will develop that will correspond to the broader unification and deeper modernization that can now be emphasized with increasing likelihood of success.

Language planning in South and Southeast Asia may be expected to be increasingly subjected to supraethnic authenticity goals on the part of governmental and intellectual elites. Whereas thus far language planning has been concerned primarily with such unification and modernization goals as mass literacy, participation, and productivity the very focus on these goals has and must contribute, ultimately, to a redistribution of attention so that authenticity too will receive the recognition it has always required as one of the three equal-but-opposite partners in the inevitable triangle that nationalism represents.

POSTSCRIPT

At the conclusion of an excursion such as ours it is obvious that many problems remain to be solved; indeed, that there are more such than were initially apparent. Even if the wisdom of hindsight has been gained, and that is none too certain, the ability to put it to use — in subsequent theoretical and empirical analyses — remains to be seen. If it is true, as Kurt Lewin claimed, that "nothing is as practical as a good theory," then certainly I would add that nothing is as provocative for theory as practical problems and efforts. The recurring dimensions and sequences, with respect to nationalism and language planning, adumbrated in the previous pages, must now withstand their most serious test: attempts by others to apply them in the vast amount of archival and documentary research on the one hand and in the crucially necessary quantitative and multivariable research on the other hand, that remains and pleads to be undertaken, I am sure that much that I have outlined will need to be changed as a result of the work that will follow. The only satisfaction to which a student can legitimately look forward, other than the satisfaction of the work process itself, is that of having been considered, rather than ignored in the work of others.

For myself, I have learned a few lessons from the foregoing examination of the trials and tribulations, pains and pleasures, of successive clusters of nationalities throughout the globe. Most of the truths that I sense or acknowledge have been recognized before and in some instances, long ago. Perhaps all I can say is that I understand them better, more richly, for having derived them and arrived at them myself. It was 1893 when a little known spokesman for a little known nationality observed:

> "Modern life is supposed to tend to break down all the barriers of nationality, of race and even of language, and to weld the nations of the earth into one mighty mass. That something like this may not be witnessed in a future stage of the world's history I am not prepared to deny . . . However, . . . side by side with the levelling tendency which annihilates distinctions and which would have one law, one language, one cosmopolitan character throughout, . . .there is a counter tendency of a natural and involuntary character constantly emphasizing distinctions and building up local differences, tending to make languages" (Southall 1893, pp. 314-315).

I believe this observation to be correct; indeed to be even more correct in the latter part of the twentieth century, than it was in the latter part of the nineteenth when it was originally formulated. The need for identity, for community, to make modernity sufferable, is greater than it was and will become greater yet, and woe to the elites—in universities, governments, and industries—who do not recognize this or, even worse, who consider it to be only a vestigial remnant of nineteenth-century thinking.

The search for a rooted community, marked by uniqueness and by greatness, corresponds to a partial need, a postponable need, an overlookable need, but to a basic social need for all that, a need to which all turn or return, at one time or another. A nation that does not recognize this about itself, and a scholarship that shuts this realization off from awareness, must as a result, have less to offer modern man and modern science then is needed. It is for this reason that I am more fearful of the de-ethnicizing myths of the American and Soviet social sciences than I am of the myths of those still grasping for self-recognition and self-dignity. To call the latter "irrational" and the former "rational" (Myrdal 1970), in unabashed oblivion of the fact that one's own so-called rationality (with its "overkill" capacity) is the luxurious byproduct of a largely similar process once also dubbed "irrational" (and worse), when it too began, is to be simultaneously dangerous, heartless, and uninformed. "The significance of a social movement does not lie simply in the rationality of its ideas, nor in its success. To judge. . . nationalism only by the logic of its ideas is to miss something crucial" (Marx 1970, p. 32): its developmental necessity, its power, is creative potential. There is no maturity without adolescence—and adolescence is not only destructive and thoughtless, it is also tender and altruistic and intuitive and profoundly, humanly troubled, hopeless and hopeful at one and the same time.

It is foolish to predict the demise of adolescence, to deny its legitimacy, to ridicule it. It is doubly foolish to do so from the vantage point of an establishment bound to be counterridiculed. But it is also triply foolish, because the deniers are simultaneously denying themselves, their own inner selves, and offering this self-denial, at once stifling, self-congratulatory, and beside the point, to others who are in far different circumstances, as if it were the ultimate wisdom.

Nationalities will come and nationalities will go, but nationality behavior is here to stay and those attaining it for the first time, or attaining it anew at a broader level, will continually display the added sensitivity and insensitivity which always mark heightened experiences. This does not at all mean that the dream of "one world" is an unattainable (not to say an unworthy) dream. Quite the contrary. If merely means that levels of kinship must be recognized and that these will continue to coexist as concentric circles, each adding to and enriching the human social identity provided by the others. Nor will national languages disappear. Quite the contrary; more and more national standard languages were predicted by Deutsch towards the beginning of the Second World War (1942) and his prediction has held up very well during the past three decades. However, the increasing number of standard national languages (the codification, elaboration, and cultivation of which are goals pursued via national language planning) does not forebode the doom of international languages or, ultimately, of even one language for the entire world. "Narrower languages" and "wider languages" have always coexisted, as have narrower and wider networks of sociocultural and political-operational integration. Indeed, the greatest force working for the voluntary acquisition of languages of wider communication in educated circles today (Denison 1970), is the realization that one's national language is safe-but-insufficient (Fishman 1969). Widespread diglossia patterns are reemerging throughout the world today and nowhere as strongly as where speakers of small languages feel certain that their national and linguistic place in the sun is not threatened thereby.

When the fate of the world hangs in the balance, as it does today, only our faith in the emotional and intellectual capacity of man can carry the day. Nationalities and languages have been planned in the past and their bearers have subsequently gone on to other, more inclusive problems. This is happening again today. It will happen again in the future. It is part of the social drama of humanity. Would that we could help it happen with less wear and tear and with more mutual acceptance among all concerned.[52]

Notes to Part I

1. The best sources for reviewing the terminological variation in this general field of inquiry are Carr (1939), Snyder (1954), and Zernatto (1944). I have found the greatest conceptual clarification with respect to *terminology* in the work of Akzin (1964), Wirth (1936), and Znaniecki (1952) and my own usage, in terms of the distinctions that it draws and the processes to which it refers, is most directly similar to theirs. Readers seeking other useful introductions to the study of nationalism should certainly consult such justifiably well-known general works as those by Deutsch (1953, rev. ed. 1966), Doob (1964), Emerson (1962), Kedourie (1961), Kohn (1944 and 1955), Shafer (1955), and Snyder (1964). All of the above have highly useful bibliographies, as do Pinson (1935) and Deutsch (1956). The new *International Encyclopedia of the Social Sciences* has informative articles on nationalism and related topics by Kohn (1968), Kazemzadeh (1968), Rustow (1968), and Levine (1968).

2. As here employed *ethnic group* subsumes such prenational societies as are commonly designated by the terms clan, band, tribe, etc. It is to this more general sense of the term that Akzin refers (1964) when he states that "... the point at which the ethnic group has both exceeded purely local dimensions and become of significance in the political sphere ... is the point at which the appellation ... nationality can be applied to it," or "the ethnic group at the point when it begins to loom ... as an active factor ... is referred to as a ... nationality" (ibid., both on p. 29).

3. A few examples of recent and relatively nonjudgmental definitions of this term may be of help in pointing out certain differences in emphases between authors. Znaniecki comes closest to my own use in stating "we shall define the term nationalism as the active solidarity of 'national culture' society" (1952, p. 21). Kedourie draws upon older discussions of "national will" when he states "[Since] national self-determination is, in the final analysis, a determination of the will ... nationalism is, in the first place, a method of teaching the right determination of the will" (1961, p. 81). There is a touch (and sometimes more

NOTES TO PART I   87

than just a touch) of mocking rejection in Kedourie's treatment of nationalism which is evident in the above definition. Rosenblatt (1964) is representative of those who are concerned with differentiating between nationalism and either less formalized or more rabid ethnic behaviors, viz: "Nationalism, more often than ethnocentrism, involves loyalty to a politically distinct entity, membership in an elaborately organized and relatively populous social grouping, adherence to a formalized ideology, and performance of relatively stereotyped allegiance-expressing behavior" (p. 31). I consider Rosenblatt's reference to "membership in a politically distinct entity" to be an unproductive restriction, since it unjustifiably singles out one of several possible goals of nationalism as a necessary attribute. In addition, like the historian Kedourie, the psychologist Rosenblatt does not stress the ethnocultural mainsprings which serve as point of departure for all other nationalist behaviors. Finally, while the furtherance of ethnic self-interest is recognized by Wirth (1936) in his definition of nationalism, he tends to specify the latter quite narrowly as "the ideology of nationality" rather than as a rather broadly organized system of interrelated and elaborated ethnic beliefs, values, and behaviors. Lieberson's recent sociological definition (and confrontation between ethnic and class differences as well as similarities) nevertheless mistakenly limits nationalism to state-forming ethnic groups.

4. Rustow (1968b) provides a conveniently brief indication of the varying meanings of the term *nation*. The treatment of this topic is more extensive in Carr (1939), where varying usage in English, French, German, and Russian is reviewed. The most extensive review of the different connotations of the term, from ancient times through to the modern era, is that of Zernatto (1944). It is partly because of the excessively many connotations of the term (sometimes referring to the polity, as in the American pledge of allegiance to "one nation, under God, indivisible," sometimes to all of the inhabitants of a polity, and sometimes to any relatively large and solidary cultural group), that many writers have so clearly come to prefer *nationality* (rather than *nation*) for the more specific designations for which I have reserved it in this paper. Znaniecki noted (1952) that from the middle 1930's and throughout the forties "in view of this terminological confusion, the editors of several encyclopedias have omitted the term 'nation' altogether" (International Encyclopedia, Encyclopedia of the Social Sciences, Encyclopaedia Britannica, Handwörterbuch der Staatswissen-schaften)." In more recent years the term has again come to be much used with at least some tendency to favor the kind of usage to *nationality* that I prefer.

5. The contrast between *traditional, transitional,* and modern populations, not only in terms of beliefs, attitudes, and behaviors related to broader and more authentic ethnicity but in terms of identification with nonlocals, media participation, literacy, and political participation more generally, is convincingly

presented in Daniel Lerner, *The Passing of Traditional Society* (Glencoe, Ill.: Free Press, 1958). Contrasts of this kind are inherent in much of the recent and extensive social psychological and sociological literature on the development and modernization of the "new" nations. The political historian Akzin depicts the prenationalist era as one in which " . . . the relative immobility of the large masses of mankind, coupled with their lack of literacy, kept their outlook geared to the immediate social group with which they experienced close personal contact (village, clan, tribe), thus making them regard as strangers all those who . . . lived beyond these narrow confines" (1964, pp. 49-50). Akzin's reference to the role of illiteracy in maintaining the particularism that he describes anticipates our subsequent discussion of the contribution of literacy in the vernacular to the formation of broader affiliative bonds between

In like manner, Lerner's description of traditional society (particularly in the Moslem Near East) anticipates several points that will figure again in our discussion below: "Traditional society is non-participant—it deploys people by kinship into communities isolated from each other and from the center, . . . it develops few needs requiring economic interdependencies, . . . people's horizons are limited by locale and their decisions involve only other *known* people in *known* situations. Hence there is no need for a trans-personal common doctrine formulated in terms of shared secondary symbols—a national 'ideology' which enables persons unknown to each other to engage in political controversy or achieve 'consensus' by comparing their opinions" (1958, p. 50).

Perhaps the most perceptive discussion of the interaction between tradition and modernity and of the *resilience* of the former even in current social life is that of Shils (1971).

6. The importance of communicational discontinuities in curtailing broader unity may be great even where local societies are rather highly developed in many other ways. Thus Aristotle believed that communities suffered if they consisted of fewer than 10 or more than 10,000 inhabitants (*Ethics* IX, 10, 3) and the considerably larger barbarian communities were, for him, not real communities at all (*Politics,* VII, 4). Obviously, both technological and ideological change are required to enable small and discontinuous social units such as those known to Aristotle, which normally "identified only with themselves," to begin ". . . to identify with other social units . . . In the protonationalist phase social cohesion begins to expand. Groups formerly in conflict with each other begin to see common elements with respect to a more esoteric and differentially defined social unit. While a traditional response would define all outside groups as threatening, a protonationalist response differentiates the external social force and distinct social units act together . . . against a mutual external threat" (Friedland 1968, pp. 16-17).

7. "The essence of the integrative relationship is seen as *collective action to promote mutual interests* . . . It is both the *range* of functions in which they engage corporately, as well as the particular *kind* of functions that is important" (Jacob and Toscano 1964, p. 5), and, we might add, that differs widely.

8. I have *not* consulted the original German version in order to determine the term that Herder used which Kohn translated as "nation." Echoes of the view expressed by Herder are still commonly heard in nonnationalist (or even antinationalist) anthropological and linguistic circles as providing the rationale for the collection of ethnographic, folkloric, and linguistic data on small and vanishing cultures before their individuality is lost forever. For an enlightening discussion of the anti-French and antirationalist origins of Herder's views and of their roots in earlier and comtemporary philosophical and literary thought see Kedourie's chapter 2, 3, and 4 (Self-determination, State, and Individual, and The Excellence of Diversity; 1961, pp. 20-61).

9. "Among the long-forgotten masses of Anatolia the 'real Turk' was happily discovered, unaware that his language and customs . . . were about to become a political asset. The intelligentsia was urged to learn the history, folklore and traditions of the Turkish masses" (Karpat 1964, pp. 269-270).

10. The distinction between seekers of a genuine and total past and seekers of a usable and eclectic past has been made by many students of protest movements in differentiating between nativist and revivalist movements, on the one hand, and cargo cults and nationalisms, on the other (see, e.g., Depres 1967, 1968 for summaries of such distinctions). In connection with nationalism Gellner claims that "ultimately the movements invariably contain both elements, a genuine modernism and a more or less spurious concern for local culture, or rather the re-employment of what had been a traditional culture for the enrichment and the trappings of a new education-rooted way of life" (1964, p. 171).

11. Znaniecki concludes the cited passage with the unwarranted observation that "This doctrine is a joint product of ethnographers and of historians", thereby slighting the large variety of possible interactions between "gehobenes Primitivgut" and "gesunkenes Kulturgut" in the formation of doctrines of this kind.

12. Such nationalistic pleas to prospective allies were a favorite device of Napoleon in attracting popular support and give evidence of the widespread existence of latent nationalist sentiments in Central and Eastern Europe even in the early years of the nineteenth century. Thus, in setting up the Grand Duchy of Warsaw in order to enlist Polish support for his invasion of Russia, he urged a

Polish delegation to "show yourselves worthy of your forefathers. They ruled the house of Brandenburg; they were the masters of Moscow; they took the fortress of Widden; they freed Christianity from the yoke of the Turks" (cited by Kedourie 1961, p. 94).

13. While popular evolutionary thought may underlie or strengthen some of the search for ancient origins that typifies modern nationalism, it is also strikingly true that Western social and political theory had come to be concerned with interpreting the losses and gains attributable to modernization long before Darwinism came to the fore. While Durkheim was by no means the first to suggest that the difference between the old and the new was *a difference in the basis of solidarity* (which difference, in turn, was derived from the division of labor) his impact on his own contemporaries and subsequent elites in Central and Eastern Europe and in Africa and Asia was quite striking. Similarly noticeable was the impact upon Durkheim himself of the social philosophy of several French writers (in particular Rousseau, Descartes, Comte, and Saint-Simon) whose views had contributed to earlier formulations of the impact of modernity on European society.

Durkheim recognized "only two kinds of positive solidarity which are distinguishable by the following qualities:

1. The first binds the individual directly to society without any intermediary.

In the second he depends upon society, because he depends upon the parts of which it is comprised.

2. Society is not seen in the same aspect in the two cases. In the first, what we call society is a more or less organized totality of beliefs and sentiments common to all the members of the group: this is the collective type. On the other hand, the society . . . is a system of different, special functions which definite relations unite (p. 129) . . . It is the division of labor which, more and more, fills the role that was formerly filled by the common conscience. It is the principal bond of social aggregates of higher types" [1893] 1933, p. 173).

Clearly Durkheim believed that both types of solidarity were found in all societies but that there was a secular trend from the first to the second as societal complexity increased.

14. Gellner observes that "in simple societies culture is important, but its importance resides in the fact that it reinforces structure. In modern societies culture does not so much underline structure; rather, it replaces it" (1964, p. 155). It is the latter condition which Gellner believes to be the peculiar characteristic of affilative behavior of modern nationalism which is "marked by features such as the non-intimate, mass nature of the loyalty-evoking group, the

definition of membership by (in effect) culture, and the fact that membership is direct and not mediated by intervening subgroups" (1964, p. 173).

15. Depres (1967) has stressed that one of the outcomes of technologically based social similarity in plural societies is that "interdependent units tend to comprise culturally differentiated rather than socially differentiated" clusters of persons. This observation gives us a glimpse of how uniformation and diversification may not only be concomitant aspects of the very same social changes but how an increase in the one (social uniformation) may lead to greater stress on the other (ethnocultural uniqueness) as a principle or device of mobilization. As we will subsequently see, those language planning efforts that are guided even in a general way by nationalist authenticity strivings must also balance these two simultaneous trends. On the one hand, indigenous national languages must be quickly developed to render them usable for modern governmental, industrial and scientific functions that are highly similar (i.e., supraethnic or nonethnic) throughout the world. On the other hand, the languages so developed must also follow (and, at times, even devise) patterns that are thoroughly authentic and unique. In a way, these strictures are evocative of those imposed by Stalin's dictum that Soviet minority cultures might be national in form provided they were socialist in content (J. Stalin, "O politicheskikh zadachakh universiteta narodov vostoka," *Sochineniia*, 7 [18 May 1925]).

16. As examples, note " ... the national movements [in Eastern and Central Europe] would not have arisen ... if it had not been for the growth of the capitalist system and the industrial revolution" (Carr 1939, p. 112), and " ... the great transoceanic expansion of European commerce and economy at the close of the Middle Ages was closely related to the rise of national states along the Atlantic seaboard ... The economic differentiation of nationalities ... has been striking" (Hayes 1960, p. 34).

17. As examples, note "The repeated association between deliberate economic development and extreme nationalism is surely not accidental. Nationalism presents an essentially nonrational unifying force that may ease and rationalize the hardship of personal change [during economic development] " (Moore 1965, pp. 36-37), and "Since the Industrial Revolution nationalism has drawn much of its strength from successively lower levels of material civilization ... That the difference in poverty is so great and that the world's poorest peoples are so numerous ... are perhaps the fundamental facts behind much of today's nationalistic insistence on national separateness and economic and political

barriers" (Deutsch [1953] 1966, p. 191), and "And why does this situation [nationalism] obtain? . . . The erosion of the given, intimate structure of traditional society, an erosion inherent in the size, mobility and general ecology and organization of industrial society, or even of a society moving in this direction" (Gellner 1964, p. 157).

18A. Two examples that span 120 years are the following: "Nationalism . . . would redeem modern man from his fearful loneliness and from the malaise of living in the impersonal mechanized world of industrial society" (Michelet [1846] 1946, p. 44) and "The vision of progress towards a common industrial society that the 18th century foresaw, and that people like Mill and Tocqueville in the 19th century came to fear, is plainly being realized in the 20th century. But it also seems plain that this thesis has its antithesis in the rise of modern nationalism . . . a tendency to emphasize differences in the midst of a common movement toward similar institutions and modes of existence . . . [and a] need for a sense of identity in a world where ancient bonds of kinship and community are weakening and the correlative demand for some principle of integration among large numbers of people" (Sutton 1968, pp. 1-2).

The relatively more psychological emphases of the first statement, above, and the more sociological emphases of the second, still represent the poles toward which most comments relating nationalism to modern economic development tend to gravitate. For additional psychological formulations (linking the appeal of nationalism with feelings of anxiety and alienation, fear of failure and incompetence, bewilderment at loss of traditional ways as well as compensatory identification stemming from early and continuing frustrations), see such valuable summaries as Doob 1964, Katz 1965, and Rosenblatt 1964. Those who are particularly interested in this level of analysis may also find many stimulating formulations in older studies such as those by Pillsbury 1919 and Katz 1940.

18B. "Exponents of the economic interpretation of nationalism would do well to take a long-range view of history and especially to ponder an interesting contrast between 'results' of economic development at the beginning of the Christian era and 'results' of economic development in our age. At the earlier time a remarkable expansion of commerce, acceleration of industry and development of capitalism were attended by the swift expansion of tribal states and city-states of diverse nationalities into a multi-lingual cosmopolitan state known as the Roman Empire; localism was transformed into imperialism; nationalism, if it existed at all, was weak. The contrast certainly suggests that economic development of itself does not create nationalism or cosmopolitanism but that it merely speeds up a political tendency which for other reasons is under way" (Hayes 1931, pp. 297-298). Without questioning Hayes' conclusion it should be pointed out that several students of Roman history have, indeed, pointed to a mass Roman nationalism as a major force during the early period of Roman expansion and to an elitist Roman nationalism during the subsequent periods of Empire. "The Roman who was a Spaniard or African or an Italian was also a 'Roman' " (Barrow 1949, p. 116). That such Roman nationalism did not commonly go far beyond elitist ranks is viewed as a weakness of the regime attributable, basically, to the absence of economic, industrial, and technological change sufficiently massive and continuing to penetrate, mobilize, and Romanize the countryside.

19. "Certain long-drawn-out armed conflicts such as the series of wars between Christians and Moslems in Spain, between Russians and their neighbors, the Hundred Years War across France, did much to arouse national consciousness among those concerned" (Akzin 1964, p. 45). The difference between "national(ity) consciousness" and nationalism, particularly in terms of massive and organized activity has already been mentioned. In the absence of sufficient economic-technological development, even long-drawn-out wars did not truly long involve the entire populace (as do the citizen armies of today), nor long disrupt them from returning to their particularistic and localistic forms of economic, social, and cultural integration (as do modern wartime controls). As a result, nationality consciousness due to protracted hostilities had no post-emergency operative base and, therefore, unlike modern nationalism, it tended to evaporate outside of the area of localized conflict, as well as soon after the cessation of hostilities, and to remain merely as raw material for future nationalist exploitation (Braunthal 1946). As a result, e.g., several regional Spains, rather than a single united Spain, emerged from the "reconquista" and these have not fully united to this very day owing to the uninterrupted force of regional life and the general lack of major scale instrumental integration (Menéndez-Pidal 1945, Linz 1970).

20. The relationship between nationalism and religion and the purported rise of nationalism as a result of the decline of religion are both very involved topics that cannot be adequately treated in an essay of this kind. Nevertheless, because the ties between nationalism and religion are of significance for an understanding of nationalism in a number of developing countries as well as for an understanding of some of the language planning problems there encountered, a few observations concerning these matters are justified at this point.

Recently, Myrdal has stated that the extensive interpenetration of nation-alism with religion in South and Southeast Asia represents a major contrast with the predominantly secular and even anticlerical nature of nationalism in Europe (1968, pp. 119, 2112, etc., although contradicted elsewhere). This view of the purported secularism (and the, presumably, greater rationalism) of European nationalism essentially follows in the path of Durkheim's dictum: "If there is one truth that history teaches us beyond doubt it is that religion tends to embrace a smaller and smaller portion of social life" ([1893] 1933, p. 169); and is in agreement with Kohn's "universal sociological law" ("religous groups lose power when confronted with the consciousness of a common nationality and speech" [1932, p. 229]). Similar general formulations can be found in Emerson (1962, p. 158); Kedourie (1961, p. 101); Minogue (1967, p. 147) and others. Znaniecki includes the development of a secular culture and a secular literature among the defining characteristics of societies that have attained nationality status (1952, p. 21). A more cautious formulation is that by Inglehart and Woodward, who merely claim that language and nationality "seems" more important than religion as a basis of political cleavage in modern societies; but this is true only insofar as it becomes linked with differences in social mobility" (1967, p. 32). Baron, the only scholar who has attempted a truly intensive and comparative analysis of modern nationalism and religion, is even more cautious (1947). His position seems to be that there has rarely been a major establishment of the one without the other (actually, that their concepts are fully intertwined) and that whichever has been the weaker of the two has always attempted to draw strength from the other, without being controlled by it. The fact that European polities have increasingly become religiously neutral in their international dealings should not blind us to the fact that "all major Continental nationalities, except the long-divided Germans and Hungarians, overwhelmingly belong to a single denomination" (p. 17). As a result, religion, polity, and nationality have become for the most part complementary terms covering the same human groups when viewed from an intrapolity perspective.

The examples of religious *preservation, cultivation,* and *dependence upon* ethnic and nationality differences are legion, including all European religious groups during all periods of European history. For early examples of predominantly national forms of Christianity note the patriarchate of Alexandria (Hardy 1946) and the Armenian Church, which first "adopted Monophysitism out of opposition to Persian [i.e., Nestorian] Christianity. They used it finally as a barrier to defend their nationality" (Woodward 1916, p. 48). Furthermore, "among Eastern Christian Churches, some (e.g., Armenian, Coptic, Syrian) retained an ethnic character, making of religion a strong supporting element both of the fact of nationality and of sentiment laden national consciousness. Others–the Russian, Bulgarian, Rumanian, Serbian– developed . . . an increasingly autocephalous structure because the mother Greek Orthodox Church was not regarded by worshippers and clergy as sufficiently close from an ethnic viewpoint" (Akzin 1964, pp. 47-48). "Roger Bacon and Bartholomew, known as Anglicus, were among the first [13th century] to call attention to the nation[ality] as a factor in state and society" (Akzin 1964, p.

14). "Catholic clerics, being the main intelligentsia in medieval society, were also the main promoters of national literature and recorders of national history" (Baron 1947, p. 13). "At the Council of Constance the spirit of nationalism was not only present, but received concrete expression in its most menacing form in the method of voting by nations" (Powers 1927, p. viii). The nationality-promoting role of Hus, Wycliffe, and Luther among Protestant leaders has frequently been pointed out and is too widely known to require citation here. The Greek hierarchy played a similar role from the eighteenth century on regarding itself "as the guardian of the Greek nation from both the Latins and the Turks, and considering this nation distinguished not only by its Orthodox religion but also by the Greek language" (Sherrard 1959, p. 178). Judaism, of course, "must be considered an ethnic religious system because its institutions and practices are closely tied to the land of its origin . . . and so preserve the distinctive identity of the community" (Sopher 1967, pp. 5-6).

Corresponding references pertaining to nationalist exploitation of religion are literally too numerous (and perhaps too self-evident) to merit citation. From the Gothic ruler's choice of Arianism rather than Catholicism (Woodward 1917) to the Croatian, Slovenian, Slovak, Polish, and Irish uses of Catholicism to establish their separateness and pursue their independence, there has been a constant reliance by European secular leaders on their particular religious traditions, institutions, and hierarchies to serve nationalist purposes in general and the causes of the newly developing national languages in particular (Grentrup 1932). Above and beyond the foregoing there is the more general reliance of European nationalism on such fundamental Judeo-Christian religious concepts as "chosen people," "promised land," and "sacred language." These enabled nationalists to immediately draw upon a bountiful source of established images and associations implying divine sanction, to the end that it rang true to say that "The day when France, remembering that she was, and must be, the salvation of mankind, will place her children around her, and teach them France, as faith and as religion, she will find herself living and firm as the globe" (Michelet [1846] 1946, p. 241).

Hayes (1942), more than most students of this particular problem, has documented the constant interdependence of religion and nationalism in Europe from earliest times. "A mere history of doctrinal aspects of schism and heresy will hardly make clear why, for example, the Monophysite heresy of the fifth century found embodiment in schismatic national churches for Egyptians, Armenians and Syrians" (p. 4). However, just as religion made use of national sentiments in the prenationalist past so has nationalism made use of religious sentiments, in more modern days. Hayes indicates Napoleon's awareness of the power of religious sentiments (for eliciting national feeling on his behalf) to such an extent that it "made a Catholic of me when I had finished the war of Vendée, made a Muslim of me when I had established myself in Egypt . . . If I governed a Jewish people I would re-establish the Temple of Solomon" (p. 10). Chateaubriand, believing that "the most appropriate instinct in man, the most beautiful, the most moral *c'est l'amour de la patrie"* concluded, as a result, that "the Church is to be cherished because it is the best teacher of nationalism" (pp. 9-10). Finally, in the view of "such atheistic or agnostic ultra-nationalists as Maurice Barrès, Charles Maurras and Gabriele d'Annunzio, the Catholic Church . . . should be preserved because it represents the national tradition" (p. 10). Lest it be assumed that only religion can thus be exploited to serve nationalist ends today, note Lipset's remarks concerning a similar use to which socialism has been put (1968, pp. 102-107).

The upshot of the foregoing, it seems to me, is that European religions were long the carriers of ethnicity and nationalism at the same time that they pursued their respective universalistic truths. While the last 200 years of European history have been marked by the greater prominence of nationalism as a unifying and organizing force, particularly in political affairs, the relationship between the two has merely been reversed (nationalism now being an important carrier of religious imagery and religious distinction) rather than weakened. By the time of the industrial revolution the European multinationality state had already made an ally of religion and had learned to control it rather than be controlled by it. "For each melting pot is not merely fusing religion into the state church, it is also fusing the church itself into the world of the state" (Zangwill 1917, p. 66). Submerged nationalities, therefore, struggled primarily against secular forces and rarely against fundamentally religious ones. If a long-term change has occurred between religious and secular predominance in political affairs, it came with the Reformation and Counter-Reformation in the sixteenth and seventeenth centuries (see, e.g., Powers 1927, p. 202, theses 21 and 25), rather than with the rise of nationalism in the eighteenth and nineteenth. Thus, the distinction between Europe and Asia is not so much the relative absence of secular nationalism in the latter as much as the relative absence of secularism per se, either among those against whom nationalism must struggle, or among those it seeks to influence. In addition, of course, Western states (and in the East, especially China and Japan) have developed *civil* religions that interlock with the more traditional religions, in very substantial ways (see, e.g., Bellah 1967, Yang, 1961).

21. "[Nations] are connected more with the concepts of honor than with the idea of wealth. The nation is not an economic group" (Sulzbach 1943, p. viii). The last Minister for Nationalities of the Austro-Hungarian Empire, having witnessed himself the seemingly endless sequential progression of nationality movements concluded, more evenhandedly, that "if we study the intellectual and moral struggles of the heroic period of nationalism we distinctly recognize

that we face not only the introduction of a new method of economic production but, at the same time, the establishment of a new scale of moral values" (Jaszi 1929, p. 258). In this same vein another observer has noted that "the materialistic explanation does not hold good for a nationalist movement like, for example, the Polish whose moving spirits were the gentry and whose source of inspiration was the historic past and memories of an aristocratic freedom, and hardly an economic grievance against the foreign rulers or the rapid pace of social change" (Talmon 1965, p. 18). Talmon, like Jaszi, does not deny "the great influence of economic forces on the forms of national consciousness and the patterns of nationalist strategy" but concludes that "economic factors alone cannot be considered to have been the matrix of nationalism" (ibid, p. 17).

22. The notion of locating nationalism within a nexus of interrelated causes and effects occurred to Acton over a century ago when he considered the revolutionary theories of his age. "There are three principal theories of this kind," he wrote, "impugning the present distribution of power, of property and of territory, and attacking respectively the aristocracy, the middle class, and the sovereignty. They are the theories of equality, communism and nationality. Though sprung from a common origin, opposing cognate evils and connected by many links, they did not appear simultaneously. Rousseau proclaimed the first, Babeuf the second, Mazzini the third" ([1864] 1907, p. 273.

23. A very similar linkage is posited by Kohn when he concludes that "As a phenomenon of modern European history the rise of nationalism is closely linked with the origins of popular sovereignty, the theory of government by the active 'consent of the governed,' the growth of secularism, the lessening of the older religious, tribal, clannist, or feudal loyalties, and the spread of organization, industrialization and improved communication" (1968, p. 64).

24. In an equally (though oppositely) one-sided approach most communist social theoreticians have tended to concentrate on only two aspects of the interactions of nationalism with other processes: (a) the "positive" contribution of nationalism to the breakdown of feudalism and, therefore, to the emergence of both the bourgeoisie and the working class, and (b) the "negative" contribution of nationalism, under bourgeois dominance, to the inevitable international unification of the working class. In practice there has been a trend toward increasingly nationalist brands of communism since the end of World War II (Snyder 1968, pp. 304-319). An Asian observer comments as follows: "As long as communism worked in cooperation with nationalism it continued to flourish, but once the clash occurred its fate was more or less sealed, for nationalism is still the most powerful force" (Singhal 1967, p. 283).

At the level of theory no post-World War II revisionist integrative statement of the relationship between nationalism and communism (see, e.g., Glezerman 1970, Potekhin 1958, Rodinson 1968) has yet attained widespread recognition rivaling in any way that formerly accorded the writings of Marx, Engels, Lenin, and Stalin on this topic. Marx and Engels were largely guided by considerations of parsimony that led them to prefer the nationalism of a few superstates over that of an endless procession of microstates (in each of which the proletariat would be smaller, weaker, and more easily influenced by fabricated, pseudonationalist diversionary antagonisms). This view is summarized in Engels 1866 and in Rjasanoff 1916. Subsequent theory was more sophisticated, providing for an evolutionary-transformational approach to the development of a nationality. Thus in 1913 (in *Prosvescheniye* nos. 3-5; subsequently included in the collection entitled *Marxism and the National Question* [1942]) Stalin outlined a stagewise progression from the clan, through the tribal community (still based largely on kinship), the ethnic group, and the narodnost (a not yet fully unified or precisely defined linguistic-territorial-economic cooccurrence) to the nation/ality. However, the basic task of such theory was neither descriptive nor predictive, but, rather, manipulative. Just as Lenin had admonished his disciples to "consider each national demand, national separation, from the vantage point of the class struggle of the workers" in order not "to confuse the right of self-determination with the actual usefulness of it" (Dadrian 1968, p. 35), so Stalin frankly observed that " . . . the interests of the proletariat and the rights of a nation . . . are two different things" (*Works*, v. 2, p. 322). For orthodox international communism nationalism is obviously no more than an exploitable distraction, at best, particularly in view of the contratheoretical fact that in modern times "vertical cleavages have been more important than horizontal ones" (Binder 1964, p. 152). For the language policy consequences of such ambivalence see Desheriev et al 1965 (for a defense) and Weinreich 1953b (for an indictment). A studied attempt to present a balanced view is that of Lewis, 1972.

25. Several examples of such early total or partial rejections are given by Kohn (1968, p. 64). This problem of elite formations and reformations has been particularly emphasized by Kedourie (1961), Minogue (1967), and other historians and philosophers, schooled as they are in the textual analysis of the writings of great men, even though they have been aware that societal circumstances favorable to the elites under study were as necessary as the felicity of their formulations. For a more judicious recognition of the role of elites, one that relates them to social and economic changes affecting the masses, see Friedrich (1963).

26. The mid-nineteenth century German nationalist spokesman and activist Friedrich Ludwig Jahn stressed his contributions along these very lines in the concluding passage of his *Selbstverteidigung* (written in the third person): " . . . [he] served his Fatherland throughout his life . . . to turn away all things un-German and foreign (*Undeutschheit und Ausländerei*) and led the confused back to the path of virtue and honor." Jahn composed his own epitaph: "I held fast to the idea of German unity, as if it were an unhappy love" (Snyder 1952, p. 41).

27. "Karel Havlicek, a popular leader of the Czech national movement had a daily column in his paper under the heading 'The Irish Repeal Movement' in which he described from day to day the situation of the unhappy island and the growing force of the nationalist movement [there] . . . in a time when censorship made all political action impossible [in the Austro-Hungarian Empire]" (Jaszi 1929, p. 260).

28. "The philippic of Björnstjerne Björnson, the great Norwegian poet, against the policy of Magyarization of Count Albert Opponyi [was widely distributed and] aroused more indignation in the hearts of the oppressed nationalities than the policy of assimilation itself" (Jaszi 1929, p. 267).

29. The intended contrast is between Zangwill's oft quoted (but never authenticated) phrase that "a nation is a body of people who feel they are a nation" and Buber's more differentiated view [1933]: "A people is a phenomenon of life, nationality (which cannot exist without national feeling) is one of consciousness, nationalism is one of superconsciousness" (Cited by Baron 1947, p. 3)." Actually, Zangwill's usage is well aware of the action potential of nationalism, viz: "Nationality degenerates into nationalism. Fire is a good servant but a bad master, and the same flame that vivified sub-nationality turns nationality into a belligerent fireship" (1917, p. 49).

30. Thus, French unity was traced back to ancient Gaul in Théophile Lavalée's *Histoire des Français depuis le temps des Gaulois* (Paris 1830), and German unity to the struggle against Rome in the second century B.C. in Johann Sporschil's *Geschichte der Deutschen von den ältesten Zeiten* (5 vols. Regensburg, 1859-60). One of the first such historical creation of greater unity was Francesco Guicciarcini's *La Historia di Italia* published in Florence in 1561, three full centuries before the attainment of Italian unity.

31. The allusion here is to Minogue's apt characterization of Rousseau's view of society around that time (1967, pp. 41-42). Minogue concludes "He was, in fact,

dominated by an overpowering nostalgia for the past." It is this nostalgia that nationalism modernizes and activates.

32. Thus, after the unsuccessful revolution of 1848, Prague Germans, nevertheless, commented on the fact that "the Czech national colors and dress were much in view, talking Czech in public was becoming *bon ton* . . . The Students' League broke up, and a 'Slavia' ranged itself (as yet fraternally) by the side of a 'Teutonia'; the Czechs left the literary society 'Concordia' and formed the 'Svornost.' Innocuous intellectual activities of a 'folk-character,' hitherto countenanced by the Germans, were assuming a political complexion" (Namier 1944, p. 100). A similar straw in the wind appeared "at the occasion of a splendid ball in Zagreb [1840, at which] Croatian ladies pinned to their bosoms a star on whose points the names . . . Dalmatians, Croatians, Montenegrins, Slavenians [sic], Bulgarians and Serbs were engraved. In the center of the star the following words were to be read: 'God help us to union!' " (Jaszi 1929, p. 262).

33. Kolarz presents a long list of nationalist leaders who were themselves born outside of the group or area to which they subsequently devoted their efforts, or whose parents were "foreigners" who had socialized their children into their own (i.e., the parental) cultural tradition, rather than into the tradition of the people in whose midst they resided. For an account of the ethnic self-redefinition of such "foreign" elites (as well as the refusal of others to do so) see Lindman (1963) or Wuorinen (1931).

34. The peculiar perspective and sensitivity coming from years of life in exile is revealed by Michael Collin's statement: "I stand for an Irish civilization based on the people and embodying and maintaining the things—their habits, ways of thought, customs—that make them different—the sort of life I was brought up in . . . Just the sort of donkey and just the sort of cart that they have at home . . . Nobody who has not been an exile will understand me, but I stand for that" (cited by Minogue 1967, pp. 22-23).

35. It is probably an exaggeration to claim as does Trevor-Roper, that "all great nationalist leaders have been only half-national themselves. Their followers may be—generally are—true nationals: authentic, autochthonous, monoglot, aborigines of the tribe, bigoted fundamentalists of the faith. But the leaders, it is well known, tend to be marginal in their nationality, perhaps inspired by secret doubts of their nationality" (1962, pp. 20-21). The above seems to stand at the opposite extreme of the reality of incipient nationalism from Pye's claim that "before the nation can develop, leaders must emerge who have found

integrity in their own quests for identity and who can hence speak in terms that will bring meaning to other people's search for identity" (1961, p. 219).

36. For a basic discussion of the difference between "intelligentsia" and "intellectuals" in a context pertinent to incipient nationalism see Vladimir Nahirny 1962.

37. There is little available in the way of an analysis of the nonintellectual elites upon which all nationalist movements were and are also dependent. The political, military, financial, commercial, and industrial risk takers who are among the first to foresee the possible gains of a reorganization of society and its institutions of power on the basis of nationality have been characterized by Deutsch as including "some of the least secure among the powerful with some of the most powerful among those who . . . [are] just ceasing to be powerless" (1957, p. 88). As for the kinds of individuals most likely to follow the lead of such risk takers and innovators, Moore suggests those who "are marginal to the traditional order . . . young wives in traditional Chinese households . . . the Indian caste untouchables, the younger sons in a system of male primogeniture, merchants 'unclassifiable' in feudal Japan, dispossessed landlords subsequent to land reform, the indigenous . . . landless poor" (1965), p. 42). Moore's comments return us to the basic discontent upon which nationalism operates and which the elites attempt to channel. The aptness of elitist formulations may well be a minor factor in explaining the variance in nationalist success when contrasted with the real pressures for mass participation in organized ameliorative efforts along ethnically advantageous lines.

38. "The process of urbanization has usually been very closely related to the breakdown of at least some of the more traditional ascriptive criteria of status, whether tribal, estate or regional ones, and to the development of somewhat more flexible and variegated social strata; to the upsurge of social mobility through occupational, educational and political channels, and to the develop-ment of a great variety of forms of social organization, ranging from various functionally specific enterprises to various civic and voluntary associations and professional groups . . . All these processes have created a status system of great fluidity and ambiguity. The assurance of a fixed given position which spilled over into most of an individual's institutional roles was being continually undermined . . . by the very nature of the system of social organization . . . [and by] continual changes and structural differentiation. Hence, although these developments usually opened up new perspectives of advancement and change of status, status necessarily became also a focus of insecurity, awareness and

political conflict" (Eisenstadt 1966, p. 11). "We have identified education, urban experience and occupation (especially industrial experience) as three of the most powerful influences determining individual modernity" (Smith and Inkeles 1966, p. 369). Several investigators, among them Lerner (1958) and Deutsch (1953), have effectively used indices of urbanization in lieu of indices of industrialization, mobilization, or modernization that are so much more difficult to obtain.

39. The appeal of social psychological variables such as these in connection with the urban locus of nationalist movements is apparent in the writings of a large group of scholars, classical and modern, such as Hertz (". . . The personality and prestige that the individual cannot attain in his own name may be accessible to him in the form of collective personality in which he has a share" [1944, p. 274]), Rosenblatt ("Needs to be related to something supra-individual, to have goals or to 'belong', are greater among deracinated or marginal individuals" [1964, p. 134]), Simmel (". . . Individuals [previously] liberated from historical bonds now wished to distinguish themselves from one another . . . It is the function of the metropolis to provide the arena for this struggle and its reconciliation. For the metropolis presents peculiar conditions . . . the opportunities for the development of both of these ways of allocating roles to men" [Hatt and Reiss 1957, p. 645]), and Wirth ("In view of the ineffectiveness of actual kinship ties [in the city] we create fictional kinship groups" [1938, p. 62]).

Whether all of the above reactions to urbanization always occurred "naturally" or were also, at least in part, derivative, is open to question in view of the concurrent intellectual condemnation of the city. "Nothing promotes an appreciation of nature more than urban growth" (Minogue 1967, p. 75).

40. "The centre, or the central zone, is a phenomenon of the realm of values and beliefs. It is the centre of the order of symbols, of values and beliefs which goven society . . . As long as societies were loosely coordinated, as long as much of the economic life of the society was carried on outside any market or almost exclusively in local markets, the central value system invariably became attenuated in the outlying reaches . . . The emergence of nationalism, not just the fanatical nationalism of politicians, intellectuals and zealots, but as a sense of nationality and an affirmative feeling for one's own . . . is a very important aspect of this process of the incorporation of the mass of the population into the central institutional and value systems" (Shils 1961, pp. 117, 124 and 128).

41. Just prior to World War II, Wirth was still able to observe that "the foreign born and their children constitute nearly two-thirds of all the inhabitants of cities of one million and over. Their proportion of the urban population declines as the size of the city decreases, until in the rural areas they comprise only about

one-sixth of the total population" (1938, p. 59). While Wirth is pointing primarily to the results of modern immigrations involving largely rural and recently urban populations, the underlying factors involved are not too different from those that brought previously urbanized populations to foreign cities in multiethnic states before the rise of nationalism.

42. "Not until the emancipation of the serfs in Austria in 1848 and in Russia in 1861, were the silent people able to . . . enter other social classes or, above all, take work in the towns" (Kolarz 1946, p. 16).

43. That several cities underwent this process not once but several times is evident from the fact that "The Slovaks can prove that in 1920 only 16% of the population [of Bratislava=Poszony=Pressburg] was Magyar, whilst the Hungarians, basing their claims on the census of 1910, can show that 40% was then Hungarian and only 18% Slovak . . . The Germans . . . refer to the census of 1880 wherein 65% of the population is shown to have been German" (Kolarz 1946, p. 16). In the interim "some of the town dwellers who had [originally come from the land and had] gone over into the camp of the ruling strata changed their language and nationality" not once but twice or even oftener (ibid., p. 15).

44. "It is the decisive nature of the metropolis that its inner life overflows by waves into a far flung national arena . . . The most significant characteristic of the metropolis is this functional extension beyond physical boundaries" (Simmel, in Hatt and Reiss, p. 643).

45. See, e.g., Deutsch (1953, p. 101), Hayes (1960, p. 81), Lerner (1958, p. 71), and Wirth (1938, p. 62), all of whom stress that the city facilitates communication from elites to masses in view of its higher density of interaction networks, communication channels and media, and communication occasions.

46. "It is in the distant provinces . . . where the inhabitants move about less and experience fewer changes of forture and status that the genius and customs of a nation should be studied" (Rousseau, cited by Namier 1952, p. 26).

47. As sensitive a commentator as Gellner considers it fruitful to observe that there is substantial error in each of the "three principle components" of the doctrine of nationalism. "One is a piece of philosophical anthropology: men have 'nationality' as they have a nose and two eyes and this is a central part of their being. The second is a psychological contention: they wish to live with those of the same nationality and above all resent being ruled by those of another one. The third is an evaluative contention, and adds that this is rightly

so" (1964, p. 150). Gellner concludes that "nationalism is not the awakening of nations to self-consciousness: it invents nations where they do not exist" (ibid., p. 168). Deutsch on the other hand views the process of nationality formation as being entirely rational: "When there is a significant high level of important transactions, many of which bring joint rewards, the people who have experienced these mutual transactions will like them. When these transactions are highly visible, easy to identify and differentiate, people . . . form images of the community or of the group involved in the transaction" (1964b, p. 54).

48. In this connection, Sorel observes: "The myth must be judged as a means of acting on the present; any attempt to discuss how far it can be taken literally . . . is devoid of sense" (1961, p. 125).

49. The point I wish to stress is that differences are not naturally "divisive" (nor are similarities unifying) until highlighted as such. It is not the experience of difference that is divisive but the interpretation given to the experience. Thus, the "highly differentiated and clustered world of settlements, nodes of transport, centers of culture, areas and centers of language, divisions of castes and class, barriers between markets, sharp regional differences in wealth and interdependence" (Deutsch 1953, p. 187) are only *potentially* divisive in the sense that they do not further integration. These must first interact with conflict or competition in order to be experienced as justifications for differentiation (Katz 1965, p. 566). The nationality level of society facilitates such interpretive experiences between groups since "sociologically a nationality is a conflict group. The self- and group-consciousness generated by nationalistic movements corresponds to the nature of the inter-group relationship that exists between one nationality and another" (Wirth 1936, pp. 224-225).

The insufficiency of "consciousness of differences" for the purposes of maintaining differentiation is well documented by Hugelman (1931), who traces German national feeling as far back as the reign of Charlemagne, and by Heinz Zatchek (1936), who extensively catalogs the many expressions of antipathy between natives and "foreigners" during the period of the late middle ages. Yet, because these cases had no ideology of nationalism behind (or immediately ahead of) them, most of them proved to be inferior in strength and influence to the integrative experiences that subsequently followed. They did not feed into larger secondary systems that could maintain themselves once the initial irritations had receded into the past (Hayes 1960, p. 29). On the other hand, *some* of these irritations came to be cumulatively interpreted by members of those groups whose self-interests and self-concepts had come to be *organized*, at least in part, in mutually contrastive terms. It then seemed far more significant than it had previously that "at the start of the Second Crusade in 1147, the French army of Louis VII and the German army of Conrad III were kept separate lest they battle each other instead of the Muslems" (Hayes 1960, p. 28). Indeed this seemed particularly significant over 600 years later to Thomasius when he proclaimed (about 1687) " . . . If our German forefathers were to rise from the dead and come amongst us they might think they were in a foreign land. Everything French seems to be in fashion—French food, French clothes, French speech and even French diseases" (Blackall 1959, p. 13). Over a century and a half later, Herder elaborated nearly 800 years of Franco-German conflict into a philosophy with immense and almost immediate political ramifications (although "his own interest was predominantly spiritual-aesthetic: he was fighting the cultural and literary predominance of France and politics hardly entered" into his awareness (Talmon 1965, p. 106). Thus, while Fichte was exaggerating somewhat when he claimed (1807) that " . . . Men cannot *fit* themselves into a new nation once a communal existence [*das Volkseyn*] has entered their natural existence and consciousness" (cited by Namier 1952, p. 22), he was, by and large, not far from what might be a currently acceptable formulation concerning indigenous populations that have undergone long-term and pervasive nationalist ideologization. For a veritable catalog of selective remembering and forgetting of past animosities see Braunthal 1946.

50. Apropos the relevance of superordinate threat note, e.g., Wuorinen's observation that after the mid-century intensification of Russification efforts in Finland "Finn and Swede-Finn stood shoulder to shoulder. They thus proved beyond challenge that much of the 'language fight' had involved grievances and prejudices of no lasting import and . . . had not destroyed the higher loyalty toward nation[ality] and country as a whole" (1950, p. 474). (For further details concerning the threat of Russification as a moderating influence in Finn vs Swede-Finn differentiation see Lindman 1963 and, particularly, Wuorinen 1931). Note, however, that superordinate threat was important in *two* ways. It brought the Finns and Swede-Finns of Finland *closer together* (which is not, of course, to say that they have ever been fully integrated ethnoculturally), on the one hand, and increased their differentiation from the Russians, on the other hand. Common enemies have played a similar role in unifying the Spanish kingdoms (the Moors), the Flemish lowlands (the Spanish), the Scottish districts (the English), the German principalities (the French), etc.

51. An examination of the varying relationships between nationality and polity will also enable us to avoid the dangers foreseen by Wirth: "As long . . . as we continue to confine ourselves to a particularistic analysis of the nationalism of different countries and epochs, on the one hand, and treating nationalism as a single undifferentiated phenomenon, on the other hand, there is little prospect of scientific advance on this subject" (1936, p. 724). A further danger that is worth guarding against, however, is that of establishing purely classificatory

"types of nationalism" which do not provide for transitions, transformations, or links from one to the other. To the lengthy list of older classificatory typologies (many of which have been mentioned in passing above) the more recent additions by Snyder (1964), Haas (1964), and Chilcote (1969) should be noted.

52. This shortsighted view of "naturalness" even applies to the very link between nationality and polity itself. Thus, while Kedourie is certain that "nationalists consider that political and cultural matters are inseparable and that no culture can live if it is not endowed with a sovereign state exclusively its own" (1961, pp. 116-117) he overlooks thereby the counterarguments of a large number of nationalist leaders on all continents and the stable counterpolicies of several more-enlightened multiethnic states. Tagore's view of the relationship between polity and community is encountered among spokesmen for other nonpolitical nationalist movements: "A nation, in the sense of the political and economic union of a people, is that aspect which a whole population assumes when organized for mechanical purposes. Society as such has no ulterior purpose. It is an end in itself. It is a spontaneous self-expression of man as a social being . . The political side. . . is only for a special purpose. It is for self-preservation. It is merely the side of power, not of human ideals" (1920, p. 9). Depres comments on the difference between cultural and political goals as follows: " . . . . . a nationalist movement has as one of its distinguishing characteristics a professed ideology which makes a chauvinistic appeal to a shared tradition of one type or another. Theoretically, an independence movement may or may not share this goal" (1967, p. 10), to which I would merely add, "nor vice versa."

53. That these varying meanings and the words themselves continued to be troublesome for many is evident from the comment that "never have the names *Nation* and *State* been so repeated as today. These two words were never pronounced under Louis XIV and the idea [nation] itself did not even exist . . . This comes from the Parlement and the English" (René Louis de Voyer [d'Argenson], *Journal*, June 26, 1754, p. 262; cited by Barzun 1932).

54. Snyder too refers to the fact that "a common sovereignty provides common institutions" as a result of which "the nation developed within the chrysalis of the state . . . in the Western Atlantic world" (1964, p. 58). Katz discusses "institutional nationalism" at length and contrasts it, as transitional, between statism per se and cultural nationalism. "Institutional nationalism centers around certain societal purposes and national goals. Thus, American nationalism may consist in part of belief systems about the political institution of democracy, and the economic institution of free enterprise, and the related institution of technology as the expression of American national purpose. Value systems

centering around these institutions can exist independently of values about the national state itself, but they are often linked to one another or even fused. Thus, nationalism has an input from the dominant institutions of the society. Advancing national interests means extending these institutions" (Katz 1965, p. 360). It should not be supposed that *all* long established multinationality states necessarily foster the development of institutionally based state-nationality. This outcome is a result not only of common institutions but of internal processes of change, centralization, and in common mobilization or ideologization of the populations involved.

55. The primacy of state (or, in our terms, nation) over nationality obviously influenced and shaped the nature of other integrative forces in Western Europe in addition to the force of nationalism. Thus, Barker observes (in his review of the Reformation and nationality) "There is what I should call Etatism, as well as nationalism, in our English Reformation, and in the beginning there is more etatism than nationalism, although there was always some nationalism there. In other words, the English Church began as a State Church, rather than a national church, but in the course of time the position was gradually changed and inverted" (Barker 1932, p. 340).

56. Engels was the first collectivist spokesman to interpret nationality and nationalism as a malevolent by-product of the bourgeois state. Since that time socialist, communist, and other collectivist movements have been disrupted on several occasions, both by the nationalism of state-nationalities (where long stabilized states have formed broader nationalities) and by the nationalism of nationality-states (when recently integrated nationalities have sought or gained states of their own). Nevertheless, we still find Rocker claiming that "the nation is not the cause, but the result of the State. It is the State which creates the nation, not the nation the state . . . And with the State will disappear also the nation—which is only the state-folk—in order that the concept of humanity may take on a new meaning" (1937, pp. 200, 536). Even capitalists ridiculed state-nations that were of recent vintage and had not yet fully digested the groups upon which they had fed. Zangwill quotes The *(London)* Times as referring to "That maze of cross-bred Celts, Sumarians, Hellenes, Iranians, Semites and Caucasians shot through with Turanians, which we call the Turkish people" (1917, p. 49). The tone is much the same as that employed in current popular references to African state-nations. Thus, even the state-nation is legitimate only if it is old.

57. Countless others wrote in a similar vein, particularly in England, throughout the nineteenth century. At the time the Irish, Scottish, and Welsh seemed to be fairly well incorporated into the lower rungs of British society and "an

underemphasis on nationality became intellectually fashionable in England" (Akzin 1964, p. 18) until well into the twentieth century. Among leading intellectuals, only Byron, John Stuart Mill, and Disraeli seem to have spoken up on behalf of the claims of the newer nationalities during the nineteenth century and even they were less than completely evenhanded about the principle of nationality to which these nationalities referred. Thus, J. S. Mill strongly criticized the nationality principle as "tending to make men indifferent to the rights and interests of any portion of the human species, save that which is called by the same name and speaks the same language as themselves. These feelings are characteristic of barbarians . . . In the backward parts of Europe and even (where better things might have been expected) in Germany, the sentiment of nationality so far outweights the love of liberty that the people are willing to abet their rulers in crushing the liberty and independence of any people not of their race and language" (in "The French Revolution and its Assailants," *Westminster Review* (April 1849), cited by Namier 1952, p. 32). All in all, however, Mill was more inclined than were most of his contemporaries to recognize that the nationality-forming potential of common political ante-cedents depended on their historical priority in comparison to other integrating sentiments. "When nations, thus divided, are under a despotic government which is a stranger to all of them. . . and chooses its instruments indifferently from all, in the course of a few generations identity of situation often produces harmony of feeling and the different races come to feel toward each other as fellow countrymen. But if the era of aspiration to free government arrives before this fusion has been effected, the opportunity has gone by for effecting it" (reprinted 1910, p. 366).

58. The vehemence of Engels' remarks is perhaps understandable if we recognize, as he did, that the fractionated nationalist movements presented a grave danger to the ideal of a parsimonious victory of the proletariat. "There is no country in Europe where there are not different nationalities under the same government. The Highland Gaels and the Welsh are undoubtedly of different nationalities to what the English are, although nobody will give to these remnants of peoples long gone by the title of nations any more than to the Celtic inhabitants of Brittany in France . . . The European *importance,* the *vitality* of a people is as nothing in the eyes of the principle of nationalities; before it, the Roumans [sic] of Wallachia who never had a history, nor the energy required to have one, are of equal importance to the Italians who have a history of 2000 years, and an unimpaired national vitality; the Welsh and Manxmen, if they desired it, would have an equal right to independent political existence, absurd though it be, with the English! The whole thing is absurdity. The principle of nationalities, indeed, could be invented in Eastern Europe alone, where the tide of Asiatic invasion, for a thousand years, recurred again and again, and left on the shore those heaps of intermingled ruins of nations which

even now the ethnologist can scarcely disentangle, and where the Turk, the Finnic Magyar, the Rouman, the Jew, and about a dozen Slavonic tribes live intermixed in interminable confusion" (Engels, 1866; also reprinted in the Appendix to N. Rjasanoff 1916). For continuing evidence of the struggle of small Slavic groups against such views see Glaskow 1971.

59. "The upper classes of the more backward peoples adopted the culture and language of the higher civilization, thus changing their nationality . . . Poland, where Lithuanian, White Russian, and Ukrainian nobles changed over to Polish nationality, provides here a no less striking example than Hungary where Slovak, Rumanian and other nobles merged into the Magyar nobility" (Kolarz 1946, p. 13). In a sense, the upper classes underwent reethnization. As a result of favorable social and economic changes they were incorporated into a new and broader unity. Nationalism performed a similar function for the masses, with an accompanying stress not only on broader unity but on authenticity as well. The second-time-around de-ethnization and reethnization of estranged intellectuals returning them to the fold undoubtedly contributed additional intensity to nationalism in Southern and Eastern Europe.

60. ". . . The peoples without history were peoples without town life . . . The towns without their habitat did not bear the imprint of their national language and customs . . . The cultural centers of the inarticulate peoples were necessarily located outside their proper sphere" (Kolarz 1946, p. 44). This last comment pertains to the fact that when the first nationalist elites of the submerged Central, Eastern, and Southern European nationalities began to organize they were forbidden to engage in the educational, cultural, and political activities which they considered essential for the purposes of mass mobilization. As a result, many of the most outstanding among them were forced to leave (or flee) to foreign centers of intellectual activity, many of which (e.g., Vienna, Budapest, Odessa, Constantinople, Lvov, and even Paris, London, and Geneva) long had very sizable colonies of expatriate intellectuals who created, studied, and intrigued *there* while maintaining clandestine contacts with their homelands. The experience of prolonged foreign residence and intergroup contact undoubtedly contributed to the "theoretical ethnicity" evolved by many exiled or self-exiled intellectual spokesmen for the peoples without history.

61. Herder contended that "the empire of the Ottomans and the Grand Mogul are corrupt states which comprise a multitude of nations; while the States of China, of the Brahmins, and of the Jews are wholesome states which, even if they perish, leave the nation intact, because it has been able to withstand intermixture with other nations" (Kedourie 1961, p. 59). The Jewish tradition, of course, accepts the distinction-between-peoples as God-given-without-

invidiousness, in that each nation has its own mission: "When the Most High divided to the nations their inheritance, when he separated the sons of Adam, he set the bounds of the people" (Deuteronomy 32:8).

62. The intensity of anti-French and antiforeign feelings in Germany and Italy was so great (particularly as a result of the long frustrated political unification of both of these nations whose historicity was acknowledged even in the West) that in both of them the nation-state philosophy was clearly dominant by the eighteenth century, if not earlier, even though their contacts with Western intellectual circles were infinitely greater than those obtaining for Hungary, Poland, or Greece. Thus, German philosophers and literati ridiculed the rationality of French and British social and political thought and declared it to be a mechanistic outcome of the ethnic and cultural mongrelization of their underlying populations. However, when a unified Germnay finally appeared it was not at all the nation-state that had been prophesied and so long ideologized. It not only included many non-Germans (Alsatians, Lorrainers, Danes, Poles, etc.), but it failed to include all of the Germans (particularly those that remained under Habsburg rule). A large proportion of the population it coveted in order to become a true nation-state was scattered throughout predominantly Slavic and increasingly nationalistic "peoples without a history" to the east of them. The resulting tensions between German reality and German theory produced well-known catastrophic consequences for Germany and her neighbors.

The Italian case is also an interesting hybrid, but in this instance the outcome was in accord with Central European thought, whereas the view propounded was in accord with Mazzini's basic dedication to Western notions of popular sovereignty. However, the "mission of Rome" was such an entrenched element in Italian thought and the plebian fractionization of Italian daily life so shocking a reality to Italian intellectuals that the conflict between the nation-state and the state-nation remained as constant themes in postunification Italy, even as they had been before. Thus, the libertarian Mazzini could exclaim that since the world had twice before been united by Rome, Imperial and Papal, ". . . why should not a new Rome, the Rome of the Italian people . . . arise to create a third and still vaster unity?" (cited by Namier 1952, p. 30) while the authoritarian Massimo d'Azeglio could proclaim "We have made Italy; now we must make Italians" (cited in Sturzo 1927, p. 13). For further analyses of German and Italian nationalism as hybrid expressions of state-nation and nation-state cross-pressures see Pflanze 1966.

63. The Habsburg Empire itself presents many particularly interesting similarities relative to some of the current "new nations" in that, on the one hand, it was still very far from fostering a state-nationality and, on the other hand, its ruling classes normally resisted any efforts to fractionate it into a number of

nationality-states. Akzin comments that in the latter decades of the Empire nation-state views were quite predictably held "by writers belonging to non-dominant nationalities who sought the dissolution of the Empire, whereas many of those belonging to dominant nationalities (German-Austrian, Hungarian) tended to value the state mainly because of its role as an instrument in service of the [ir particular] nation" (Akzin 1964, pp. 17 and 44), thus leaving no very articulate body of opinion to function on behalf of the state as a whole, i.e., as a supranational object of patriotism or nationism.

64. The extent to which American scholars have largely had the nation-state context in mind when criticizing nationalism is evident from comments by Pillsbury ("The nation is cause, the state effect," 1919, p. 773) and Gellner ("It is not the aspirations of nations which create nationalism; it is nationalism which creates nations," 1964, p. 174). Kohn rejects this ". . . 'closed' nationalism [which] stresses the nation's autochthonous character, the common origins (race, blood), the rootedness in the ancestral soil" as being "romantic, anti-Western and anti-Enlightenment . . . Their ideal society was to be found in the tribal or premodern past, in emphasis on *Eigenart* or *samobytnost*" (Kohn 1968, p. 66). Among the scholars who have been most aware of the social and historical contextualization of both processes one must mention Lemberg 1964 and Symmons-Symonolewicz 1965, 1968 and 1971, neither of whom has attained the recognition he deserves. Like Passerin d'Entrèves they stress that "In those parts where amalgamation of state and nation had long been achieved, patriotism could find expression in the proud assertion of the liberty won and sanctioned by means of free institutions which were held out for the admiration of the world. . . . But where nations were still broken up into a multiplicity of political units, patriotism could not but take the shape primarily of a demand for unity and independence" (1967, p. 179). Generally speaking, the transition from one process into the other is little recognized.

65. There have been few major treatments of pan movements as a general phenomenon in the years since the Second World War. Among the more helpful brief reviews, the ones by Kazemzadeh (1968), Kohn (1962; see chapter on "The Global Awakening of Peoples") and Snyder (1964; see chapter on "Nationalism and Supranationalism") should be mentioned because of their bibliographic usefulness particularly with respect to Pan-Slavism and Pan-Germanism in Europe and Pan-Turkism and Pan-Arabism in parts of the Moslem world. Pan-Africanism in particular still lacks sufficient integrative empirical investigation but will probably receive more attention if the notion itself obtains broader social and political support, (See Decraene 1961, Mazrui 1963, Legum 1965, Geiss 1967, Hazelwood 1967, Markakis 1967, Langley 1969, Walshe 1970, and Waters 1970.)

66. "Pre-Soviet Pan-Slavism had two distinct stages: the non-political, cultural, democratic one, in which Czech and Slovak intellectuals played the dominant part; and the conservative nationalist, political one, led by an unusual combination of [largely Russian] intellectuals, bureaucrats and the military" (Kazemzadeh 1968, p. 367). Recent French and Portuguese efforts to declare their colonial possessions as being essentially extensions of their respective "metropolitan" cultures are other recent examples of state-nation pan movements.

67. " . . . [Initially] Pan-Slavism stimulated scholarly interest in Slavic antiquity, spurred linguistic and archeological studies, encouraged the collection of folklore, and gave the Czechs, Slovaks, Serbs, Croats and Bulgars a sense of worth and importance through membership in a vast and glorious community" (Kazemzadeh 1968, p. 367). Jan Kollar, the Slovak nationalist poet, wrote that " . . . if the various branches of the Slav race were of metal, he would make a unique statue of them. From Russia the head, from Poland the breast, from Bohemia the arms and from Servia the legs. Before such a colossus Europe would kneel down" (Jaszi 1929, p. 256). In an earlier period, very similarly, "The Catalans tended to look upon their Aragonese and Valencian neighbors as closely akin to themselves. The Valencians talked a variety of the same language, and both Aragon and Valencia had been their associates in the great medieval federation and formed part of the Crown of Aragon to which Catalonia belonged" (Elliot 1963, p. 43).

68. Vivid personal experiences of broader ethnocultural unity are described by many writers in recollections of their childhood. Thus, Chaudhuri recounts how nationalist agitation came to his attention in 1905, when he was still a child, after Lord Curzon had proposed the administrative partitioning of Bengal, as follows: " . . . my father asked us to bathe in the river first and then in a state of cleanness tie the thread round our wrists as a token of the brotherhood of all Bengalis. We were to observe that day as a day of national mourning and fasting." This recollection is immediately joined to one which stresses authenticity. "We also put away all our clothes manufactured in England and put on dhotis made in the Indian mills" (Chaudhuri 1951, p. 219).

69. "Most significantly, however, appeals are made to the unity and identity of the indigenous populations, particularly with respect to external social units resident in the country" (Friedland 1968, p. 19).

70. Speaking primarily of interwar East and West Africa one investigator comments: "There was a resuscitation in some countries of traditional clothing and where (as in Tanganyika) genuine traditional clothing was inappropriate a neotraditional costume was invented or borrowed" (Friedland 1968, p. 21).

71. With respect to the period of the late 1860's in Bengal, Roy reports: "Many again not only learnt to speak Hindi but vaunted *Nagrai* shoes (of the kind used only recently by the village people in U[pper] P[radesh] and Bihar) and *Sikha* (a tuft of hair at the back of the head)" (1962, p. 243.)

72. One aspect of growing nationalist sympathies in late nineteenth century Burma " . . . was a protest against the use of footwear in the precincts of pagodas and monasteries; this protest gained such general support that Europeans had to comply with it" (Furnivall 1956, p. 143).

73. "The unique superiority of the Aryan culture lay in the fact that it had developed entirely independent of any other existing civilization and unaided by the precepts or examples of any earlier or contemporary culture" (McCully 1940, p. 249, paraphrasing an anonymous article in *Bengal Magazine,* 1875-76, 4, pp. 367-368).

74. "Is it not now a well established fact that at all events we were among the first civilized nations and that our forefathers were poets and philosophers when those from whom are descended the great nations of Europe had hardly risen above the hunting or nomad state, or had even acquired a distinctive national name?" (McCully 1940, p. 248, paraphrasing an unsigned article in the *National Magazine,* 1875-76, 1, p. 338).

75. " . . . While every other ancient nation which had created a great civilization—the Egyptians, Chaldeans, the ancient Greeks, the Romans—had disappeared, we, the Hindus had survived; this could only mean that we were a chosen people who were destined, or rather ordained, to have a future more glorious than even their past" (Chaudhuri 1951, p. 221).

76. "The 20th century has added another revolutionary dimension to nationalism. Nationalism has also become a socially revolutionary movement, demanding equal economic and educational opportunities for all . . . and the active promotion of the welfare of the socially underprivileged . . . By the middle of the 20th century all 'young' nationalist movements had also become socialist movements" (Kohn 1968, p. 64).

77. " . . . A new vigorous industrial pattern, a new social and industrial consciousness, and a new way of organizing and doing things . . . have created a new climate . . . have annihilated many tribal, linguistic, ethnic barriers and divisions . . . [and are] largely responsible for the unification of African tribes" (Sithole 1959, p. 74). Also see Eastman 1971.

78. "Typically, the introduction of Western techniques of medicine cuts the death-rate and population begins to increase rapidly. This creates difficulties which a traditional system of agriculture cannot deal with, and men are therefore driven away from their villages into cities, mines and plantations which grow up in the wake of Western economic enterprise . . . Their situation is transformed in a way difficult for Europeans to understand, for in Europe this transformation has been spread over several centuries" (Minogue 1967, p. 84).

79. "Some natives are recruited into a local police force; others are trained as clerks in local government or industry, and, therefore, become literate . . . A few lucky or pertinacious young men [ultimately] set out for universities of the imperial country . . . Often it may happen that for several generations the European educated are content to operate within a European framework. But the time always comes when this educated elite makes a bid for power and when it does so it commonly uses the rhetoric of nationalism" (Minogue 1967, pp. 84-85). Kautsky notes that colonialism "produces the [native] intellectuals and yet, by its very existence, it frustrates them and hence arouses their opposition" (1962, p. 49). The Angolan case is particularly instructive in this connection (Wheeler 1969) because of the role of the *assimilados.*

80. "When the transition to independence is also accompanied by extensive efforts at economic revolution, various intermediate social structures that shared or captured loyalties in the pre-industrial system are undermined. Nationalism . . . is offered as a source of identity to substitute for the tribe or village . . . . *Nationalist ideology provides a rationale for the multitude of changes in way of life"* (Moore 1965, p. 34).

81. After the failure of the Boxer Rebellion the classical Chinese tradition came to be viewed by young radicals "as something in which one might rummage for things of current value; it had never been anything like that in previous times." Even the name of the country was changed, in order to foster a new and greater unity, from ". . . *T'ien hsia,* a cultural realm [below heaven] in which everything of value was cultivated by the mandarin class . . . to *Chung-Kuo,* the all-inclusive [middle Kingdom] state, the nation" (Minogue 1967, pp. 90-91). Conversely, the Japanese victory over Russia (1905) had a strongly positive impact on elites throughout Asia in their efforts to arrive at more modern but yet indigenous self-concepts. Tagore's evaluation of the Japanese victory was that it "broke the spell under which we [Asians] lay in torpor for ages" (1920, p. 50). Another Indian observer commented "What? An Eastern Nation facing a Western Nation on a field of battle? What? The White people were not then resistless? They had been met and overthrown by a coloured race, by men like themselves? A thrill of hope ran through Asia. Asia invaded, Asia troubled by white 'spheres of

influence,' with settlements of white people, insolent and dominant, rebelling against Eastern laws, rejecting Eastern customs with contempt, humiliating coloured nations in their own lands, and arrogating powers to which they had no right. Despair changed into hope. Asia awoke, and with Asia, India" (Besant 1926, pp. 159-160).

Blond's reconstructed account of the Japanese reaction to the Russian fleet's request to negotiate conveys the deep emotion of the moment as well as the deep emotion that such tales are intended to elicit at every successive recitation: " . . . an international code signal was run up [the mainmast of the *Nicholas I*] : XGH. The signals officer of the watch immediately translated: We ask to negotiate.

"Togo made no move. He seemed to turn to stone. The officers surrounding him were equally motionless, equally silent. They looked at the Russian ships, still under heavy Japanese fire. But more than one mouth was opened in amazement or to utter an exclamation at what came next.

"The other Russian ships, acting almost together, were striking their colors. And when the Russian flags had disappeared below their bridges, another flag was run up on every ship: The Rising Sun, national emblem of Japan. The Russians had struck their colors and run up their enemy's flag to make it quite clear that they were surrendering. It was a heartbreaking spectacle. Even on Togo's bridge there were officers whose hearts were thumping uncomfortably, officers with lumps in their throats and tears in their eyes. 'Admiral, they are surrendering,' said his chief of staff in a voice that was unsteady, almost shrill. 'Does not the spirit of Bushido require us to cease fire?'

"Togo took one more look at the signal flying from the mast of the *Nicholas I* and at the Japanese flags on the other ships. 'Cease fire,' he said.

"And he ordered all the ships to form a wide circle around the enemy. This scene was played out on May 28, 1905, at a quarter to eleven in the morning, in waters situated approximately eighteen miles southwest of Liancourt rocks" (Blond 1960, pp. 221-233).

Even the Japanese victories over the allies at the beginning of World War II were regardéd as providing a valuable lesson for indigenous populations by nationalists seeking to unify and activate them (see Singhal 1967, p. 278).

82. The interdependence of nationalism and religion is even more evident throughout Asia than it was in Europe. Not only were religious leaders and functionaries at the very forefront of most nationalist movements (see Furnivall 1956, pp. 142-144 and 201 in connection with Burma; McCully 1940, pp. 260-267 and infra in connection with India; Heyd 1950, infra, in connection with Turkey; Nuseibeh 1956, infra, in connection with Arab nationalism in general and Egypt in particular) but the very notion of nationalism other than in an ethnoreligious context was commonly rejected as a Western abberation that was

either abhorrent or impossible under local conditions. Zurayq, the great Egyptian-Arab nationalist of the nineteenth century, proclaimed that " . . . true nationalism can in no sense be incompatible with true religion, because in its essence it is naught but a spiritual movement, which aims at the regeneration of the inner forces of a nation and the realization of its mental and spiritual potentialities. Nationalism, being a spiritual movement, must go hand in hand with religion and derive from it strength and life. . . True religion. . . emanates with nationalism from the same spring" (Nuseibeh 1956, p. 92). The very conception of India as the "motherland," symbolized by the figures of the goddesses Durga, Vani, and Lakshimi, represented an effort to develop a religious basis for nationalism, or the assumption that the religious sentiment of the Hindus was far easier to arouse than any national feeling. Tagore, e.g., held that India was "a plant which would never thrive but in the soul watered by the hand of Faith—a nationality of religious union" (McCully 1940, p. 267, paraphrasing an article published by Tagore in 1895). Finally, Muhammad Iqbal, one of the principal forerunners of the drive for an independent Pakistan, "explicitly repudiated the Western concept of the nation as . . . territorially defined . . . , holding the latter incompatible with both Islam in general and the special position of Islam in India" (Emerson 1902, p. 107).

All in all India must be viewed as a mixed case, making for less explicit use of religion in pursuit of national sociocultural integration than do the nations of Islam or Theravada Buddhism. Thus Jinnah fully supported Iqbal's view (see above) noting (in 1940) that "the British people, being Christians, sometimes forget the religious wars of their own history and today consider religion as a private and personal matter between man and God. This can never be the case in Hinduism and Islam, for both of these religions are definite social codes which govern not so much man's relations with his God, as man's relations with his neighbor. They govern not only his law and culture but every aspect of his social life" (cited by Bolitho 1954, pp. 126-127).

Along similar lines Smith points out that "Islamic history is calculated to begin not the year Muhammad was born . . . , nor when he began to receive divine revelations, but when the Muslim community came to power in a state of its own. The year 1 A.H. marks the establishment of Islam as a religio-political sovereignty in al-Madinah" (1954, pp. 22-23). Cady makes a related point with respect to Buddism in Burma. "The most important positive basis on which popular allegiance to the King was acknowledged by the leading ethnic peoples of Burma (the Burmans, Mons, Shans and Arakanese) was that royalty functioned as the promoter and defender of the Buddist faith . . . a function which was regarded by Burmans as the very *raison d'être* of the State" (1958, p. 8). Mehden cites numerous details concerning the usefulness of religion in the Burmese and Indonesian nationalist movements (1968) as does Hajime (1967) with respect to Japan and Kumar (1969) with respect to India.

From the foregoing it seems clear that religion and nationalism have not only served each other in Asia (as they had in Europe), but that they are commonly presented as one and the same to the masses as a means of pursuing and maintaining the political independence and stability of multiethnic states whose boundaries have been, in part, inherited from colonial days and, in part, from precolonial multiethnic empires. Certainly, one cannot speak about nationalism in Asia as an ideological replacement either for localistic tradition as a whole or for religion more specifically, it being so widely felt that " . . . reformation, in order to be true and abiding, must mean not only the introduction of new civilization, but a revival of the old culture as well. It must not be a mere introduction of Western customs, but also a resuscitation into new life of the lingering vitality still to be found [in the larger ethnoreligious community] " (McCully 1940, p. 254; paraphrasing an article by Keshub Chundra Sen published in 1871).

83. For similar claims in other parts of Africa as well, see Wm. H. Friedland and Carl G. Rosenberg (eds.), *African Socialism,* (Stanford: Stanford University Press, 1964). Also note Myrdal's reference to India's "rich mythology about the ancient village as a perfect democracy with a rational cooperative organization of production and community life, where caste observance was less rigid and degrading, and women enjoyed a higher status" (1968, p. 77). For a more recent integrative summaries re the indigenous and roots of economic modernization ideologies see Jumba-Masagazi (1970), Gregor (1967), Hanna and Gardner (1969), and Auma-Osolo and Osolo-Nasubo (1971).

84. Although Herder, Mazzini, and even the great Slavic nationalists influenced them, African and Asian nationalists were obviously more taken with Western European liberal nationalism (with its emphasis on the state as the provider of unity of institutions, universal civil rights, and universal social services) than by Eastern European ethnic cultural nationalism (with its emphasis on the mononationality state as a protector of monocultural authenticity). They however, did provide additional rationale for the rejection of "foreign influences." (For many interesting details and formulations, see Ali Mazrui's "Some Sociopolitical Functions of English Literature in Africa," in J. A. Fishman, C. A. Ferguson and J. Das Gupta, eds., *Language Problems of Developing Nations* (New York: Wiley, 1968), pp. 183-198.) Kolarz remarked about the Germans, Russians, Poles, Italians, and Magyars (vis-à-vis the new nationalities) that they "always play . . . the roles of both Jekyll and Hyde. They are both oppressors and liberators, bringers of darkness and bearers of light" (1946, p. 50). The same observation holds true vis-à-vis the West as a whole and much Asian or African nationalism.

85. "With the coming of mines, towns and cities, the different tribes of Africa found themselves thrown together. Tribesmen who had never had anything to do with one another found themselves living together in one area, working side by side with one another . . . With the coming together of these tribes the horizons of many Africans have been greatly extended" (Sithole 1959, pp. 68-69).

86. "This general pattern— of an African town separate from and economically and politically subordinate to a European town, the two towns being closely linked in regard to their economies and administrative systems but unbelievably remote in respect to their human relationships—has an obvious bearing on the genesis of African nationalism" (Hodgkin 1956, p. 73). For extensive treatments of the economic nexus of modern African and Asian nationalisms see Wildenman and Parkalla 1966 and Johnson 1968.

87. "The exuberant growth of associations in African towns is a point which has often been noticed. There are three ways in which these Tribal Associations contribute to the development of African nationalism. They provide a network of communications entirely under African control . . . , they tend to foster or keep alive an interest in tribal songs and dances, history, language and moral belief . . . , they play an active part in [financing] the education of an African elite" (Hodgkin 1956, p. 87).

88. "The membership [of TANU, the nationalist party, in post-World War II Tanganyika] was vast but concentrated in the towns and in rural centers of population where, most often, the influence of the modern economy was felt most strongly. Among nomadic tribes TANU influence was much less significant" (Friedland 1968, p. 16).

89. " . . . in one essential respect at least mid-twentieth century Dakar and Lagos differ from mid-nineteenth century Leeds and Manchester: the cause of their existence, the basis of their economic life, is not factory industry but commerce" (Hodgkin 1956, p. 64).

90. "Nothing was more natural for us than to feel about Muslims in the way we did. Even before we could read we had been told that the Muslims had once ruled and oppressed us; that they had spread their religion in India with the Koran in one hand and the sword in the other; that the Muslim rulers had abducted our women, destroyed our temples, polluted our sacred places" (Chaudhuri 1951, p. 226).

91. "Characteristically, the nationalist leaders stress the moral, religious, or spiritual superiority of their culture to the materialism, utilitarianism and

technocracy of the West . . . They hail the distinctive contributions of native music, literature, art and poetry, and warn against the 'mental colonialism' that has separated the intellectuals from their cultural heritage and subjected them to the alien values of the dominant European civilization" (Sigmund 1963, p. 32).

92. For examples of several such reluctant acceptances of Westernization due to the urgency of modernization, see Rustow 1957, Kumar 1969, and Nandy 1970. Elsbree reviews the attempts of the Japanese occupation force to exploit anti-Western sentiments on behalf of its Greater Asia Co-Prosperity Sphere, the subsequent switch to gratifying local nationalist aspirations (such as encouragement of publication and broadcasting in Bahasa Indonesia throughout the occupied Dutch East Indies), and, finally, the " . . . awakening . . . to the fact that nationalism was a stronger and more demanding force than they had imagined and demanded greater concessions than they had anticipated" (1953, p. 165). Japanese experience in attempting to direct submerged nationalisms against an enemy external to the supranational state (in order to deflect them from being directed against the supranational state itself which kept them submerged) was as unsuccessful as that of the Habsburg Empire mentioned above (see footnote 63).

93. The few nationality-states among post-World War II additions to the family of nations are (clearly) Somalia, Korea, (less clearly) Burma, Vietnam, Cambodia, Laos, (and least clearly) Malaysia, Israel, and the Moslem state of the Maghreb and the Near East. The Moslem states mentioned have such substantial pan-Arab ties that their ethnic individuality at the national level is still in the process of formation. Israel is faced by the problem of fusing two large streams of immigrants, those from Western and those from non-Western countries of origin. Malaysia, Burma, and new states carved out of former French Indochina all contain substantial numbers of Chinese and other minority peoples.

94. Curtin (1966) sees the dominant force in recent African politics as the desire to build nations of the state-nation type. He views the first two decades of the African revolution as a clean sweep of the state-nation type. The state is to create the nationality, not the reverse. As noted earlier this is also Kautsky's view (1962). See Mushkat 1971, Rotberg 1962 and 1966 for the opposing view that African nationalism is essentially nonethnic in origin and in purpose.

95. This may be what Silvert means when he concludes that "nationalism in contemporary underdeveloped areas develops in manners organically different from the classical British and American patterns" (1963, p. 442). My own view is that it is not so much in its early stirrings that the most striking differences are found between the two as in their respective relationships to subsequent state formation. The British and American states both started with ethnically rather

homogeneous groups (i.e., they were originally nation-states) and have evolved into state-nations as they expanded to include successive other-ethnic populations under slowly modified symbols and institutions. This is *not* the case with respect to most of the states to which Silvert refers.

96. "In the latter half of the 19th century and after, Macedonian, Great Bulgarian and Pan-Slav sentiments and political movements, coexisted in south-eastern Europe (Hodgkin 1956, p. 21). "Pan-Turkism was born in the last quarter of the nineteenth century among the Tartars of the Crimea and the Volga ... [as] a reaction against the encroachment of ... Russian nationalism ... Although theoretically [Ismail Bey Gasprinski, its formulator] ... envisaged the union of all Muslim peoples, his activity was directed at Russia's Turkic masses ... [and] Pan-Slavism [was his] ... intellectual model" (Kazemzadeh 1968, p. 369). Also see Zarevand, in press (French translation 1930).

97. "During the period of Arab nationalist opposition, first to Turkish and later to British and French rule, one could find layers of Druse, Lebanese, Greater Syrian and Pan-Arab nationalism imposed one above the other" (Hodgkin 1956, pp. 21-22). The modern Indian case is a better example than Pan-Arabism of a relatively successful pan movement since, except for the fringe areas which became Pakistan, Burma, and Ceylon, the efforts of Gandhi and the Indian Union Party to convince millions that "the past of India, with all its cultural variety and greatness, was a common heritage of all the Indian people, Hindu, Moslem, Christian and others, and their ancestors had helped to build it" (Nehru 1953, pp. 6-7) have thus far succeeded tolerably well, at least at the political-operational level. That this outcome was based, in part, upon the reality as well as upon the ideal of Hindu sociocultural integration is evident from such observation as "Ambala in Upper India was over 1100 miles from Calcutta ... But nothing struck the Bengali as strange and made him feel that he was in a new country. Instead he saw the same plains, the same people working in the fields, the same well-irrigation, the same village congeries, the same naked peasantry, and the same women with veiled heads and armlets to the elbows. Such uniformity proved that India was designed by nature to form a grand national unity" (McCully 1940, p. 245; paraphrasing an article of Bholonath Chandra published in 1881). That broader and narrower loyalties cannot only coexist but be repeatedly accommodated to each other at successively higher levels of integration is a point neatly stressed by Mazrui 1969a, Ranger 1968b, and Ronen 1968; Skinner's paper (1959), and the entire symposium which it introduces, is particularly informative in this connection.

98. "Dr. Sukarno, in his days of power, promoted a state called Maphilindo ..., a pan-Malay creation ... [with] a certain cultural and political plausibility

which might give it a future" (Minogue 1967, pp. 13-14). Note, however, that Dr. Sukarno's dream of uniting *Ma*laysia, the *Phil*ippines, and *Indo*nesia (=Maphilindo) was itself merely an extension of the earlier Indonesian nationalist reference to the "medieval empire of Majapahit, which from a Javanese capital had claimed control over a large part of the Indies and of the Malay peninsula. That many of these claims lacked solid historical evidence to support them does not detract from the importance of Majapahit to modern Indonesian nationalism, and not least in the years after independence" (Kennedy 1968, pp. 82-83).

99. "The failing fortunes of Muslim states, and their inability to withstand the pressure of European imperialism, gave rise to the Pan-Islamic movement that called for the union of Muslim peoples and states against Western aggression and domination . . . It . . . preached a supranational doctrine at the same moment that Western nationalism was beginning to stir up the peoples of the Middle East . . . Jamal al Din [its founder and principal ideologist, 1838-1897] failed to sense the growth of nationalism among the Persians, the Turks and the Arabs" (Kazemzadeh 1968, p. 369). For a confirming interpretation of pan-Islamism as an early stage (rather than as a subsequent further elaboration) of Arab nationalism, see Keddie (1969).

100. "Whenever we try to talk in terms of larger units on the African continent, we are told that it can't be done. We are told that the units we would so create would be 'artificial.' As if they could be any more artificial than the 'national' units on which we are now building" (Nyerere 1961, reprinted in Sigmund 1963, p. 209). Subsequently Nyerere makes even clearer his conviction that no essential ethnic differences divide Negro Africa: "I believe that . . . the role of African nationalism is different—or should be different— from the nationalism of the past; that the African national state is an instrument for the unification of Africa and not for dividing Africa; that African nationalism is meaningless, is dangerous, is anachronistic, if it is not at the same time Pan-Africanism" (ibid., p. 211). Senghor's philosophy of "Negritude" is similarly supraethnic and supralocal in design, extolling as it does "the whole complex of civilized values—cultural, economic, social and political—which characterize the black peoples, or, more precisely, the Negro-African world . . . The sense of communion, the gift of myth-making, the gift of rhythm, such are the essential elements of Negritude which you will find indelibly stamped on all the works and activities of the black man" (*West Africa*, Nov. 4, 1961; reprinted in Sigmund 1963, p. 249), See also Irele 1969).

Notes to Part II

1. Indeed, those pursuits and processes not influenced by such ideologies were long unconcerned with the vernaculars. Since political participation, e.g., was restricted to the nobility, the upper bourgeoisie, and the intellectuals, all of whom were suitably multilingual by virtue of also controlling a classical tongue and a prestige vernacular (even when they no longer maintained their original vernaculars), it was unnecessary "before the end of the eighteenth century . . . [for] governments [to] regard the language of the people as a matter which concerned them . . . [Nor did they] attempt to destroy a language when they acquired new subjects through conquest or peaceful annexation" (Sulzbach 1943, p. 48). There are, however, many pre-eighteenth century records of governmental use of vernaculars wherever contact with the masses *was* desired.

2. Learning (or relearning) the vernacular was an integral part of the reethnization of Czech, Slovak, Polish, Ukranian, Jewish, Rumanian, Estonian, and other latter nineteenth-century and early twentieth-century protoelites drawn from middle-class (or better) sociocultural backgrounds. Thus, Arwiddson, a mid-nineteenth century leader of the pro-Finnish Swede-Finns held that "the Finns could never become a truly united nation while the upper classes were separated from the lower by a linguistic gulf. The gulf could be bridged and the people united only by reversing the process which had made the upper classes increasingly Swedish. In a word, they would have to adopt Finnish as their mother tongue" (Wuorinen 1931, p. 53). A similar linguistic reethnization was frequently necessary in late nineteenth-century India. Chaudhuri recollects that during his childhood the nationalist leader Aurobindo Ghose "spoke in English because having been educated wholly in England he could speak no Bengali at all when he came back to his country, and when he came to Kishorganj he had learnt just enough to carry on a simple conversation" (1951, p. 239).

3. Where the approximate vernacular is not that which is ideologically preferred (e.g., Sanskrit, classical Greek, classical Arabic, Irish, Hebrew), or where there are a great many mutually incomprehensible vernaculars without an established lingua franca (as, e.g., in parts of East and West Africa), the functional load of nationalism may be carried by other languages for longer or shorter periods. In most of these cases, however, there is considerable tension between two tendencies, on the one hand to revise nationalist ideology so that it will conform in a more stable fashion with the *actual* vernaculars, and, on the other hand, to augment the language planning and learning aspects of nationalist policy so that the vernaculars utilized will more quickly become the ones that the ideology requires. The successes and failures of nationalism in the revival of so-called "dead" languages or in the indigenization of distant languages is a fascinating topic which merits separate attention (see footnote 46, below).

4. In another context Kedourie observes quite correctly, that "the reading of books [in the vernacular] became a political, a revolutionary activity" (1961, p. 103).

5. The earliest European arguments on behalf of *vernacular education* (rather than merely on behalf of more widespread literacy) can be traced back at least to the early fifteenth century. Nevertheless, such education long remained rare, indeed it was not until 1548 that "Louis Le Roy first lectured in French at a University and became the first author of a treatise on metaphysics in the vulgar language" (Kohn 1944, p. 132). Even then it was necessary to argue that there was no question of disregarding Hebrew, Greek, or Latin but only "de cheminer plus seulement en sa voye domestique, c'est à dire escripre françoise, comme François que nou somme" (Geoffroy Tory of Bourges in his Champfleury 1529; cited by Kohn 1944, p. 131). At roughly the same time the number of German books published annually in Protestant Germany was still only 116, i.e., half the number of Latin books (246). As late as 1714, the number of Latin books remained fairly constant although the number of German books published annually had increased to 419. In 1780 the two figures were 198 (Latin) and 1,917 (German) (see: Karl Biederman, *Deutschland im achtzehnten Jahrhundert* [Leipzig: Weber, 1859], vol. II, p. 504).

By the end of the eighteenth century elementary education in the vernacular was becoming sufficiently common among the "historic peoples" of Western Europe for coterritorial minorities to recognize the disadvantage under which their children labored and to agitate for change. "Is it not strange that the Welsh differ in their method of teaching children from every other nation in the world? There is no other country, to our knowledge, which does not first teach its own language to the children, apart from Wales" (Morgan John Rys 1793; cited by

W. R. Jones 1966, p. 39). A century later this identical argument had spread to Eastern Europe and half a century thereafter, to substantial parts of Africa and Asia. In all cases, however, the definition of the "nation's own language" is ideologically rather than merely "naturally" determined.

6. The educational use of the vernacular, particularly in higher education, seems, generally, to have lagged behind its use in particular legal pronouncements and in military announcements *intended to reach the common man.* Thus, "in the 1360's King Edward III prescribed the use of English instead of Latin or French, in the lower courts of England" (Hayes 1960, p. 60). Even earlier (842) the Oaths of Strasbourg presented significant evidence of the official use of the vernaculars for strategic purposes "Louis the German (King of the East Franks) and Charles the Bald (King of the West Franks) swore loyalty to each other. As they did, Louis used the *lingua romana* (Roman-French) so that his brother's retainers might understand him; and Charles spoke *lingua teudesca* (Deutsch-German) for the same reason. But these languages were certainly not yet . . . Kingdomwide in usage" (Shafer 1955, p. 77). Nevertheless, such precedents did not always lead to consistent followups, due primarily to the fluctuating dependence of royal power upon popular support. In 1539 Francis I found it necessary to order that only French be used in legal acts and pronouncements (thus excluding both Latin and regional languages such as Provençal), although such orders had also been given by earlier monarchs. Similarly, Philip II of Spain was advised during the century of Spanish world power to use "clear Castilian instead of an obscure and barbarous Latin" and that civil law should be expressed "en lengua común y popular" (Simón Abril 1550? ; cited by Kohn 1944, p. 153). The great and final decision on behalf of the vernacular came with mass armies, mass involvment in political and legal affairs, improved communication networks, and mass education systems, rather than with any of the earlier precedents of the kinds mentioned above.

7. "Furtherance of the modernization ideals requires the extended use of the indigenous languages. No real 'emotional integration' of the new nations, and, therefore, no secure national consolidation is possible as long as the members of the tiny upper class in charge of administration, law enforcement and modernized business and industry communicate in a European language and the masses speak only their native tongue" (Myrdal 1968, p. 81).

8. The objectively instrumental role of language in the reorganization of economic and political systems is one of the major foci of Deutsch's *Social Communication and Nationalism* (1953). His many indices of mobilization all have in common the fact that they highlight exposure to vernacular communi-

cation from elitist groups attempting the activation and unification of specific populations. More recently Myrdal has both indicated the indispensability of the vernaculars in national modernization in South Asia, as well as the problems of large-scale political integration likely to flow from their utilization (1968, pp. 81-89, 1639-40, etc.). Friedrich, among political scientists, has consistently maintained the view that "In any elaborate sense, community means . . . language" since it conveys "emotions, thoughts and other expressions of selfhood which bind. . . [interlocutors] into a community that is continuously reborn through speaking and listening" (1963, pp. 43 and 40). His formulation contains echoes of the nationalist emphases on subjective function, i.e., on the *particular* languages that are involved in the emotional rebirth and in the authentic preservation of a nationality. The connection between both kinds of functions is recognized (even if not stressed) by each of the above mentioned authors, as well as by observers in the developing nations per se. Chatterji, e.g., states " . . . we have the need for an [all-] Indian language, which we must have for both utility and sentiment" (1943, p. 23). Exactly the same point has been made by Ajarchukwu (1960), Ola (1960), Whiteley (1969), Harries (1969), and others in Africa. Social science recognition of the link between instrumental and in sentimental interdependence, particularly in the work of Daniel Katz (1940, 1965) and others of the University of Michigan group who have more recently been studying "the national role" in individual behavior, has not yet been directed expressly toward language, but could easily be so directed.

9. The vernacular also figured as a symbolic rallying cry (among several others of a religious nature) in most of the premodern European efforts at broader sociocultural integration beginning with the Arab invasion of the Iberian Peninsula. Thus, under their military leader Jan Zizka, the Hussites went into battle in 1420 with the [Catholic] Holy Roman Emperor and his allies in order "to liberate the truth of the Law of God and the Saints, and to protect the faithful believers of the Church, and the Czech and Slavonic languages" (cited by Kohn 1944, p. 111).

At similarly early dates the Catholic Churches of various countries recognized language as a natural indicator of nationality. Thus at the Council of Constance (1414), at which nation[ality] (rather than state) was the basis of representation, the English prelates claimed to represent a true nationality, as defined on the basis of "peculiarities of language, the most sure and positive sign and essence of a nation in divine and human law" [" . . . diversitatem linguarum, quae maximam et verissimam probant nationem et ipsius essentiam, jure divino pariter et humano"]. Conversely, the Portuguese objected to "the inclusion of prelates from Sicily and Corsica with the Aragonese in the Spanish nation on the ground that, although subjects of the King of Aragon, they spoke another language and were therefore, 'truly of a different nation' " (Loomis 1939, pp.

525-526). An even earlier example of the seemingly natural identity of separate peoplehood with separate language is found in Llywelyn II's thirteenth-century plea to Henry III ("I therefore seek, being a Prince, that I likewise shall have my Welsh law, and proceed according to that law. By common right, we ought to have our Welsh law and custom, as the other nations [*nationes*] in the King's Empire have–and in our own language." [Jones-Pierce 1950, p. 52]). Such examples can be multiplied almost without end both from even earlier periods as well as from after the Reformation, when language became an increasingly common referent in conjunction with minority efforts to differentiate between recognized states and unrecognized nationalities.

10. Language has undoubtedly appealed to many social scientists who have sought a more objective criterion of nationality than "will," "consciousness," or other common designata of nineteenth century nationalism. Thus, even in recent years, we find the view "that the most conspiciuous dimension of familiarity and difference, the dimension with the most points on it and the sharpest discontinuities, is language. [Therefore,] language is one of the most important factors in delimiting a national or ethnic group" (Rosenblatt 1964, p. 37). The realization that language boundaries–particularly when we refer to spoken language–can be every bit as vague and as ambiguous as other sociocultural boundaries, has not penetrated far into social science circles.

A major pre-World War II review of nationalism in Europe concludes that "all nationality movements on the continent [with the dubious exception of the Scottish] seem to be connected with language" (Chadwick 1945, p. 2). Minogue's commentary on this conclusion would be widely accepted today, namely, that "any single test of nationality breaks down . . . Yet in a metaphorical sense language remains the most promising candidate. A nation [ality] *does* consist of people who speak the same language" (1967, p. 31), thus once more, turning to the objective rather than facing squarely the subjective features of our concern.

If the sufficiency of language as a badge of nationality is questioned today, it is more likely to be partially due to the fact that language in and of itself does not unite England and the United States nor divide Switzerland, and partially on the grounds that people should not insist on being united politically on the basis of so inconsequential a factor as language. The "linguistically neutral" Swiss federation (where strong language-nationality links exist within each of the cantons) arose in premodern days and has not been successfully copied in modern times. The first rejection confuses nationality and nation (or even state) and seems to argue unjustifiably that if two groups speaking the "same" language do not clamor to be part of the same nation (or state) then their language cannot be a significant aspect of their respective groupness. The second rejection confuses the observer's values with those of his subjects.

In 1766 Turgot remonstrated with Du Pont de Nemours for having confounded the idea of the nationality with that of the state and went on to define "nation[ality] as a community of language" (cited by Kohn 1944, p. 229). Similarly, Stalin sought to reach a compromise between the demands of proletarian internationalism on the one hand and pre-Soviet nationalist appeals on the other, by stating that one of the characteristic features which distinguishes nationality from state is that "a national[ity] community is inconceivable without a common language" of its own ([1913] 1942, p. 241). Whereas the bourgeois state *was* the enemy of the proletariat the nationality was not, since it *was* the proletariat.

11. Wilhelm von Humboldt expressed this view most succinctly, as follows: "Their speech is their spirit and their spirit is their speech. One cannot express too strongly the identity of the two" (cited by Rocker 1937, p. 228). The formalization of this view in more recent years has become known as the Whorfian (or the Sapir-Whorf) hypothesis (Fishman 1960). Its original presentations are indicative of the nationalist contexts in which the conviction arose that language must be taken "not merely as a set of words and rules of syntax, not merely as a kind of emotional reciprocity, but also as a certain conceptualization of the world" (Minogue 1967, p. 120). Thus, Schleiermacher held that "only one language is firmly implanted in an individual. Only to one does he belong entirely no matter how many he learns subsequently . . . [for] every language is a particular mode of thought and what is cogitated in one language can never be repeated in the same way in another. . . Language, thus, just like the Church or state, is an expression of a peculiar [i.e., of a distinct way of] life" (cited by Kedourie 1961, p. 63). That such views quickly lent themselves to sweeping invidious comparisons is obvious from Hamann's observations that "Every people reveals its mode of thought through the nature, form, rules and mores of its speech. . . The legalism of the Jewish people, which rendered it so blind at the time of the divine visitation, is fully revealed in its language" (Johann Georg Hamann, *Schriften*, vol. II, [Berlin: 1821]; cited by Baron 1947, p. 132).

The continued emotional hold of this view, in the absence of confirmatory evidence, notwithstanding repeated efforts to provide such via controlled experiments, is evident from the fact that most cultural anthropologists today would doubtlessly agree with Vossler's intuitive claim that "there rests in the lap of each language a kind of predestination, a gentle urge to this or that way of thinking" (1932, p. 137).

12. Although Herder's devotion to linguistic and cultural authenticity and diversity was certainly sincere, it was equally certainly anti-French, at least in origin (Barnard 1969, Clark 1955, Wells 1959). It is interesting, therefore, to

find a very similar view being expressed at approximately the same time by the French philosopher Limoge, who in a letter of 1790 to Bishop Gregoire of the National Assembly, observed that "the spiritual wealth of the nation was stored in its language and could only be tapped by those understanding it; the true spirit and character of a nation could only be expressed in the national tongue" (paraphrased by Shafer 1955, pp. 122). Certainly Herder was not alone in his recognition of the link between language and national authenticity. His contribution to this view and its subsequent espousal and intensification by generations of German philosphers and scholars must not be overlooked. Herder, Wilhelm von Humboldt, the Schlegel brother, the Grimm brothers, Bopp, Schleicher, Dier, and many others " . . . established the attitude of the German mind to the language of its own people and to other languages. The whole of modern philology is essentially and almost exclusively a German product" (Vossler 1932, p. 130). For continued German (post-Nazi) concern with such topics see Polenz (1967), Pielow (1967), Kochs (1966).

13. The unimportance of the distinction between languages and dialects, from the point of view of this argument, is revealed by the following claim on behalf of preserving Swiss-German: "Unsere Mundart ist mehr als eine Verkehrs- und Umgangssprache: Sie ist Ausdruck einer ganz bestimmten Gesinnung. Sie wächst über andere Dialekte hinaus, weil in der Schweiz die Mundart daurend die Umgangssprache aller Stände geblieben ist . . . ; bei uns bildet sie ein Merkmal sozialer Einheit und ist Sinnbild unseres demokratischen Denken" (Sommer 1945, p. 100). Thus, the same arguments utilized to distinguish between recognized varieties ("languages") were easily transferred to distinguish between less privileged ones, the status of the latter as languages (rather than as dialects) coming to be a reflection of *the societal success of the argument presented* rathern than of the distance between any variety of reference and any other. Modern sociolinguistic theory takes full cognizance of the fact that the distinction between "language" and "dialect" is essentially linguistically arbitrary and societally reversible by treating both within one and the same theoretical framework (Fishman 1971).

14. The last two lines are rendered in a much subdued fashion in Chamberlain's widely known English translation, viz:
> "That is thy land;
> That, German, is thy Fatherland."
(See J. F. Chamberlain, "Literary Selections as an Aid in Teaching Geography," *Journal of Geography* [September 1916], p. 12.) Arndt's German orginal may have been inspired in part by the last two lines of a poem entitled "Now or Never" that appeared in the *Rheinische Merkur,* No. 130, October 19, 1814:

"Und wo der Teutschen Sprache Laute tönen/Erblühe nur ein Reich des Kräftigen und Schönen!"

15. Where no indigenous literature is as yet being created in the vernacular the link between language, literature, and nationalism is sometimes forged via well-planned translations from world literature. In this connection note Hodgkin's reference to translations from Racine and Marx in Wolof (1956, p. 176) and similar scattered references to such translations in Krio, Akan, and other smaller West African languages. Similar programs of creating nationalist literatures in translation have been conducted by the Soviets (e.g., see Wurm 1954; Wurm, Waterson, and Simpson 1960).

Conversely, where earlier mass movements had succeeded, at least in part, on the basis of particularly moving and influential vernacular literatures, subsequent pan movements on behalf of a supranationality or state language may face unusual difficulty. Thus, "the regional languages [of India] developed as the literary vehicles of a popular religious revival extending over centuries . . . The *bhakti* movement which popularized Hinduism and made it intelligible to a mass public was a movement conducted in the language of each region . . . a millenium ago . . . The *bhakti* poets went out of their way to adhere to the native or *desi* meters characteristic of language as it was spoken and thereby capture its flavor and make more effective emotional contact with would be devotees . . . It was for this reason that the regional languages provided the obvious outlet for the burst of new cultural creativity which followed the 19th century influx of Western social and political thought . . . [and which explains] the resistance to Hindi on the part of the votaries of other languages, notably Tamil, Bengali and Marathi, which have a far more impressive and more ancient literary heritage" (Harrison 1963, pp. 281-283). A very similar point is made for Irish in terms of the wealth of Irish literary (and other sociocultural) authenticity created in English over a span of centuries. As a result most Irishmen would prefer to cherish Irish "as a museum piece, playing at most the role enjoyed by Latin in American colleges of a generation ago . . . The utmost that can now be hoped for in reviving the use of Gadhalic would be the creation of a bilingual bureaucratic upper class, ruling over an English speaking mass—a paradoxical reversal of the conquest" (Clarkson 1950, p. 46). A foreign (and foreign-speaking) ruling class, has been viewed as a particular misfortune since Biblical days: "Lo, I will bring a nation upon you from afar, O house of Israel, saith the Lord; it is a mighty nation; it is an ancient nation, a nation whose language thou knowest not, neither understandest what they say" (Jeremiah 5:15).

16. The major advocate of this extrapolation was Fichte, who not only championed the sociocultural distinctness of speech communities ("Those who

speak the same language are linked together before human intervention takes a hand, . . . they are by nature one indivisible whole," [Minogue 1967, p. 64]), as did Herder and others, but also their political-operational distinctness. "Just as it is true beyond doubt that, wherever a separate language is found, there a separate nation[ality] exists, which has the right to take independent charge of its affairs and to govern itself; so one can say, on the other hand that, where a people has ceased to govern itself, it is equally bound to give up its language and to coalesce with its conquerors" (Hayes 1931, pp. 215-216). The anti-French context of German language nationalism of the time is even clearer in Schlegel's statement that "A nation[ality] that tamely looks on whilst it is being despoiled of its idiom forfeits the respect due to independence; it is degraded in the ranks of civilization" (Hayes 1931, pp. 225-226.) German thought relating language to political integration went so far as to imply double political loyalty to bilinguals, viz Ludwig Mises (1919). The struggle against French among English literati, coming as it did in premodern times, left many fewer scars (note: "Theyr longage [French] In redynge is douse and dylycate./ In theyr mother tonge they be so fortunate./ They have the bybyll and the apocalypys of devynyte,/with other nobyll bokes that in Englyche may not be" [Anon., *The Kalender of Shepherdes*, 1506]. "Shall English be so poore, and rudely-base/ as not be able (through mere penury)/ to tell what French hath said with gallant grace,/ and most tongues else of lesse facunditie?/God shield it should . . . " [John Davies of Hereford, prior to 1618]).

17. Voltaire himself provides us with insight into the state of affairs in elitist German circles against which Fichte, Herder, and their associates cried out. "When Voltaire was in Berlin as a guest of Frederick II he wrote to his friends in Paris that he felt as though in France. French was spoken exclusively and German was only fit for the horses. The king's brother advised a Prussian nobleman to learn French since he surely could not want to be 'a German beast' " (Hertz 1944, p. 84). Frederick himself "did not hide his contempt for German literature and German writers. In these, resentment against their lowly position became confounded with resentment against the French language and literature which the privileged classes and their imitators affected to cultivate. It was literary men, with literary preoccupations, who thus endowed language with political significance" (Kedourie 1961, p. 60). If we extend the designation "literary men" to include a variety of protoelites it is obvious that the situation of Germany vis-à-vis France was long quite similar to that subsequently experienced by submerged nationalities in Central, Eastern, and Southern Europe, vis-à-vis Germany, Austro-Hungary, and Russia, or in parts of contemporary Africa and Asia today vis-à-vis the West.

18. Peoples throughout the world and in all ages have viewed themselves as uniquely possessing the gift of speech or, at least, of proper speech. The Greek designation of all non-Greeks as barbarians presumably "had its source in the idea of stammering or inability to speak in a comprehensible way, the Greek word *barbaros* [being] akin to the Sanskrit expression *barbara*, which meant 'stammering' "(Kohn 1944, p. 7). Similarly the ancient Hebrews viewed their Egyptian masters as having been a "stammering" or, at the very least, a "wild-speaking" people (Psalms, 114:1) from whom they were delivered because they (the Hebrews) had remained true to their names, their language, and their customs. "The name *Slav* is derived from *slovo*, which, in all Slav languages, means 'word'—they were the 'worded ones,' who could understand each other, whereas the Germans who merely mumbled *(mye-mye)*, were *Myemtsy* . . . dumb" (Namier 1944, p. 102). The word *Hausa* (the self-name of a numerous people of Northern Nigeria) means "language" in the vernacular of its native speakers, although there is the possibility that it refers to the fact that they adopted Arabic as their language of religion and higher learning rather than to their vernacular. Both *Hausa* and *Bahasa* (Indonesia) probably share the Arabic root for *language* or *tongue*.

19. Compare "I should also like to call attention to the illogical position of men who drop their own language to speak English, of men who translate their euphonious Irish names into English monosyllables, of men who read English books and know nothing about Gaelic literature" (Hyde; cited by Kohn 1944, p. 147) with "Is it not the chief object of our literary ambition, at present, to be able to compose an article in good English and to deliver an eloquent speech in the same language? And can we who have not even a smattering of the Aryan tongue honestly claim the denomination of Arya? Is it not a painful, a shameful necessity that compels me, at the present moment, to advocate the cause of Aryan learning in a foreign language" (A. Mitra, 1879-80; cited by McCully 1940, p. 257). In our own day advocates of Swiss-German have similarly argued, vis-à-vis High German, "Zukünftige Geschlechter werden uns Dank Wissen wenn wir ihnen diese lebendige Schutzwehr gegen fremdes Wesen und fremden Geist gesund erhalten" (Sommer 1945, p. 101). Mazrui cites many such views (opposing the currently accepted Western languages of wider communication) by various African spokesmen (1973) and appends the full text of a statement by Obote (1967).

20. "Philological research has proven beyond doubt a close relation between the Greeks, Romans and Indo-Aryan peoples . . . This relationship existed also in thought . . . Indo-Aryans (now called Hindus) were the originators of civili-

zation . . . Egypt, Greece and Rome were their pupils and recipients" (McCully 1940, pp. 247-248; paraphrasing an unsigned article in *The Arya* 1882-1883, I, 21-23). Somewhat later young Bengalis began to justify their use of Bengali (rather than English) for advanced, modern purposes on the ground that "the English language was only a borrowing from Bengali" (Chaudhuri 1951, p. 410). Note also the Great Sun Language theory whereby all (modern European) languages are derived from Turkish (Szabe 1952).

21. Prior to the cited passage Elsbree observes: "One of the characteristics of national movements in Southeast Asia has been that they have not developed out of native languages . . . The process in Southeast Asia clearly has been that of the state creating a national language rather than that whereby the national language forms the basis of the state" (1953, pp. 120-121). The experience of India with Hindu, Malaysia with Malaysian, Indonesia with Indonesian, the Phillipines with Pilipino, and Pakistan with Urdu, are all of this type. However, this formulation would seem to be somewhat less applicable to Vietnam, Thailand, Burma, Ceylon, and one or two other nations with clearer ethnic preponderance (e.g., Korea, Cambodia, Laos). Thus, as earlier in Europe, both types of processes seem to be in evidence in Asian modernization and, again, they tend to be cyclically interrelated, the one flowing into and eliciting the other.

22. Perhaps the outstanding example of the flexibility of language planning and language decisions on behalf of largely unideologized populations is the Illyria movement of the mid-nineteenth century on behalf of the Southern Slavs. An Illyrian nationality was to be united, an Illyrian language was to be formulated, and an Illyrian nation was to be created out of the Croats, Slovenes, Macedonians, and several other smaller Balkan Slavic groups that shared a common ritual language. Napoleon had succeeded in briefly establishing an Illyrian duchy sixty years earlier, but it was not until the advent of pan-Slavism that an indigenous protoelite discovered Illyria for its own purposes. Illyrianism easily attracted foreign intellectual support. "Indeed, the interest of German romanticists in 'Illyrian' literature was even greater than their attachment to Czech literary excavations. Southern Slav literature was even further off the main tracks of Western European literature, and, therefore, appeared still more romantic and politically more innocent" (Kohn 1955, pp. 419-420). However, the case of Illyria is not as unique as it might appear to be. The Dravidasthan movement which once sought to unite all southern (non-Aryan) India via a Tamil-based koine (McCully 1940, p. 270) is also of this type, as is Sukarno's proposed union of Malyasia, the Philippines, and Indonesia into a single "Malphilindo." In each case the prior continuities and discontinuities were not sufficiently established or clear-cut to rule out a large number of alternative

sociocultural and political-operational integrative possibilities, each of them with a language rationale among its components. The practical failure of many schemes is no more a real indication of their "irrationality" than is the success of their competitors any valid indication of their "rationality." Success and objective rationality are two quite separate dimensions in sociopolitical behavior and history.

23. Seyssel goes on to "admonish Louis XII to follow the example of Rome. 'What did the people and the princes of Rome do when they held the world empire and aspired to perpetuate and eternalize it? They found no way as sure and as certain as that of magnifying, enriching and sublimating their Latin language, which at the beginning of the empire had been very meager and very crude" (Kohn 1944, p. 130), thus turning the diglossia argument in his own favor. Latin was but a vernacular in its own day and age and if it too required cultivation in order to become the great instrument of culture that it subsequently came to be, might not a vernacular like French, which currently must live in the cultural shadow of Latin, aspire to the same greatness if it too were properly developed? This antidiglossia argument we will see, was, subsequently, essentially repeated by adherents of other and still less recognized vernaculars. Thus Thomasius argued "The Greeks had not written their philosophy in Hebrew nor the Romans in Greek—each of these great nations had used its vernacular because they rightly envisaged philosophy as a subject for all men. The French philosophers of recent times had followed the ancients in using the vernacular for their writings. Why should the Germans, by not doing so, suggest to other nations that philosophy and learning could not be written in their language?" (Cited by Blackall 1959, p. 13).

24. "While French spread throughout the world as a universal language it had the greatest difficulty in gaining admission as a language of instruction in French schools even in the lower grades . . . Even the few educators who accepted the demands for teaching French, however, did not regard it as a desirable end in itself; they saw in it an introduction and an aid to the better teaching of Latin. In the Collège de France it was explicitly forbidden to comment in French on Latin or Greek texts . . . Even at the time of the Revolution no chair of French language existed [in any university in France]" (Kohn 1944, pp. 229 and 231). Little wonder then that when the jurist Christian Thomasius posted a German notice on the official bulletin board of the University of Leipzig (1687) stating that he proposed to offer a course in German, his act was viewed as "a symbolic gesture reminiscent of Luther's nailing his theses to the door of the Church. Some 30 years later in looking back at this action, Thomasius declared that nothing had so horrified the University of Leipzig since its foundation and the screens [i.e., the bulletin board on which he posted his notice] might well have

been reconsecrated with holy water as a result" (Blackall 1959, pp. 12-13). The revolutionary implications of disturbing the established diglossia patterns via offering education in the vernacular was at least implicitly recognized by many who advocated the vernacular. Thus the German linguist Gottsched (in 1739) attacked "the 'lovers of darkness' and the 'enemies of the fatherland' who refused to countenance scholarly work in the vernacular. Like the ancient Egyptians they would make a mystery out of learning and so keep those who have not studied classical languages—that is to say the large mass of the nation—in bestial ignorance" (Blackall 1959, p. 116).

25. Advocates of various panmovements also recognized both the need for and the possible consequences of language planning. A modernized version of classical Arabic was advocated by some pan-Arabists as a crucial compromise between the uniform (but inaccessible and archaic) classical Arabic and the diverse (and diversifying) colloquial varieties (Nuseibeh 1956, pp. 74-76). Chinese communist recognition that a uniform written language (i.e., one not tied to the diverse spoken vernaculars) is of immense unifying value was anticipated, for their own panpurposes, by early Christian missionaries such as S. Wells Williams who cautioned that "separate systems of writing would tend to break up the people into little clans and states," and E. J. Eitel who pointed out that "to tamper with the ideographs was tantamount to denationalizing the Chinese" (De Francis 1950, pp. 217-218). Recent Soviet pan policy in Central Asia of developing selective integrative vernaculars but of stressing the unifying and leading role of Russian (see e.g., Allworth 1965, Quelquejay and Bennigsen 1961, Rakowska-Harmstone 1970) was anticipated by the Finnish Social Democrats in 1906 when they declared that "(1) The development of Finnish into a fully satisfactory literary and educational medium and its elevation to the position of an official language has ever been and still is important for the educational, moral and material progress of the Finnish speaking workers . . . ; (2) Swedish is indispensable for the advance of the Swede-Finn people in Finland. It is also an important channel through which educational influences and Social Democratic ideas may be brought to us . . . for these reasons the Party Congress favors the retention and further cultivation of Swedish; (3) . . . the Russian language . . . and modern Russian literature dealing with the ideal of liberty should be spread in Finland" (Wuorinen 1931, p. 211).

26. " . . . The French used cultural relations as an object of low bargaining. We must refuse all bargaining. This refusal could lead to the reshaping of our programs. We may even have to envisage the use of a language other than French, and thus look toward other civilizations, countries, and friends" (Bourguiba 1961; published in Sigmund 1963, p. 143).

27. "Korais saw his task as two-fold: the revival of the Greek language and the education of the modern Greeks through the study of the works of their classical ancestors. The lack of linguistic homogeneity would be a stumbling-block to the unity of the Nation, since only when Greeks became aware of their ancient culture would they set about freeing themselves" (Sherrard 1959, p. 182).

28. "There were not only two [Magyar] nations [the noble and the peasant] but two Magyar languages: the language of the noble society full of foreign words which was scarcely understood by the peasants, and the popular Magyar tongue in its virginal purity and limitless capacity for development, looked down upon by the lord with a pitiful smile" (I. Acsady, 1903; cited by Jaszi 1929, p. 263). Similarly, "in 1790 the French national assembly published a manifesto which sought to arouse in all districts a holy emulation to banish jargons, the last remains of feudalism and monuments of slavery" (De Francis 1950, p. 212).

29. " . . . there is a growing tendency for a local [industrial town] vernacular to be accepted as a worker's lingua franca—Wolof in Dakar, Bambara in Bamako, Yoruba in Lagos" (Hodgkin 1956, p. 121). Compare this observation with Delgado de Carvalho's "that the road net of the time [eighteenth century] constituted one form of the industrial movement. The circulation of workers brought on the disappearance of the dialects. Where workmen from different provinces congregated for great works, the use of French soon prevailed" (1962, p. 91). Nevertheless, French was initially primarily a lingua franca rather than a national standard.

30. For the extreme case note "Lutfi's view [referring to Ahmad Lutfi al Sayyid the major Egyptian nationalist theorist of the nineteenth century] (that) Arabic had ceased to develop since the latter Abbasid period; its forms had been fixed and the gap had widened between the written and the spoken language. Nothing less than a deliberate renovation (of the written language) was needed" (Ahmad 1960, p. 103). A similar goal, but of less serious dimensions, was commonly espoused by European nationalist movements that initially found/created older written traditions and then proceeded to modify the modern (planned) written language in the direction of one or another spoken variety. For nationalist views *opposing* the approximation-uniformation of writing and speaking in instances where the two are much closer to each other than in the Arabic case note Chapter 7 ("Die Einwände der Reformgegner") of Lendle 1935.

31. This quotation, dealing as it does with Illyrian, was selected in order to stress the similarity between the planning problems faced by *Ausbau* languages

(Kloss 1952 and 1967) of greater and lesser differentiability. The quotation continues " . . . of developing the grammatical skeleton from the literary treasures of the past. There was a widespread conviction at that time that the Illyrian 'mother tongue' already existed" (Kohn 1955, p. 243).

32. Note the similarity of the condition of German in 1700 to that of Finnish in 1880. "The absence of formal instruction in Finnish in the schools meant . . . that Finnish did not lend itself easily to the demands of polite society or of the world of letters . . . " (Wuorinen 1931, p. 65). The popular emphasis on elaboration is formulated by Bentham in his "list of the several qualities desirable in language" as follows: "On the highest point stands *copiousness*. It is only in proportion as it is copious that a language contributes anything to its end" ([1820] 1962, p. 310).

33. "Primarily due to the influence of Commonwealth President Manuel Quezon, Tagalog—the language of his youth and of most Filipinos living in the environs of Manila—was selected as the basis for the national language to be known as Pilipino. Tagalog then was the native tongue only of some 19 percent of the population, as contrasted with Cebuano, which was spoken at home by one out of every four Filipinos" (Rauenholt 1963, p. 192).

34. E.g., "[Leibnitz proposed] the establishment of what he called a 'teutshgesinte Gesellshaft' whose function shall be to encourage the production of serious works (*Kernschriften*) in the German language" (Blackall 1959, p. 4), or "Composed of political leaders such as Sukarno and Hata as well as literary figures the [Indonesian language] Commission added to the language several thousand new terms [during the Japanese occupation period] many of them in the technical field in which all the languages of this area are weak" (Elsbree 1953, pp. 122-123).

35. "In every country the diffusion of the *national* language was essentially a military necessity, it was imposed from above by means of compulsory education and, in many regions, it was nothing but an artificial creation" (Delaise 1929, p. 165). Also, for an earlier period note Baron's contention that "only Peter the Great's act of daring, followed by ruthless supression of opponents, simplified alphabet and ritual so as to re-establish a measure of conformity between the religious and secular languages" (1947, p. 166).

36. "We whose life is more peaceful, and who have more opportunity to cultivate letters, must use all our strength to enrich and to refine our language. In parliament and in country assemblies we must speak Magyar, and it is

shameful that we cannot clothe fine thoughts in fine language" (Ribinyi 1775; cited by Marczali 1910, p. 236).

37. "Meine Absichten sind nicht gewesen Neuerungen in unserer Sprache zu machen. Ich gehöre nicht unter die Zahl derer die sich einbilden, sie hätte Fähigkeit genug, ihre Muttersprache zu verbessern, andere einzurichten, und zu verschönern . . . Alles was also, meines Erachtens, ein Sprachlehrer thun kann, ist dieses, dass er die vorborgenen Schönheiten seiner Muttersprache aüfsuche, entdecke, anpreise und bey seinen Landsleuten in Schwang bringen helfe" (Gottsched, in the introduction to his *Sprachkunst* 1748; cited by Blackall 1959, p. 115).

38. "Seventeenth-century French grammarians . . . claimed that the *ordre direct* was the 'natural order' . . . as the 18th century unfolds we find Batteux and others recognizing emotional as well as logical order. It was pointed out that Latin order was different from that of French" (Blackall 1959, p. 455).

39. Similarly, but with typically greater care to avoid invidious comparisons, Herder claimed that "Germans, like all active peoples, preferred active verbs" (Minogue 1967, p. 60).

40. In connection with foreign borrowings (which had been long opposed, but in vain, in the premodern development of English) Bentham observed "When a word has thus been transplanted and naturalized in a single state, the conception entertained.of its import by persons altogether unacquainted with the cluster to which it belonged in the language from which it was borrowed is always very obscure and imperfect in comparison with that which he has of a word which forms one of a cluster, more or less complete, originally of the growth of his own language, or fully rooted and naturalized in it" ([1820] 1962, p. 319). Southall employed his very same line of thought some seventy years later, but on behalf of Welsh language maintenance in the face of the rising tide of English: "It is a simple fact that a man cannot express himself now in English concisely, or in an effective style; he can neither generalize nor specialize, without drawing into use words originating from extraneous sources" (Southall 1893, p. 256). The ease with which this initially nonnationalist argument can be transformed for nationalist purposes is indicated by del Rosario who inveighs against foreign borrowing on the grounds that " . . . consistent and intelligent modernization of their national languages would enable the Malaysians, the Indonesians and the Filipinos to overtake and eventually surpass in science and technology the Western nations, whose national languages are burdened with large numbers of terms derived from Latin and Greek, combining forms which are no longer

consistent with the home and community languages spoken by their children. Japan, with her consistent Nippongo, is demonstrating that this can be done" (1968, p. 16).

41. Chatterji's reference to the "more elegant forms" of Hindi and Urdu as most influenced by language planning should remind us that it is the more formal varieties in general, and the written language in particular (most particularly of all, written language for public governmental purposes), that are most directly exposed to language planning. Kloss has probably exaggerated the case in claiming that only written language is subject to *Ausbau* (1952, 1967). It is probably more accurate to say that official written language and the informal spoken language represent opposite extremes of a continuum of varieties with the former extreme being at the very vortex of language planning influences and the latter being most distant therefrom (see Fishman, in press a).

42. "The literary Finnish then in use [about 1835, when Lönnrot's *Kalevala* first appeared]...was based mainly on the West Finnish dialect...heavily freighted with Swedicisms...One phase of the nationalist movement was the so-called 'Finnization' of the literary Finnish, which meant that it should be purged of Swedish words and idioms so as to render it more national and more easily understood by the common man. The supporters of this demand looked to the richer eastern Finnish dialect as the future literary language" (Wuorinen 1931, p. 75). The role of elites and of powerful literature in making and consolidating decisions with respect to such matters is indicated when Wuorinen observes, immediately following the above passage, that " Lönnrot accepted the eastern dialect as his medium but made many important changes in it in favor of the western dialect...His choice...was decisive in determining the foundation upon which the Finnish language has rested since his day" (p. 76).

43. De Valera's reaction to this suggestion was to declare that "he would willingly give up all he knew of English to talk like the natives" (Bromage 1956, p. 30).

44. Gaj (1809-1871) not only held "that this rather elementary idiom could serve as a better common denominator of Illyrian," presumably due to its having remained closer to the "proto" stage out of which (and away from which) the more accomplished southern Slav languages had developed, but his choice was also motivated by the hope "that the factors of national rivalry could thus be eliminated from the reform work" (Kohn 1955, pp. 246-247). A similar consideration was also operative in the Indonesian elevation of Bazaar Malay to the position of Bahasa Indonesia. Thus instrumental considerations are often

present from the very outset in locating the sentimental roots that nationalism requires, and particularly so in pan movements. For explicit recognition of this fact in connection with language planning see I. Kleivan 1969/70 who, not incidentally, also attends to the radio as a new instrumental factor in language planning.

45. The Arabic world popularly explains the revival and survival of their "pure, original language," after it had changed to Aramaic subsequent to the fall of Adam and Eve, by attributing the revival, on the one hand, to the miraculous powers of Ishmael, a son of Abraham, and the survival, on the other hand, to the loyalty of the inaccessible Arabs of the Hejaz (Gallagher 1963, p. 204). Lutfi's interest in reestablishing the link between written and spoken Arabic is similar to that of critics of the French Academy, such as Maurice Barrés [1862-1922], who held that "words which spring from the soil represent nice distinctions and are employed by deeply rooted people with sharpened imagination and poetic feeling" (cited by Hayes 1931, p. 196).

46. When no extant population remains that speaks the purported original vernacular then there may be no recourse but to seek broader unity and true authenticity by reviving a (classical) variety that has entirely ceased being a vernacular. Some of the efforts on behalf of Sanskrit or classical Arabic, and to an extent, those on behalf of Irish, Greek, and Hebrew, have been of this kind. All of these reveal the dangers that are hidden in the search for authenticity when a truly great past language is adopted even though it no longer is functional as a vernacular.

In the case of Hebrew the ideological and physical rejection of the diaspora plus the ingathering of exiles from all over the world made it possible for biblical, mishnaic, and medieval Hebrew (that had survived primarily as languages of liturgy, study, and writing) to give birth to a modernized (and widely accepted) vernacular. However, in Ireland, or more particularly, in Greece, neither of these antecedent ingredients were present. The Greek population still spoke a Greek vernacular when the nationalist movement began and it was therefore by no means without a useful indigenous vehicle of mass communication when that movement decided to adopt "a slightly modernized version of ancient Greek, very different from the spoken idiom" as the national language, "although it was familiar only to antiquarian scholars. They insisted upon it, because to them the rebirth of Hellas meant the rebirth of Classical Hellas, with its classical language, the language of republican freedom and of mankind's leading thought" (Kohn 1944, p. 539). Here was a language—the parent of the living vernacular, never obsolete as the liturgical language of the Church, a link with the medieval splendor of Near Eastern civilization and with the greater ancient splendors of Hellenic civilization. The West admired Ancient Greece as much as Modern Greece admired the West and the ancient language, having sufficed in its day for a civilization which enlightened Westerners regarded as the equal of their own, would surely supply now the indispensable medium for a modern Greek variety of Western culture" (Toynbee 1922, pp. 20-21). After over thirty years of struggling with the adopted amalgam of modern and ancient Greek it was decided to return to the vernacular. However, by then the problem of "how to express Western thought in Modern Greek without calling up reinforcements from the ancient language" (Toynbee 1922, p. 21), had become much more emotionally and politically (and, therefore intellectually) involved and remains so to this very day, after several additional shifts in policy between more classical and more vernacular usage.

A similar danger, albeit in a less extreme degree, is involved in the ongoing efforts to Sanskritize Hindi. These efforts "complicate what would in any case be the difficult task of choosing between words drawn from the different dialects [of Hindi] by insisting, with purist zeal, on virtually complete Sanskritization" (Harrison 1963, p. 284). In this connection Nehru's plea that "an effort must be made to discourage the extreme tendencies and develop a middle literary language on the lines of the spoken [Hindi] language in common use" (Nehru 1953, p. 454) has been ignored due to the pull of the great tradition of Sanskrit authority and authenticity. "In ancient and medieval India the unity of the entire sub-continent was preserved, such as it was, by just one factor: the existence of an elite of Brahmins who had a common culture throughout India and who spoke a common language—Sanskrit" (Naik 1965, p. 103). Both Lutfi and Nehru were confident that mass education would inevitably force the written language in the direction of the spoken but, as yet, this has not happened to any great degree either in the case of written Arabic or in that of written Hindi.

Most nationalist movements of modern times have dealt with "Great Traditions" of their own choosing, of their own definition, of their own shaping. The "Great Tradition" was, in large part, a coproduct of the "movement," every bit as much as "the movement" was a coproduct of the tradition." The pliability of the preferred past was an undisguised blessing not available to those movements related to Great Traditions whose classical remains were widely known and highly regarded. Where real classical pasts of worldwide renown existed the language problem was not one of choosing (or defining) the vernacular of the masses over the language of wider communication that had been adopted by assimilated elites but, rather, of choosing between a relatively indigenous (or indigenized) vernacular of the masses and the language of widely recognized and validated classical greatness and authenticity. In such cases the rejection of the immediate servile past led inexorably not to the reconstruction and elevation of a purer vernacular but of a real rather than metaphorical return to the language of authentic greatness. Such movements, therefore, are even more conflicted from the point of view of modernization than are those whose "Great Tradition" is less evidential and more in need of interpretive recreation. In the strained dialectic between authenticity, unity, and modernity that characterizes all modern nationalist movements the hypnotic attraction toward a valid, classical tradition and classical (or classicized) language represents a possibly disfunctional victory for the first (and more immediately sentimental) over the two remaining (and more immediately instrumental) considerations. "The language of a nation's youth is the only easy and full speech for its manhood and for its age. And when the language of its cradle goes, itself craves a tomb" (Davies 1945 [1845], p. 70).

The Arabic world has certainly evidenced the most vocal recent concern for maintaining a classical versus any vernacular link to authentic greatness. "[Arabs] are conservative classicists, even purists in all that concerns their language. They do not want to facilitate the rules of grammar, they do not welcome foreign words, even those which have a modern scientific meaning. They invent words from Arabic roots for vitamins, hormones, automobiles ... etc. This purism is the result of ... more than thirteen hundred years of literary religious memories" (Moussa 1955, p. 41-42). "The Qur'an is accepted as the highest linguistic achievement of the Arabic language in every possible respect; nobody can possibly vie with it; everybody should try humbly to emulate it. Nothing should be written which does not comply with the linguisitc, idiomatic, literary, and rhetorical conditions obtaining in the Qur'an. It would be considered almost treasonable if an Arab were to misspell a word or break one of the intricate numerous rules of Arabic grammar, especially if he were expected to have known the right form" (Shauby 1951, p. 288-289). "[For] it is the Koran, the holy book of Islam, which will always remain our guide and our inspiration, and if we keep to the purity of the language, ... then indeed we shall have accomplished a renaissance of Arabic literature" (Nusuli 1953, p. 23). "The advocates of a classical or unadulterated Arabic have [therefore] won an overwhelming victory over those who would have liked very much to introduce some necessary reforms" (Chejne 1969, p. 173). That this situation is subject to change is evident from the fact that "a 'medial' Arabic, neither rigidly classical nor fully coloquial ... arose chiefly during the revolution in Egypt, starting with Naguib and Nasser ... The masses ... felt an unprecedented kinship with the new leadership ... removing a profound psychological barrier separating the illiterate masses from the educated classes of society and creating on the political plane a new sense of unity and belonging" (Sharabi 1966, p. 94).

47. The *reinforcement* of nationalist pressures upon language planning via religious influences is best indicated in conjunction with matters of spelling and orthography. Since language planning deals primarily with the written word it quickly trespasses upon that aspect of language use which has religious

associations of the greatest stability. Little wonder then that religious sanctions have so frequently been utilized for and against nationalist language planning.

The distinction between Serbian and Croatian was initially a script distinction between Roman Catholic (and, therefore, Latin script) Croatians and Eastern Orthodox (and, therefore, Cyrillic) Serbs. This distinction "repeated itself in the Ruthenian cultural evolution between the Polish-Latin alphabet and the 'old Ruthenian' Russian alphabet" (Kohn 1955, pp. 322-323), leading Ukrainians to finally opt for a Cyrillic alphabet even though a Latin one would have differentiated their language more fully from Russian efforts to absorb it. On the other hand, in the early nineteenth century, "Count Sedlnitzky, the president of the Austrian police administration and one of the most influential officials under the Emperor Francis' regime after 1815, recommended the . . . restoration of the Czech written language" in Latin letter, specifically for the purpose of translating the Orthodox prayer book. "Translation into the Western Slav languages in Latin letters appeared to the Austrian police state as an important device to fight the political danger of the pro-Russian Pan-Slav movement" (Kohn 1955, p. 159-60; quoting materials from the archives of the Imperial Royal Ministry [Fischel 1919, p. 57]). This use of Latin letters for a church text helped to firmly establish their hold on Czech and Slovak.

In the East "the most powerful argument against a change in the script is that the sacred character of the divinely revealed Qurr'an places Arabic and its script in a special category" (Nuseibeh 1956, p. 73), for "religion was as much the conveyor of the language as the language was the conveyor of religion" (Polk 1970, p. xiv). Similarly, "with the Persian script the Muslim feels his Urdu is an 'Islamic language'; with the native Nagari it becomes a Hindu speech to which he cannot give his allegiance. The Hindu will not give up his national alphabet" ["Hindi in Devanagari script . . . are *beati possidentes;*" Myrdal 1968, p. 88] . "No compromise is possible between the two scripts, so fundamentally different are they from each other" (Chatterji 1943, p. 25). "Some of the greatest books in the *Devabhasha*, the language of the Gods in India [have been published] . . . in that script. This fact was responsible for the addition of the word *Deva*, i.e., 'of the Gods, Divine, Holy,' to the word *Nagari*, for the script. So Nagari became Devanagari, the script par excellence . . . [This view is] behind the widespread practice which has become established in present day Hindi letters, according to which not only names of books and authors but also long quotations from English are given in Nagari letters, totally eschewing Roman script . . . as if it were something untouchable and not worthy of a place in the pages of Nagari Hindi" (Chatterji, in Anon. 1963, p. 10). On the other hand, those not willing to adopt such a position on the script issue are viewed as being "unwilling to give an indigenous thing prominence" and "like old Indian rulers . . . who invited alien powers to come and take over" (Raghavan, in Anon. 1963, p. 27).

Religious support has also been of great importance in the maintenance of traditional scripts for Chinese, Japanese, Armenian Amharic, various Indian vernaculars, Irish, and Hebrew, with orthographic change also being resisted for religious reasons in several of these cases.

48. Instances of nationalist abandonment of traditional religious scripts are far fewer. The Turkish case is the most famous, of course, but equally interesting and far less known is the Rumanian "adoption of the Latin alphabet, though it is incapable of conveying all the sounds of the Rumanian language . . . [owing to] the ideology of their Latin origin . . . In 1863 the use of Cyrillic was forbidden" (Kolarz 1946, p. 22). Ataturk's romanization of Turkish script was motivated not only by a desire to modernize but also by an urge to separate Turkey from her Ottoman cultural past. A similar dual function may be noted in the forced cyrillization of Central Asian languages of Moslem, Buddhist, and Confucianist, populations in the Soviet Union (Quelquejay and Bennigsen 1961; Wurm 1954; Wurm, Waterson, and Simpson 1960).

Several references to religion-based difficulties encountered in script revision and orthographic revision and in the planning of writing systems are reviewed in Fishman in press d. Quite similar religious involvements are to be found in all other aspects of language planning from code selection through codification and elaboration, to cultivation and implementations. Thus, just as modern mass nationalism has had to grapple with religious loyalties (a premodern and prenationalist basis of sentimental and functional integration) and to learn to put such loyalties to its own use, so nationalist-based language planning has had to overcome religious obstacles as well as to exploit religious advantages in connection with its simultaneous goals of reinterpreted authentification, unification, and modernization goals.

It is amply clear that in premodern times religious elites not only contributed to the ethnic authentification and unification of populations and languages but, in addition, appealed to the latent sentiments of the speakers of these languages in order to foster and strengthen their own positions as well" (Cornish 1936). A reciprocally reinforcing relationship was thus established which could later be appealed to by both religionists and nationalists for their particular purposes. The Western inspired need to choose between the two is all the more painful in the East, where no indigenous rupture between them has obtained. "The circumstances of the invention of the 36 character alphabet in A.D. 362, the role of the clergy in the adaptation and further development of Armenian letters, and, above all, the persistent incursions and devastations befalling Armenia as a nation clinging with tenacity to her ancient language and her Mother Church in which that language remains enshrined, elevated the language to a supreme altar of enduring distinction" (Dadrian 1965, p. 377). "In attempting in 1636 [the

Council of Tarragona] to prevent the further dissemination of Castilian from the pulpits, the Catalan clergy had made an important move towards safeguarding Catalonia's existence as an independent national entity" (Elliot 1963, pp. 321-322). "The clergy . . . had raised the vernacular to the stature of a written language in the first half of the 16th century. By the close of the eighteenth century the clergy represented, putting it broadly, the only group among the educated that was still Finnish in speech" (Wuorinen 1931, p. 46). "Luther . . . perfected modern German and almost created it out of the chaos of provincial dialect, because his aim was to bring the word of God, the Bible, closer to us" (Vossler, 1932, p. 129). As a result of such long continuing associations between language and religion an aura of antiquity (if not sanctity) is repeatedly discovered in modern vernaculars, which blends with the authenticity ethos of modern nationalism. "Y por siglos y siglos rompían las olas del castellano sobre las santas payas los profetas, y todavía rompen sobre ellas en larga, interminable voluptuosidad de sueño y de amor. Y de este modo, ¿en dónde habrá voz moderna, en dónde eco de lengua actual qué más corra y se dilate por los espacios de las lenguas arcáicas" (Capdevila 1940, p. 164).

49. Vossler (1932, p. 136), though far more sympathetic to nationalist language planning than Mauthner, also admits that realia are outside of the normal boundaries of the national. "There is no national language that could be entirely national . . . In some way or another it must always be concerned with some factual or technical concepts." This escape hatch, so frequently referred to in early stages of nationalist lexical elaboration, is often subsequently closed, fully or partially, either by insisting on indigenous morphs alone or by utilizing indigenous grammatical and phonological models (for pluralization, vowel harmony, etc.) to indigenize that which was initially permissibly foreign.

50. Similar to the appeal to common usage in combating excessive purism is the appeal to usage during earlier glorious periods. Thus, in the case of Arabic, Lutfi argued that "in classical times the Arabs had accepted foreign words, and some of them found their way into the Qurr'an . ,. It [the Arab] language must do the same again" (Ahmad 1960, p. 104).

51. So salient and accepted is the quest for modernization of concepts in African and Asian nationalism that Lutfi is able to turn this quest into an argument on behalf of admitting European words and expressions into scientific Arabic. "Those who rejected the European name for the European tool, he said, were really implying that it was unpatriotic to learn the modern sciences of Europe or utilize its inventions" (Ahmad 1960, pp. 116-117). Compare Lutfi's and Gökalp's eagerness for scientific terminology and lexical elaboration more generally with that of the third edition of the French Academy's *Dictionary*

(1740): "To the vocabulary was added a considerable number of words borrowed from the arts and sciences, which the Academy recognized as having become part of the mental equipment of many speakers and writers; but, conservative always, it murmurs a little against their too common usage" since its goal is to preserve "France from a pernicious innovation in lexicography such as is encouraged in populous and fast-growing communities of uncritical readers where there is no such wholesome check" (Robertson 1910, p. 216 and 223). Two centuries later, a historian of the French language reacted to the Academy's concentration upon the "language of literature and correct conversation" (Robertson 1910, p. 222) by stating that "the civil engineers served the interests of the language more than many members of the Academy" (Brunot 1924-37; cited by Delgado de Carvalho 1962, p. 90).

52. When this volume was in final page-proof I came across the stimulating work of Anthony D. Smith (particularly his *Theories of Nationalism*. London, Duckworth, 1971). A first reading of his publications reveals many differences between my views and conclusions and his, as well as an even larger and more important array of similarities. The true significance of these differences and similarities must, of necessity wait for a future occasion to receive proper consideration.

Bibliography

Aavik, Joh. "Der Entwicklungsgang der estnischen Schriftsprache." *Sprak-vetensdapliga Sallskapets i Uppsala forhandlingar,* 1946-1948, 93-111 (Bilaga F).

Abu-Lughod, Ibrahim. "Nationalism in a New Perspective." *Patterns of African Development; Five Comparisons.* Ed. Herbert J. Spiro. Englewood Cliffs, N.J.: Prentice-Hall, 1967, 35-62.

Abun-Nasr, J. "The Salafiyya Movement in Morocco: The Religious Bases of the Moroccan Nationalist Movement." *St. Anthony's Papers,* 16 (1963), 90-105.

Acton, Lord (John E. E.). "Nationality." *The History of Freedom.* Ed. J. N. Figgis and R. V. Lawrence. London: Macmillan, 1907 (Originally published in *Home and Foreign Review,* 1862, July).

Agoncillo, Teodoro. *The Revolt of the Masses.* Quezon City: Univ. of the Philippines, 1956.

Ahmad, Jamal Mohammed. *The Intellectual Origins of Egyptian Nationalism.* London. Oxford Univ. Press, 1960.

Ajarchukwu, Nkechi. "In Quest of National Language after Independence." *West African Pilot.* 1960, Sept. 30.

Ajayi, J. F. A. "The Place of African History and Culture in the Process of Nation-Building in Africa South of the Sahara." *J. of Negro Education,* 30 (1960), 206-213.

Akzin, Benjamin. *State and Nation.* London: Hutchinson Univ. Lib., 1964.

Alisjahbana, Takdir. "The Indonesian Language, By-product of Nationalism." *Pacific Affairs,* 12 (1949), 388-392.

―――. "The Modernization of the Indonesian Language in Practice," in his *Indonesian Language and Literature: Two Essays.* New Haven: Yale Univ. Southeast Asia Studies, 1962, pp. 1-22.

―――. "New National Languages: A Problem Modern Linguistics Has Failed to Solve." *Lingua,* 15 (1965), 515-30.

Allworth, Edward. *Central Asian Publishing and the Rise of Nationalism.* New York: New York Public Library, 1965.

Al-Toma, Salih J. "Language Education in Arab Countries and the Role of Academies." *Current Trends in Linguistics VI*, 1971, 690-720.

Anderson, Eugene N. *Nationalism and the Cultural Crisis in Prussia, 1806-1815.* New York: Ferrar and Rinehart, 1939.

Anon. *A Common Script for Indian Languages.* Delhi: Ministry of Scientific Research and Cultural Affairs, 1963.

Apter, David E. *The Politics of Modernization.* Chicago: Univ. of Chicago Press, 1965.

Arendt, Hannah. "Imperialism, Nationalism, Chauvinism." *Review of Politics, 7* (1945), 441-463.

———. *The Origins of Totalitarianism.* New York: Harcourt, 1951.

Ashford, Douglas E. *Perspectives of a Moroccan Nationalist.* Totowa, N. J.: Bedminster Press, 1964.

Auma - Osolo, A. and Osolo - Nasubo, Ngweno. Democratic African Socialism: An Account of African Communal Philosophy. *African Studies Review.* 14 (1971), 265-272.

Aung, Htin. Commentary on Rupert Emerson's "The Progress of Nationalism." *Nationalism and Progress in Free Asia,* Ed. Philip W. Thayer. Baltimore: Johns Hopkins, 1953, pp. 82-95.

Auty, R. "The Evolution of Literary Slovak." *Transactions of the Philological Society* (London), 1953, 143-60.

Avtorkhanov, A. "Denationalization of the Soviet Ethnic Minorities." *Studies on the Soviet Union,* 4, No. 1 (1965), 75-99.

Bailey, Fred. *Tribe, Caste and Nation.* Manchester: Manchester Univ. Press, 1960.

Balandier, Georges. "Messianismes et nationalismes en Afrique Noire." *Cahiers Internationaux de Sociologie,* 14 (1953), 41-65 (in French).

———. "Political Myths of Colonization and Decolonization in Africa." *State and Society.* Ed. R. Bendix. Boston: Little, Brown, 1968, pp. 475-484.

Bald, Marjorie A. "The Anglicisation of Scottish Printing." *Scottish History Review,* 23 (1925-26), 107-115.

———. "The Pioneers of Anglicised Speech in Scotland." *Scottish History Review,* 24 (1926-27), 179-193.

Banton, Michael. "Social Alignment and Identity in a West African City." *Urbanization and Migration in West Africa.* Ed. Hilda Kuper. Berkeley: Univ. of Calif. Press, 1965, pp. 131-147.

Barker, Ernest. "The Reformation and Nationality." *Modern Churchman,* 22 (1932), 329-343.

Barnard, F. M. *Herder's Social and Political Thought: From Enlightenment to Nationalism.* Oxford: Clarendon Press, 1965.

———. *J. G. Herder on Social and Political Culture.* London, Cambridge Univ. Press, 1969.

Baron, Salo W. *Modern Nationalism and Religion.* New York: Harper, 1947.
Barrow, R. H. *The Romans.* Baltimore: Penguin, 1949.
Barzun, Jacques. *The French Race.* New York: Columbia Univ. Press. 1932. (Reissued by Kennikat Press, 1966).
Bascom, Wm. R. "Tribalism, Nationalism and Pan-Africanism." *The Annuals,* 342 (1962), 28-29.
Baskakov, Nikolai Aleksandrovich. *The Turkic Languages of Central Asia: Problems of Planned Culture Contact.* Translated with comments by Stefan Wurm. Oxford: Central Asian Research Centre, St. Antony's College, 1960.
Beckett, J. C. *The Making of Modern Ireland, 1603-1923.* London: Faber and Faber, 1966.
Bégouin, Louis-Paul. "Les Franglophones." *Le Travaileur,* 1970, October 6, 1.
Bell, Wendell, et al. *The Democratic Revolution in the West Indies: Studies in Nationalism, Leadership and the Belief in Progress.* Cambridge, Mass.: Schenkman, 1967.
Bellah, Robert. "Civil Religion." *Daedalus,* 96, No. 1 (Winter), (1967), 1-21.
Bendix, Reinhard. *Nation-Building and Citizenship.* New York: Wiley, 1964.
Bentham, Jeremy. "Essay on Language." *The Works of Jeremy Brentham.* New York: Russell and Russell, 1962, Vol. 8, pp. 310-320. (Originally written about 1820.)
Berg, Elliot J. "The Economics of the Migrant Labor System." *Urbanization and Migration in West Africa.* Ed. Hilda Kuper. Berkeley: Univ. of Calif. Press, 1965, pp. 160-184.
Besant, Annie. *India, Bond or Free?* New York: Putnam, 1926.
Bidwell, Charles E. "Language, Dialect and Nationality in Yugoslavia." *Human Relations,* 15 (1962), 217-225.
Biederman, Karl. *Deutschland im achzehnten Jahrhundert,* vol. 2. Leipzig: Weber, 1859.
Binder, Leonard. "Ideological Foundations of Egyptian-Arab Nationalism." *Ideology and Discontent.* Ed. David Apter. New York: Free Press, 1964, 128-154.
———. "Ideology and Political Development." *Modernization: The Dynamics of Growth.* Ed. Myron Weiner. New York: Basic Books, 1966, pp. 192-204.
bin Ismail, Tuan Syed Narir. "Strengthening Linguistic Links Will Hasten Malay Unity." *Asia Magazine* (Manila), 1966, Oct. 9, 10-13.
Blach, Jaroslva. *Die čechoslaven.* Wien and Teschen: Karl Prochaska, 1883.
Blackall, E. A. *The Emergence of Standard German as a Literary Language.* London: Cambridge Univ. Press, 1959.
Blond, Georges. *Admiral Togo* Trans. Edward Hyams. New York: Macmillan, 1960.
Boehm, Max H. "Nationalism: Theoretical Aspects." *Encyclopedia of the Social Sciences,* 11 (1933), 231-240.

Bolitho, Hector. *Jinnah: Creator of Pakistan.* London: John Murray, 1954.
Bourguiba, Habib. "Bourguibism." (Speech delivered on October 12, 1961; translated and published by the Tunisian Secretariat of State for Information), in *The Ideologies of the Developing Nations.* Ed. Paul E. Sigmund, Jr. New York: Praeger, 1963, pp. 142-143.
Bram, Joseph. *Language and Society.* New York: Random House, 1955.
Braunthal, Julius. *The Paradox of Nationalism.* London: St. Botolph, 1946
Breton, Albert. "The Economics of Nationalism" *Journal of Political Economy,* 72 (1964), 376-386.
Bro, Margueritte Harmon. *Indonesia: Land of Challenge.* New York: Harper & Row, 1954.
Broda, Rudolf. "Revival of nationalities in the Soviet Union." *American Journal of Sociology,* 37 (1931/2), 82-93.
Bromage, Mary C. *De Valera and the March of a Nation,* New York: Noonday Press, 1956.
Brown, Leon Carl. "Changing Cultures and New Loyalties in North Africa." *French-Speaking Africa: The Search for Identity.* Ed. Wm. H. Lewis. New York: Waler, 1965, pp. 95-106.
Brown, W. Norman. "Script Reform in Modern India, Pakistan, and Ceylon." *Journal of American Oriental Society,* 73 (1953), 1-6.
Bruner, Edward. "Urbanization and Ethnic Identity." *American Anthropologist,* 63 (1961), 508-521.
Brunot, Ferdinand. *Histoire de la langue française des origenes à 1900.* Vol. I-X. Paris: Colin, 1924-33 (. . . à nos jours, in 14 parts, - 1953).
Buck, C. D. Language and the Sentiment of Nationality." *American Political Science Review,* 10 (1916), 44-69.
Cady, John. *A History of Modern Burma.* Ithaca: Cornell Univ. Press, 1958.
Cahnman, Werner J. "Religion and Nationality." *American Journal of Sociology,* 49 (1944), 524-529.
Capdevila, Arturo. *Babel y el castellano.* Buenos Aires: Editorial Bosada, 1940.
Carr, E. H. (Chmn). *Nationalism: A Report by a Study Group of Members of the Royal Institute of International Affairs.* London: Oxford Univ. Press, 1939.
Catalonian Cultural Committee. *Appeal on Behalf of Catalonia.* Geneva: Catalonian Cultural Committee, 1924.
Chadwick, H. Munro. *The Nationalities of Europe and the Growth of National Ideologies.* New York: Macmillan, 1945.
Chamber, W. W. "Language and Nationality in German Pre-romantic and Romantic Thought." *Modern Language Review,* 41 (1946), 382-392.
Chamberlain, J. F. "Literary Selections as an Aid in Teaching Geography." *Journal of Geography,* 15 (1916), 9-16.
Chatterji, Suniti Kumar. *Languages and the Linguistic Problem.* London: Oxford Univ. Press, 1943.

––––. *Civilizations*, 2, No. 1 (1952), 19-32 [no title over paper.]

Chaudhuri, Nirad C. *The Autobiography of an Unknown Indian.* New York: Macmillan, 1951.

Chejne, Anwar G. "Arabic: Its Significance and Place in Arab-Muslim Society." *Middle East Journal*, 19 (1965), 447-470.

––––. *The Arabic Language. Its Role in History.* Minneapolis: Univ. of Minnesota Press, 1969.

Chilcote, Ronald H. "Development and Nationalism in Brazil and Portuguese Africa." *Comparative Political Studies*, 1 (1969), 501-25.

Childe, V. Gordon. *The Aryans: A Study of Indo-European Origins.* New York: Knopf, 1926.

Chowdhury, Munier. "The Language Problem in East Pakistan." *International Journal of American Linguistics*, 26, No. 3 (1960), 64-78.

Clark, S. D., "The Importance of Anti-Americanism in Canadian National Feeling." *Canada and Her Great Neighbor.* Ed. H. F. Angus. Toronto: Ryerson Press, 1938, pp. 392-438.

Clark, T. T., Jr. *Herder, His Life and Thought.* Berkeley: Univ. of Calif. Press, 1955.

Clarkson, Jesse D. "Big Jim Larkin: A Footnote to Nationalism." *Nationalism and Internationalism: Essays Inscribed to Carlton J. H. Hayes.* Ed. Edward M. Earle. New York: Columbia Univ. Press, 1950, pp. 45-63.

Clough, Shepard B. *A History of the Flemish Movement in Belgium: A Study in Nationalism.* New York: Smith, 1930.

Coleman, James S. "Conclusions: The Political Systems of the Developing Areas." *The Politics of the Developing Areas.* Ed. Gabriel A. Almond and James S. Coleman. Princeton N. J.: Princeton Univ. Press, 1960, pp. 552-557.

––––. *Nigeria: Background to Nationalism.* Berkeley: Univ. of Calif. Press, 1963.

Constantin, D., Emil Petrovici, and Gheorge Stefan. *La formation du peuple roumaine et de sa langue.* Bibliotheca Historica Romaniae, I. Bucharest: Editions de l'Académie de la République Populaire Roumaine, 1963.

Corkery, Daniel. *The Fortunes of the Irish Language.* Cork: Mercier Press, 1956.

Cornish, Vaughan. *Borderlands of Language in Europe and their Relation to the Historic Frontier of Christendom.* London: Sifton-Praed, 1936.

Coulton, G. G. "Nationalism in the Middle Ages." *Cambridge Historical Journal*, 5 (1935), 15-40.

Crabb, Cecil V., Jr. *Nations in a Multipolar World.* New York: Harper, 1968.

Curtin, Philip D. "Nationalism in Africa." *Review of Politics*, 28 (1966), 143-153.

Dadrian, Vahakn N. "Major Patterns of Social and Cultural Change of the Armenians." *Year Book of the American Philosophical Society*, 1965, 375-379.

———. "Nationalism, Communism and Soviet Industrialization." A paper presented at the 62nd Annual Convention of the American Sociological Association, Aug. 28-31, 1967, San Francisco. Mimeo. 45 pp.

———. "The Initial Development of the Soviet Posture on Nationalities: A Reappraisal of the Roles of Lenin and Stalin. *Indian Sociological Bulletin,* 6 1 (1968), 18-38.

Daniel, Samuel. *The Poetical Essays of Sam. Danyel.* London, 1599.

Daube, Anna. *Der Aufsteig der Muttersprache im deutschen Denken des 15 und 16 Jahrhunderts.* Frankfurt am M. -Diesterveg, 1940 (*Deutsche Forschungen,* Vol. 34).

Davies, Thomas. *Essays and Poems with a Centenary Memoir:* 1845. Dublin: Gill, 1945.

Dawson, Christopher. *The Revolt of Asia.* New York: Sheed and Ward, 1950.

de Blaghd, Earnan (Bluthe, Ernest). *The State and the Language.* Dublin: Comhdhail Naisiunta na Gaeilege, 1951.

De Francis, John. *Nationalism and Language Reform in China.* Princeton, N. J.: Princeton Univ. Press, 1950.

De Freine, Sean. *The Great Silence,* Dublin: Foilseacháin Náisiúnta Teoranta, 1965.

Decraene, Ph. *Le Panafricanisme.* Paris: Presses Universitaires de France, 1961.

Delaise, Francis. *Political Myths and Economic Realities,* New York: Viking, 1927.

de La Ramée, P. *Grammaire,* Paris: n.p. 1572.

Delgado de Carvalho, C. M. "The Geography of Languages." *Readings in Cultural Geography.* Ed. Philip L. Wagner and Marvin W. Mikesell. Chicago: Univ. of Chicago Press, 1962, pp. 75-93.

del Rosario, Gonsalo. "Consistency, Not Purity, Is the Important Factor in Language Development." *Philippine Educational Forum,* 1967, June, 1-11.

———. "A Modernization-Standardization Plan for the Austronesian-derived National Languages of Southeast Asia." *Asian Studies,* No. 6, 1 (1968), 1-18.

Denison, N. "The Use of English as a Medium of Communication in Europe." London: The Institute of Linguists, 1970. (Paper prepared for a conference on "English—a European language" April, 1970.)

de Campo. Estaban A. "José Rizal." *Journal of Southeast Asian History,* 3 (1962), 44-55.

Desheriyev, Yu., Kammari, M., and Melikyan, M. [Soviet National Linguistic Policy Seen as a Model] *Kommunist* 1965, No. 13 (September) 55-56. (In English: *Current Digest of The Soviet Press,* 1965, 17, No. 47, 14, 19.)

Depres, Leo A. "The Implications of Nationalist Politics in British Guiana for the Development of Cultural Theory. *American Anthropologist,* 66 (1964), 1051-1077.

———. *Cultural Pluralism and Nationalist Politics in British Guiana.* Chicago: Rand McNally, 1967.

———. "Protest and Change in Plural Societies." Paper presented at the 1968 annual meeting of the American Anthropological Association, Seattle, Washington.

Deutsch, Karl W. "The Trend of European Nationalism: The Language Aspect." *American Political Science Review,* 36 (1942), 533-541.

———. *Nationalism and Social Communication; An Inquiry into the Foundations of Nationality.* Cambridge: MIT Press, 1953 (second edition: 1966).

———. *An Interdisciplinary Bibliography on Nationalism, 1935-1953.* Cambridge: MIT Press, 1956.

———. *Political Community in the North Atlantic Area.* Princeton, N. J.: Princeton Univ. Press, 1957.

———. "Social Mobilization and Political Development." *American Political Science Review,* 55 (1961) 493-514.

———. "Integration and the Social System: Implications of Functional Analysis." *The Integration of Political Communities.* Ed. Philip E. Jacob and James V. Toscano. Philadelphia: Lippincott, 1964, pp. 179-208.

———. "Communication Theory and Political Integration." *The Integration of Political Communities.* Ed. Philip E. Jacob and James V. Toscano. Philadelphia: Lippincott, 1964, pp. 46-74.

———. "Nation-building and National Development; Some Issues for Political Research." *Nation-Building.* Ed. Karl W. Deutsch and Wm. J. Foltz. New York: Atherton, 1966, pp. 1-16.

Diop, Cheika Anta. "The Cultural Contributions and Prospects of Africa." *The First International Conference of Negro Writers and Artists.* Paris: Presence Africaine, 1956, pp. 349-354; also in Kohn and Sokolsky, pp. 140-148.

Djarylogasinova, R. Sh. "On the Question of Cultural Convergence of the Koreans of the Uzbek SSR with Neighboring Peoples. *Soviet Anthropology and Archeology,* 7 (1969), 26-35.

Doob, Leonard. South Tyrol: An Introduction to the Psychological Syndrome of Nationalism. *Public Opinion Quarterly,* 1962, 26, 172-184.

Doob, Leonard W. *Patriotism and Nationalism: Their Psychological Foundations.* New Haven, Conn.: Yale, 1964.

Dominian, Leon. *The Frontiers of Language and Nationality in Europe.* New York: American Geographical and Statistical Society of New York, 1917.

Draper, Theodore. *The Rediscovery of Black Nationalism.* New York: Viking, 1970.

Droz, Jacques. "Concept français et concept allemand de l'idée de nationalité." *Europa und der Nationalismus, Bericht über das III internationale Historiker-Treffen in Speyer, 17 bis Oktober 1949.* Baden-Baden, 1950, pp. 111-133.

Du Bellay, Joachim. *La défence et l'illustration de la langue françoyse.* Paris: Chamard, 1948 (originally 1549).

Dubos, Jean-Baptiste. *Histoire critique de l'établissement de la monarchie française dans les Gaules.* 3 Vols. Paris: n.p., 1735.

Durkheim, E. *The Division of Labor.* Trans. G. Simpson. New York: Macmillan, 1933 (originally published 1893).

Eastman, Carol M. Who are the Waswahirli? *Africa,* 1971, 41, 228-236.

Eddy, S. K. *The King is Dead.* Studies in the Near Eastern Resistance to Hellenism, 334-31 B.C. Lincoln, Neb.: Univ. of Nebraska Press, 1961.

Eisenstadt, S. N. *Modernization: Protest and Change.* Englewood Cliffs, N. J.: Prentice-Hall, 1966.

Ellmers. J. E. "The Revolt of the Netherlands: The Part Played by Religion in the Process of Nation-Building." A paper presented at the 6th World Congress of the International Sociological Association, Sept. 4-11, 1966, Evian (France). 9 pp.

Elliot, John Huxtable. *The Revolt of the Catalans; A Study in the Decline of Spain, 1598-1640.* Cambridge (Eng.)

Elsbree, Willard H. *Japan's Role in Southeast Asian Nationalist Movements, 1940 to 1945.* Cambridge, Mass.: Harvard Univ. Press, 1953.

Emerson, Rupert. *From Empire to Nation.* Boston: Beacon Press, 1962.

Engels, F. "What Have the Working Classes to Do with Poland?" *Commonwealth,* 1866, March 24, March 31, May 5.

Epstein, A. L. "Urbanization and Social Change in Africa" (followed by comments and reply). *Current Anthropology,* 8 (1967), 275-295.

Estienne, H. *Deux dialogues du nouveau langage français, italianisé et autrement desguizé.* Ed. P. Ristelhuber. Paris: Lemerre, 1885 (orig. pub. 1578).

Etzioni, Amitai. *Political Unification.* New York: Holt, 1965.

Fallers, Lloyd. "Ideology and Culture in Uganda Nationalism." *American Anthropology,* 63 (1961), 677-86.

Farmer, B. H. "The Social Basis of Nationalism in Ceylon." *The Journal of Asian Studies,* 24, 3 (May 1965) pp. 431-440.

Fatemi, Narollah S. "The Roots of Arab Nationalism." *Orbis,* 2 (1959), 437-456.

Febvre, Lucien. "Langue et Nationalité en France au XVIIIe siécle," *Revue de synthèse historique,* 42 (1926), 19-40.

Ferguson, Charles A. "Myths about Arabic." *Georgetown University Monograph Series on Languages and Linguistics,* 12 (1959), 75-82; also in *Readings in the Sociology of Language.* Ed. J. A. Fishman. The Hague: Mouton, 1968, pp. 375-381.

———. "St. Stefan of Perm and Applied Linguistics." *Language Problems of Developing Nations.* Ed. Joshua A. Fishman, Charles A. Ferguson, and Jyotirindra Das Gupta. New York: Wiley, 1968, 253-266.

Fernandez, J. W. "Folklore as an Agent of Nationalism." *African Studies Bulletin,* 2 (1962), 3-8.

Fichte, Johann Gottlieb. *Addresses to the German Nation.* Trans. R. F. Jones and G. H. Turnbull. Chicago and London, Open Court, 1922 (originally printed 1807-1808).

Fischel, A. *Der Panslawismus bis zum Weltkrieg.* Stuttgart/Berlin: Cotta, 1919.

Fishman, Joshua A. "A Systematization of the Whorfian Hypothesis." *Behavioral Science,* 5 (1960), 323-329.

Fishman, Joshua A. et al. *Language Loyalty in the United States.* The Hague: Mouton, 1966.

———. "Nationality-Nationalism and Nation-Nationism." *Language Problems of Developing Nations.* Ed. Joshua A. Fishman, Charles A. Ferguson, and Jyotirindra Das Gupta. New York: Wiley, 1968.

———. "Some Contrasts between Linguistically Homogeneous and Linguistically Heterogeneous Polities." *Language Problems of Developing Nations.* Ed. Joshua A. Fishman, Charles A. Ferguson, and Jyotirindra Das Gupta. New York: Wiley, 1968, 53-68.

———. "National Languages and Languages of Wider Communication in the Developing Nations." *Anthropological Linguistics,* 11 (1969), 111-135.

———. *Bilingualism in the Barrio.* Bloomington: Indiana University Center for Language Sciences, 1971.

———. The Uses of Sociolinguistics [in connection with the creation and revision of writing systems]. in G. E. Perren and J. L. Trim (eds.), *Applications of Linguistics: Selected Papers of The Second International Congress of Applied Linguistics,* Cambridge, 1919. Cambridge Univ. Press, 1971.

———. "Language Modernizaton and Planning in Comparison with Other Types of National Modernization and Planning." *Language in Society.* in press a.

———. "Problems and Prospects of the Sociology of Language. *Einar Haugen Festskrift.* Ed. Nils Hasselmo et al. In press b.

———. "A Multi-factor and Multi-level Approach to the Study of Language Planning Process." *Koelner Zeitschrift für Sociologie.* In press c.

———. Historical Dimensions in The Sociology of Language. (*Georgetown Univ. Monograph Series on Languages and Linguistics,* 1972, in press d.

Flannghaile [Flannery], Tomas O. *For the Tongue of the Gael.* London: City of London Book Depot, 1896.

Fonfrías, Ernesto Juan. *Razón del idioma español en Puerto Rico.* San Juan: Editorial Universitaria, 1960.

Franke, C. *Die Brüder Grimm, Ihr Leben und Wirken.* Dresden and Leipzig: Reissner, 1918.

Freeman, Edward A. "Race and Language," in his *Historical Essays.* London: Macmillan, 1879.

Friedland, Wm. H. "Traditionalism and Modernization: Movements and Ideologies." *Journal of Social Issues,* 24, 4 (1968), 9-24.

Friedrich, Carl J. *Man and His Government: An Empirical Theory of Politics.* New York: McGraw-Hill, 1963.
———. "Nation-Building" *Nation-Building.* Ed. Karl W. Deutsch and Wm. J. Foltz. New York: Atherton, 1966, 27-32.
Furnivall, J. S. *Colonial Policy and Practice: A Comparative Study of Burma and Netherlands India.* New York: NYU Press, 1956.
———. *Netherlands India: A Study of Plural Economy.* London: Cambridge University Press, 1939.
Gadgil, D. R. *Economic Policy and Development.* Poona: Sangam Press, 1955.
Galbraith, V.H. "Nationality and Language in Medieval England." *Transactions of the Royal Historical Society,* 23 (1941), 113-128.
Gallagher, Charles F. "Language, Culture and Ideology: The Arab World." *Expectant Peoples: Nationalism and Development.* Ed. K. H. Silvert. New York: Random House, 1963, 19-231.
Gastil, Raymond. *Language and Modernization: A Comparative Analysis of Persian and English Texts.* Cambridge: Center for International Affairs of Harvard University, 1959.
Geiss, Imanuel. "Notes on the Development of Pan-Africanism." *Journal of the Historical Society of Nigeria,* 3 (1967), 719-740.
Gellner, Ernest. *Thought and Change.* Chicago: Univ. of Chicago, 1964.
———. "Tribalism and Social Change in North Africa." *French-Speaking Africa: The Search for Identity.* Ed. Wm. H. Lewis. New York: Walker, 1965, 107-118.
Gennep, Arnold Van. *Traité comparatif des nationalités.* Paris: Payot, 1922.
Gerteiny, Alfred G. "The Racial Factor and Politics in the Islamic Republic of Mauritania." *Race,* 8 (1967), 263-75.
Glaskow, W. G. The origin of the Cossacks. *East Europe.* 20 (1971), No. 6, 25-29.
Glezerman, G. "Class and Nation." *Transactions of the Sixth World Congress of Sociology,* 3 (1970), 309-318.
Glunk, Rolf. "Erfolg und Misserfolg der nationalsozialistischen Sprachlenkung." *Zeitschrift für deutsche Sprache* (Berlin), 22 (1966), 146-153.
Gökalp, Ziya. "Nation and Fatherland (Mittet ver Vatan)." *Turk Yurdu,* 1914, 6, No. 66. *Turkish Nationalism and Western Civilization, Selected Essays of Ziya Gökalp.* Ed. trans. Niyazi Berkes. London: Allen and Unwin, 1959.
———. *Turkish Nationalism and Western Civilization.* Trans. Niyazi Berkes. New York: Columbia Univ. Press, 1959.
———. "Turkish Nationalism." *The Contemporary Middle East.* Ed. Benjamin Rivlin and Joseph H. Szyliowiez. New York: Random House, 1965, 217-224.
———. *The Principles of Turkism.* Trans. and annotated by Robert Devereux. Leiden: Brill, 1968.
Goody, Jack, and Ian Watt. "The Consequences of Literacy." *Comparative Studies in Society and History,* 5 (1963), 304-345.

Greenberg, Joseph H. "Urbanism, Migration and Language." *Urbanization and Migration in West Africa.* Ed. Hilda Kuper. Berkeley: Univ. of Calif. Press, 1965.

Greenough, James B., and George L. Kittredge. *Words and Their Ways in English Speech.* New York: Macmillan, 1905.

Gregor, A. J. "African Socialism, Socialism and Fascism on Appraisal." *Review of Politics,* 29 (1967), 324-53.

Grentrup, Theodore, *Religion und Muttersprache.* Münster: Aschendorff, 1932.

Guetskow, Harold S. *Multiple Loyalties.* Princeton: Center for Research on World Political Institutions, 1955.

Guitare, Guillermo L., and Rafael Torres Quintero. "Linguistic Correctness and the Role of Academies." *Current Trends in Linguistics.* 4 (1968), 562-604.

Guryceva, M. S. "The Initial Stage in the Formation of the French National Language." *Problems in the Formation and Development of National Languages.* Ed. M. M. Guxman. Translated from the Russian orginal (published Moscow 1960) by the Center for Applied Linguistics, ms.

Haas, Ernest B. *Beyond the Nation-State: Functionalism and International Organization.* Stanford: Stanford Univ. Press, 1964.

Hadas, Moses. "The Religion of Plutarch." *Review of Religion,* 6 (1942), 270-282.

———. "From Nationalism to Cosmopolitianism in the Greco-Roman World." *Journal of the History of Ideas,* 4 (1943), 105-111.

———. "Aspects of Nationalist Survival under Hellenistic and Roman Imperialism." *Journal of the History of Ideas,* 11 (1950), 131-139.

Haim, Sylvia. *Arab Nationalism,* Berkeley: Univ. of Calif. Press, 1962.

Hajime, Nakamura. "Basic Features of the Legal, Political and Economic Thought of Japan," *The Japanese Mind.* Ed. Charles A Moore. Honolulu: East-West Center Press, 1967, 143-163.

Hall, Robert A., Jr. *The Italian questione della lingua: An Interpretive Essay.* Chapel Hill: Univ. of North Carolina Press, 1942.

Halpern, Ben. "Zionism and Israel." *Jewish Journal of Sociology,* 3, No. 2 (1961), 155-173.

Hamzaoui, Rachad. *L'Académie Arabe de Damas et le problème de la modernisation de la langue arabe.* Leiden: Brill, 1965.

Handman, Max S. "The Sentiment of Nationalism." *Political Science Quarterly,* 36 (1921), 104-21.

Handelsman, Marcel. "Le rôle de la nationalité dans l'histoire du Moyen Age." *Bulletin of the International Committee of Historical Sciences,* October, 1929, no. 7.

Hanna, Sami A., and George H. Gardner. *Arab Socialism: A Documentary Survey.* Leiden: Brill, 1969.

Hanna, Willard A. *Eight Nation Makers.* New York: St. Martin's, 1964.

Hardy, E. R., Jr. "The Patriarchate of Alexandria: A Study in National Christianity." *Church History,* 15 (1946), 81-100.

Harries, Lyndon. "Language Policy in Tanzania." *Africa* [London], 39 (1969), 275-279.

Harrison, Selig S. *India: The Most Dangerous Decades.* Princeton, N.J.: Princeton Univ. Press, 1960.

———. "Hindu Society and the State: The Indian Union." *Expectant Peoples: Nationalism and Development.* Ed. K. H. Silvert. New York: Random House, 1963, 267-299.

Hartz, Louis. *The Founding of New Societies.* New York: Harcourt, Brace & World, 1964.

Haugen, Einar. "Linguistics and Language Planning." *Sociolinguistics.* Ed. Wm. Bright. The Hague: Mouton, 1966, 50-71.

———. *Language Planning: The Case of Modern Norwegian.* Cambridge, Mass: Harvard University Press, 1966.

———. "Language Planning in Modern Norway." *Readings in the Sociology of Language,* Ed. Joshua A. Fishman. The Hague: Mouton, 1968, pp. 673-687.

Hayes, Carlton J. H. "Two Varieties of Nationalism: Original and Derived." *Association of History Teachers of the Middle States and Maryland: Proceedings,* 1928, No. 26, 71-83.

———. *France, a Nation of Patriots.* New York: Columbia Univ. Press, 1930.

———. *The Historical Evolution of Modern Nationalism.* New York: Smith, 1931 (2nd ed., 1948).

———. *Essays on Nationalism.* New York: Macmillan, 1937.

———. "The Church and Nationalism: A Plea for Further Study of a Major Issue." *Catholic Historical Review.* 28 (1942), 1-12.

———. *Nationalism: A Religion.* New York: Macmillian, 1960.

Hazelwood, Arthur (ed.). *African Integration and Disintegration.* London: Oxford Univ. Press, 1967.

Herder, J. G. *Sämtliche Werke.* Berlin: B. Suphan, 1877-1913. 33 Vols.

Hertz, Frederick. *Nationality in History and Politics.* New York: Oxford Univ. Press, 1944.

Hettlich, E. L. *A Study in Ancient Nationalism: The Testimony of Euripides.* Williamsport, Pa.: Bayard, 1933.

Heyd, U. *Foundations of Turkish Nationalism: The Life and Teachings of Ziya Gokalp.* London: Luzac and Harvill, 1950.

———. *Language Reform in Modern Turkey.* Jerusalem: Israel Oriental Society, 1954.

———. *Revival of Islam in Modern Turkey .* Jerusalem: Magnes Press of the Hebrew University, 1968.

Hibino, Yutaka. *Nippon Shindo Ron: or, The National Ideals of the Japanese People.* Trans. A. P. McKenzie. London: Cambridge Univ. Press, 1928.

Hitchens, Keith. "The Rumanians of Transylvania and the Congress of Nationalities." *Slavonic and East European Review,* 48 (1970), 388-402.

Hodgkin, Thomas. *Nationalism in Colonial Africa.* London: Frederick Muller, 1956.

Holl, K. "Das Fortleben der Volkssprachen in Kleinasien in nachchristlicher Zeit." *Hermes,* 43 (1908), 240.

Hourani, A. "Arab Nationalism," in his *Syria and Lebanon.* London: Oxford Univ. Press, 1946, 96-104.

Hughes, A. J. *East Africa: The Search for Unity.* Baltimore: Penguin, 1963.

Hugelman, Karl G. "Die deutsche Nation und der deutsche Nationalstaat im Mittelalter." *Historisches Jahrbach,* 51 (1931), 1-29, 445-484.

Hu Shih. *The Chinese Renaissance: The Haskell Lectures, 1933.* Chicago: Univ. of Chicago Press, 1934.

Hyde, Douglas. *Revival of Irish Literature and Other Addresses.* London: Fisher Unwin, 1894, 117-37.

Ingelhart, Ronald F., and Margaret Woodward. "Language Conflicts and Political Community." *Comparative Studies in Society and History,* 10 (1967), 27-45.

Inkeles, A. "Industrial Man: The Relation of Status to Experience, Perception and Value." *American Journal of Sociology,* 6 (1960), 1-37.

Irele, A. "Negritude or Black Cultural Nationalism." *Journal of Modern African Studies,* 1969, 3 (no. 31).

Izzeddin, Nejla. *The Arab World,* Chicago: Univ. of Chicago Press, 1953, 19-21.

Jabri, Chafic. "Modern Literary Trends in Islamic Countries." *Colloquium on Islamic Culture.* Princeton, N.J.: Princeton Univ. Press, 1953, 19-21.

Jacob, Philip E., and Henry Teune. "The Integrative Process: Guidelines for Analysis of the Bases of Political Community. *The Integration Political Communities.* Ed. Philip E. Jacob and J. V. Toscano. Philadelphia: Lippincott, 1964, 1-45.

Jakobson, Roman. "The Beginnings of National Self-Determination in Europe." *Review of Politics,* 7 (1945), 29-42.

Janowsky, Oscar I. *Nationalities and National Minorities.* New York: Macmillan, 1945.

Jaszi, Oscar. *The Dissolution of the Habsburg Monarchy.* Chicago: Univ. of Chicago Press, 1929.

Jernudd, Björn, and Jyotirindra Das Gupta. "Towards a Theory of Language Planning." *Can Language Be Planned?* Ed. Joan Rubin and Bjorn Jernudd. Honolulu: East-West Center Press, 1971.

Johannson, Arwid. "Zu Noreens Abhandlung über Sprachrichtigkeit." *Indogermanische Forschungen,* 1 (1892), 232-255.

Johnson, Harry G. "A Theoretical Model of Economic Nationalism in New and Developing States." Chapter I in *Economic Nationalism in Old and New States.* Ed. H. G. Johson. London: Allen and Unwin, 1968.

Johnson, Samuel. *A Dictionary of the English Language.* 2 vols. London, 1755.

Jones, D. Gwenallt. "National Movements in Wales in the 19th Century." *The Historical Basis of Welsh Nationalism.* A. W. Wade-Evans et al. Cardiff: Plaid Cymru, 1950, 99-129.

Jones, Richard F. *The Triumph of the English Language.* Stanford: Stanford Univ. Press, 1953.

Jones, W. R. *Bilingualism in Welsh Education.* Cardiff: Univ. of.Wales Press, 1966.

Jones-Pierce, T. "The Age of the Princes." *The Historical Basis of Welsh Nationalism.* A. W. Wade-Evans et al. Cardiff: Plaid Cymru, 1950, 52-59.

Joseph, Bernard. *Nationality, Its Nature and Problems.* London: G. Allen and Unwin, Ltd., 1929.

Jumba-Masagazi, A. H. K. *African Socialism, A Bibliography.* Nairobi: the East African Academy, 1970.

Kahl, J. A. "Some Social Concomitants of Industrialization and Urbanization." *Human Organization,* 18, 2 (1959), 53-75.

Kahn, Robert A. *The Multinational Empire: Nationalism and National Reform in the Habsburg Monarchy, 1848-1918.* 2 vols. New York: Columbia Univ. Press, 1950.

Karpat, Kemal H. "Turkey: The Mass Media." *Political Modernization in Japan and Turkey.* Ed. Robert E. Ward and Dankwart A. Rustow. Princeton, N.J.: Princeton Univ. Press. 1964, 282-285.

Kartodirdjo, Sartono. "Some Problems on the Genesis of Nationalism in Indonesia." *Journal of Southeast Asian History,* 3 (1962), 67-94.

Karve, I. "On the road." *Journal of Asian Studies,* 22 (1962), 13-29.

Katz, Daniel. "The Psychology of Nationalism." *Fields of Psychology.* Ed. J. P. Guilford. New York: Van Nostrand, 1940, 163-181.

———. "Nationalism and Strategies of International Conflict Resolution." *International Behavior: A Social Psychological Analysis.* Ed. Herbert Kelman. New York: Holt, 1965, 356-390.

Kautsky, John H. "An Essay in the Politics of Development." *Political Change in Underveloped Countries: Nationalism vs. Communism.* Ed. John H. Kautsky. New York: Wiley, 1962, 1-122.

Kazemzadeh, F. "Pan Movements." *International Encyclopedia of the Social Sciences,* 11 (1968), 365-370.

Kearney, Robert N. *Communalism and Language in the Politics of Ceylon.* Durham, N.C.: Duke Univ. Press, 1967.

Keddie, Nikki R. "Pan-Islam as Proto-Nationalism." *Journal of Modern History,* 41 (1969), 17-28.

Kedourie, Elie. *Nationalism.* New York: Praeger, 1960 (revised, 1961).

Kendall, P. L. "The Ambivalent Character of Nationalism among Egyptian Professionals." *Public Opinion Quarterly.* 20 (1956), 277-289.

Kennedy, J. *Asian Nationalism in the Twentieth Century.* New York: Macmillan, 1968.

Kerns, O. P. "The Revival of Irish, a Case Re-stated." *The Irish Ecclesiastical Record,* March 1954.

Khouri, Mounah. A. *Poetry and the Making of Modern Egypt (1882-1922).* Leiden: Brill, 1971.

Kilson, M. L., Jr. "The Analysis of African Nationalism." *World Politics,* 10 (1957-58), 484-497.

―――. "Nationalism and Social Classes in British West Africa." *Journal of Politics,* 20 (1958), 368-387.

Kinross, Lord (Balfour, Patrick; Baron Kinross). *Atatürk: The Rebirth of a Nation.* London: Weidenfeld and Nicolson, 1964.

Kirk-Greene, Anthony H. M. "The Hausa Language Board." *Afrika und Übersee,* 47 (1964), 187-203.

Kleivan, Helge. "Culture and Ethnic Identity: On Modernization and Ethnicity in Greenland." *Folk,* 11-12 (1969/70), 209-234.

Kleivan, I. "Language and Ethnic Identity: Language Policy and Debate in Greenland." *Folk* 11-12 (1969/70), 235-285.

Kloss, Heinz. *Die Entwicklung neuer germanischer Kultursprachen von 1800 bis 1950* Munich: Pohl, 1952.

―――. "Abstand Languages and Ausbau Languages." *Anthropological Linguistics,* 9, 7 (1967), 29-31.

Kochs, Theodor. "Nationale Idee und nationalistisches Denken im Grimmschen Wörterbuch." *Nationalismus in Germanistik und Dichtung.* Ed. Benno von Wiese and Rudolf Henss. Berlin: Erich Schmidt, 1966, 273-284.

Kohn, Hans. *Nationalism and Imperialism in the Hither East.* London: Routledge, 1932.

―――. *The Idea of Nationalism: A Study in Its Origins and Background.* New York: Macmillan, 1944 (paperback: 1961).

―――. *Nationalism: Its Meaning and History.* Princeton: Van Nostrand, 1955.

―――. *The Age of Nationalism: The First Era of Global History.* New York: Harper, 1962.

―――. "Nationalism." *International Encyclopedia of the Social Sciences,* 11 (1968), 63-70.

Kolarz, W. *Myths and Realities in Eastern Europe.* London: Lindsay Drummond, 1946.

Koppelman, H. L. *Nation, Sprache und Nationalismus.* Leiden. Sijthoff, 1956.

Krader, Lawrence. *Formation of the State.* Englewood Cliffs, N.J.: Prentice-Hall, 1968.

Kumar, Ravinder. "Community or Nation? Gandhi's Quest for a Popular Consensus in India." *Modern Asian Studies,* 3 (1969), 357-376.

Kuper, Leo. *An African Bourgeoisie: Race, Class and Politics in South Africa.* New Haven: Yale University Press, 1965.

Kurman, George. *The Development of Written Estonian.* Bloomington: Indiana University, 1968 (*Uralic and Altaic Series,* Vol. 90, Research Center for the Language Sciences).

La Motte-Fouqué, Friedrich de. *Etwas über den deutschen Adel.* Hamburg: 1819.

Landes, David S., and Charles Tilly. "History as Social Science: Excerpts from the Report of the History Panel of the Behavioral and Social Sciences Survey." *Social Science Research Council Items* 25, no. 1 (1971), 1-6.

Langley, J. Ayo. "Pan-Africanism in Paris, 1924-36." *Journal of Modern African Studies,* 7 (1969), 69-94.

Leibnitz, G. E. *Deutsche Schriften.* Ed. E. Guhrauer. Berlin, 1838, vol. 1.

Legum, C. *Pan Africanism.* New York: Praeger, 1965.

Lemberg, Eugen. *Nationalismus.* 2 vols. Hamburg: Rowohlt, 1964.

Lendle, O. C. *Die Schreibung der germanischen Sprachen und ihre Standardisierung.* Copenhagen: Levin and Munksgard, 1935.

Lengyel, Emil. *Nationalism: The Last Stage of Communism.* New York: Funk and Wagnall's, 1969.

LePage, Robert B. *The National Language Question: Linguistic Problems of Newly Independent States.* London: Oxford University Press, 1964.

Lerner, Daniel. *The Passing of Traditional Society.* Glencoe, Ill.: Free Press, 1958.

Levine, Donald N. "Cultural Integration." *International Encyclopedia of the Social Sciences,* 7 (1968), 372-380.

———. "The Flexibility of Traditional Culture." *The Journal of Social Issue,* 24, No. 4 (1968), 129-142.

Lewis, Glyn. *Multilingualism in the Soviet Union.* The Hague: Mouton, 1972.

Lieberson, Stanley. Stratification and Ethnic Groups. *Sociological Inquiry,* 40 (1970), 172-181.

Lindman, Kerstin. "Finland's Swedes: An Introduction and a Bibliography." *Scandinavian Studies,* 35 (1963), 123-131.

Linz, Juan. "Early State-Building and Late Peripheral Nationalisms against the State: The Case of Spain," ms. for the UNESCO Conference on Nation-Building, Cérisy, Normandie, August, 1970.

Lipset, Seymour Martin. *Revolution and Counterrevolution: Change and Persistence in Social Structures.* New York: Basic Books, 1968.

Little, Kenneth. *West African Urbanization: A Study of Voluntary Associations in Social Change.* London: Cambridge Univ. Press, 1965.

Lloyd, P. C. *Africa in Social Change.* Baltimore: Penguin, 1967.

Lockwood, W. B. "Language and the Rise of Nations." *Science and Society,* 18 (1954), 245-252.

Lohia, Ram Monohar. "Hindi—Here and Now." *Seminar,* 68 (April 1965), 27-31.

Loomis, Louise. R. "Nationality at the Council of Constance," *American Historical Review,* 44 (1939), 508-527.

Lonsdale, J. M. "Some Origins of Nationalism in East Africa." *Journal of African History,* 9 (1968), 110-46.

Macpherson, James. *Fragments of Ancient Poetry (1760).* Los Angeles: University of California at Los Angeles, 1966.

Madan, Indar Nath. "Sanskritization." *Seminar,* 68 (April 1965), 24-27.

Majumdar, R. C. "Nationalist Historians." *Historians of India, Pakistan and Ceylon.* London: Oxford University Press, 1961, 416-428.

Malón de Chaide, Pedro. *La Conversión de la Madalena, donde se ponen los tres estados que tuvo, de pescador, de penitente, i de gracia.* Valencia: Salvador Fauli, 1794 (originally published: 1588).

Manning, Clarence A. "The Menace of Linguistic Nationalism." *The South Atlantic Quarterly,* 44 (1945), 13-22.

Marczali, Henry. *Hungary in the Eighteenth Century.* London: Cambridge Univ. Press, 1910

Markakis, John. "Education and the Emergence of Nationalism in Africa." *Dialogue,* 1 (1967), 9-20.

Martin, F. X. (ed.) *Leaders and Men of the Easter Rising: Dublin 1916.* London: Methuen, 1967.

Marx, Gary T. Review of Theodore Draper's "The Rediscovery of Black Nationalism." New York: Viking, 1970. *Saturday Review,* 4 July 1970, p. 32.

Mauss, M. "La Nation." *Année Sociologique,* 3rd series, 1953/54. Paris, P.U.F., 1956, 5-68.

Mazrui, Ali A. "On the Concept of 'We Are All Africans.'" *The American Political Science Review,* 57 (1963), 88-97.

———. "The National Language Question in East Africa." *East African Journal,* 4, No. 3 (1967), 12-19.

———. "Violent Contiguity and the Politics of Retribalization in Africa." *Journal of International Affairs,* 23, 1 (1969a), 89-105.

———. "Pluralism and National Integration." *Pluralism in Africa.* Ed. Leo Kuper and M. G. Smith. Berkeley: Univ. of Calif. Press, 1969b, 333-349.

———. *The Political Sociology of The English Language.* The Hague, Mouton, 1973.

McCartney, Donal. "Hyde, D. P. Moran and Irish Ireland." *Leaders and Men of the Easter Rising: Dublin 1916.* Ed. F. X. Martin. London, Methuen: 1967.

McClelland, David C. *The Achieving Society.* Princeton: Van Nostrand, 1961.

McCormack, William. "The Forms of Communication in Vïrasaiva Religion." *Traditional India:* Structure and Change. Ed. Milton Singer. Philadelphia: American Folklore Society, 1959.

McCully, B. T. *English Education and the Origins of Indian Nationalism.* New York: Columbia, 1940.

McGee, W. J. "Some Principles of Nomenclature." *American Anthropologist,* 8 (1895), 279-286.

McNeill, Wm.*The Rise of the West.* Chicago: Univ. Of Chicago Press, 1963.

Mehden, Fred R. von der. *Religion and Nationalism in Southeast Asia.* Madison: Univ. of Wisconsin Press, 1968.

Meillet, Antoine. *Les Langues dans l'Europe nouvelle.* Paris: Payot, 1928. (Avec un appendice de L. Tesnière sur la statistique des languages de l'Europe.)

Mencken, H. L. *The American Language.* New York, Knopf: 1936 (4th edition). First edition, 1919.

Menéndez-Pidal, Ramón. *Castilla, la tradición, el idioma.* Buenos Aires: Espasa-Calpe, 1945.

Mercier, Paul. "Remarques sur la signification du 'tribalisme' actuel en Afrique Noire." *Cahiers Internationaux de Sociologie,* 31 (1961), 61-80.

Merkl, Peter H. *Political Continuity and Change.* New York: Harper & Row, 1967.

Michelet, Jules. *The People.* Trans. C. Cooks. London: Longmans, 1946 (originally published in 1846).

Mill, John Stuart. *Utilitarianism, Liberty and Representative Government.* New York: Dutton, 1910.

Miller, Harry. *Prince and Premier.* London: Faber, 1959.

Milne, J. G. "Egyptian Nationalism under Greek and Roman Rule." *Journal of Egyptian Archaeology,* 14 (1928), 226-234.

Miner, Horace M. "Urban Influences on the Rural Hausa." *Urbanization and Migration in West Africa.* Ed. Hilda Kuper. Berkeley: Univ. of Calif. Press, 1965, 110-130.

Minn Latt, Yekhauŋ. *Modernization of Burmese.* Prague: Oriental Institute, Academia Publishing House of the Cezechoslovak Academy of Sciences, 1966.

Minogue, K. R. *Nationalism.* New York: Basic Books, 1967.

Mises, Ludwig. *Nation, Staat und Wirtschaft: Beiträge zur Politik und Geschichte der Zeit.* Vienna: Manzsche Verlag, 1919.

Montague, R. "The 'Modern State' in Africa and Asia." *Cambridge Journal,* 5 No. 10 (1952).

Moore, Barrington, Jr. *Social Origins of Dictatorship and Democracy: Lord and Peasant in the Making of the Modern World.* Boston: Beacon Press, 1966.

Moore, Wilbert E. *The Impact of Industry.* Englewood Cliffs, N.J.: Prentice-Hall, 1965.

Moussa, Salama. "Arab Language Problems." *Middle Eastern Affairs,* 6 (1955).

Mushkat, Marion. Some Characteristics of Colonialism and its Produce, African Nationalism. *African Studies Review,* 1971, 14, 219-241.

Myrdal, Gunnar. *Asian Drama: An Inquiry into the Poverty of Nations,* 3 vols. New York: Pantheon, 1968.

———. "Cleansing the Approach from Biases in the Study of Underdeveloped Countries." *Studium Generale,* 23 (1970), 1249-1266.

Nahirny, Vladimir C. "The Russian Intelligentsia: From Men of Ideas to Men of Convictions." *Comparative Studies in Society and History,* 4 (1962), 403-435.

Naik, J. P. *Educational Planning in India.* New Delhi: Allied, 1965.

Naim, C. M. "The Consequences of Indo-Pakistani War for Urdu Language and Literature." *Journal of Asian Studies,* 1965, 269-283.

Namier, L. B. *1848: The Revolution of the Intellectuals* (from: Proceeding of the British Academy, 1944, Vol. 30.). London: Geoffrey Cumberlege, Amen House, 1944.

———. "Nationality and Liberty." *Avenues of History.* L. B. Namier. London: Hamish Hamilton, 1952. (Originally published as a paper of the Tenth Conference of the Accademia Nazionale de Lincei, Rome, 1948.)

Nandy, S. K. "Is Modernization Westernization? What about Easternization and Traditionalization?" *Transactions of the Sixth World Congress of Sociology,* 3 (1970), 267-280.

Natarajan, S. "Pertinent facts." *Seminar,* 68 (April 1956), 12-17.

Nehru, Jawaharlal. *An Autobiography.* London: Bodley Head, 1953.

Neustupny, J. V. "Basic Types of Treatment of Language Problems." *Linguistic Communications* (Monash University), 1 (1970), 77-100.

Newth, J. A. "Nationality and Language in Turkmenia." *Soviet Studies,* 15, 4 (1964).

Nielsen, Erik W. "Asian Nationalism." *Practical Anthropology,* 1964, 211-225.

Noreen, Adolf. "Über Sprachrichtigkeit." *Indogermanische Forschungen,* 1 (1892), 95-157. (Tr. From Swedish to German by Arnid Johansson with substituted German examples.)

Noss, Richard. *Language Policy and Higher Education.* (Vol. III, part 2 of a series entitled Higher Education and Development in South East Asia.) Paris: UNESCO and the International Association of Universities, 1967.

Nugroho, R. "The Origins and Development of Bahasa Indonesia." *PMLA,* 72,2 (1957) 23-28.

Nuseibeh, Hazem Zaki. *The Ideas of Arab Nationalism.* Ithaca: Cornell Univ. Press, 1956.

Nusuli, Muhyiddin. "Modern Trends of Literature in the Muslim Countries." *Colloquium on Islamic Culture.* Princeton, N.J.: Princeton Univ. Press, 1953, 22-23.

Obote, Milton. "Language and National Identification." *East African Journal,* 4, No. 3 (April 1967), 3-6.

Ó Cuív, Brian, "The Gaelic Cultural Movements and the New Nationalism." *The Making of 1916.* Ed. Kevin B. Nowlan. Dublin: Stationery Office, 1969.

O'Hickey, M. P. "The True National Idea." Dublin: Gaelic League (Gaelic League Pamphlets, No. 1), 1898.

————. *An Irish university, or Else–*. Dublin and Waterford: Gill, 1909.

Ola, C. S. "Now Is the Time for One Language." *Daily Express* (Lagos), 30 Sept. 1960.

Omar, Asmah Haji. "Standard Language and the Standardization of Malay." *Anthropological Linguistics*, 13 (1971), 75-89.

O'Reilly, John M. *The Threatening Metempsychosis of a Nation*. Dublin: Gaelic League (Gaelic League Pamphlets, No. 24, 1900.

Ostrower, Alexander. *Language, Law and Diplomacy*, Philadelphia: Univ. of Pennsylvania Press, 1965.

Paden, John N. "Language Problems of National Integration in Nigeria: The Special Position of Housa." *Language Problems of Developing Nations*. Ed. J. A. Fishman, C. A. Ferguson, and J. Das Gupta. New York: Wiley, 1968, 199-214.

Panikkar, K. M. *Asia and Western Dominance*. London: Allen and Unwin, 1955.

————. *A Survey of Indian History*. Delhi: Asia Publishing House, 1962.

Park, R. E., and E. W. Burgess. *Introduction to Sociology*. Chicago: Univ. of Chicago Press, 1924.

Parker, Guy J. "Indonesian Images of Their National Self." *Public Opinion Quarterly*, 22 (1958), 305-24.

Passerin d'Entrèves, Alessandro. The Notion of the State: An Introduction to *Politics Theory*. Oxford: Clarendon, 1967.

Pfaff, Richard H. "Disengagement from Traditionalism in Turkey and Iran." *Western Political Quarterly*, 16 (1963), 79-98.

————. "The Function of Arab Nationalism." *Comparative Politics*, 2 (1970), 147-168.

Pflanze, Otto. "Characteristics of Nationalism in Europe, 1848-1871." *Review of Politics*, 28 (1966), 129-143.

Phipps, Wm. E. "The Influence of Christian Missions on the Rise of Nationalism in Central Africa." *International Review of Missions*, 57 (1908), 229-32.

Pielow, Winfried. "Nationalistische Muster im Lesebuch." *Nationalismus in Germanistik und Dichtung*. Ed. Benno von Wiese and Rudolf Henss. Berlin: Erich Schmidt, 1967, 248-260.

Pietrzyk, Alfred. "Problems in Language Planning: The Case of Hindi." *Contemporary India*. Ed. B. N. Varma. London: Asia Publishing House, 1965, 247-270.

Pinson, Koppel S. *Pietism as a Factor in the Rise of German Nationalism*. New York: Columbia, 1934.

————. *Bibliographical Introduction to Nationalism*. New York: Columbia, 1935.

————. "Pietism–a Source of German Nationalism." *Christendom*, 1 (1936), 266-280.

Pillsbury, Walter B. *The Psychology of Nationality and Internationalism*. New York: Appleton, 1919.

Polenz, Peter von. "Sprachpurismus und Nationalsozialismus. Die 'Fremdwort' Frage gestern und heute." *Nationalismus in Germanistik und Dichtung.* Ed. Benno von Wiese and Rudolf Henss. Berlin: Erich Schmidt, 1967, 79-112.

Polk, William R. "Introduction." *The Modern Arabic Literary Language.* Jaroslav Stetkevych. Chicago: Univ. of Chicago Press, 1970.

Ponsionen, J. A. *The Analysis of Social Change Reconsidered: A Sociological Study.* The Hague: Mouton, 1962.

Post, Gains. "Rex Imperator." *Traditio,* 9 (1953), 296-320.

Potekhin, I. "The Formation of Nations in Africa." *Marxism Today,* 2, No. 10 (1958), 308-314.

Potter, D. "The Historian's Use of Nationalism and Vice Versa." *American Historical Review,* 67 (1962), 924-950.

Powers, George C. *Nationalism at the Council of Constance (1414-1418).* Washington, D.C.: Catholic University of America, 1927.

Purcell, Victor. "The Crisis in Malayan Education." *Pacific Affairs,* 26 (1953), 70-76.

———. "The Influence of Racial Minorities." *Nationalism and Progress in Free Asia.* Ed. Philip W. Thayer. Baltimore: Johns Hopkins, 1953, 234-245.

Pye, Lucian W. "Personal Identity and Political Ideology." *Behavioral Science,* 6 (1961), 205-221.

Quelquejay, Chantal, and Alex Bennigsen, *The Evolution of the Muslim Nationalities of the U.S.S.R. and Their Linguistic Problems.* London: Central Asian Research Center, 1961.

Rabelais, François. *Pantagruel.* vol. III Ed. A. Lefranc. Paris: Champion, 1922 (orig. published 1532).

Rakowska-Harmstone, Teresa. *Russia and Nationalism in Central Asia: The Case of Tadzhikistan.* Baltimore: Johns Hopkins, 1970.

Ranger, T. O. "Connections between 'Primary Resistance' Movements and Modern Mass Nationalism in East and Central Africa." *Journal of African History,* 1968a, 9, 3, 437153, 4, 631-41.

———. "Nationality and Nationalism: The Case of Barotseland." *Journal of the Historical Society of Nigeria,* 4 (1968b), 227-246.

Rauenholt, Albert. "The Spoils of Nationalism: The Phillipines." *Expectant Peoples: Nationalism and Development.* Ed. K. H. Silvert. New York: Random House, 1963, 178-195.

Raun, Alo, and Andrus Saareste. *Introduction to Estonian Linguistics* (also: Ural-Altaische Bibliothek, XII). Wiesbaden: Harrassowitz, 1965.

Reiss, H. S. *The Political Thought of the German Romantics, 1793-1815.* Oxford: Blackwell, 1955.

Reissman, Leonard. *The Urban Process: Cities in Industrial Societies.* New York: Free Press, 1964.

————. "Urbanization: A Typology of Change." *Urbanism in World Perspective.* Ed. Sylvia F. Fauss. New York: Crowell, 1968, 126-144.

Remeikis, T. "The Evolving Status of Nationalities in the Soviet Union." *Canadian Slavic Studies,* 1 (1967), 404-423.

Rendessi, Mehdi. "Pages peu connues de Djamal al-din al-Afghani." *Orient,* 6 (1958), 123-128.

Riggs, Fred W. *Social Change and Political Development.* Bloomington: Indiana Univ., 1964. (Mimeo: Prepared for the Seminar on Political Behavior in Non-Western Countries. Ann Arbor, Michigan, July-August, 1964.)

Rjasanoff, N. "Karl Marx und Friedrich Engels über die Polenfrage." *Archiv für die Geschichte des Socialismus und der Arbeiterbewegung* (Leipzig), 6, (1916), 175-221.

Robertson, D. Maclaren. *A History of the French Academyy 16355 (4)–1910.* New York: Dillingham, 1910.

Rocker, Rudolf. *Nationalism and Culture.* London: Freedom Press, 1937.

Rodinson, Maxime. "Sur la Théorie marxiste de la nation." *Voies Nouvelles,* 2 (May 1968), 25-30.

Rojo, Trinidad A. *The Language Problem in the Philippines.* New York and Manila: The Philippine Research Bureau, 1937.

Ronen, Dov. "Preliminary Notes on the Concept of Regionalism in Dahomey." *Etudes Dahoméennes,* 1 (1968), 11-14.

Ronsard, Pierre de. *Oeuvres Complètes.* Ed. Paul Laumonier. Paris: Lemerre, 1952 (orig. pub. 1553-1584).

Rosenblatt, Paul C. "Origins and Effects of Group Ethnocentrism and Nationalism." *J. Conflict Resolution,* 8 (1964), 131-146.

Rosenthal, E. I. J. *Islam in the Modern National State.* London: Cambridge Univ. Press, 1965.

Ross, Ronald J. "Heinrich Ritter von Srbik and 'Gesamtdeutsch' History." *Review of Politics,* 31 (1969), 88-107.

Rotberg, R. I. "The Rise of African Nationalism: The Case of East and Central Africa." *World Politics,* 15 (1962), 75-90.

————. African Nationalism: Concept or Confusion? *Journal of Modern African Studies,* 1 (1966), 33-46.

Roy, Naresh Chandra. *Federalism and Linguistic States.* Calcutta: Mukopadhyay, 1962.

Rubin, Joan, and Björn, Jernudd (eds.) *Can Language Be Planned?* Honolulu; East-West Center Press, 1971.

Rustow, Dankwart A. "New Horizon for Comparative Politics." *World Politics,* 1957, 530-549.

————. "Language, Modernization and Nationhood." *Language Problems of Developing Nations.* Ed. Joshua A. Fishman, Charles A. Ferguson, and Jyotirindra Das Gupta. New York: Wiley, 1968a, 87-106.

—— "Nation." *International Encyclopedia of the Social Sciences,* 11 (1968b), 7-14.

Salmon, Vivian. "Language-Planning in Seventeenth-Century England, Its Contexts and Aims." *In Memory of J. R. Firth.* Ed. C. E. Bazell, J. C. Catford, M. A. K. Halliday, and R. A. Rubins. London: Longmans, 1966, pp. 370-397.

Sapir, Edward. "Language and National Antagonisms." *When People Meet.* Ed. Alain Locke and Bernard J. Stern. New York: Progressive Education Association, 1942, 649-662. (Excerpted from his "Language," in *Encyclopedia of the Social Sciences,* 9 [1933], 155-169.

Sayigh, Rosemary. "The Bilingualism Controversy in Lebanon." *The World Today,* 21, 3 (1965), 20-30.

Scalapino, Robert A. "Ideology and Modernization–The Japanese Case." *Ideology and Discontent.* Ed . David Apter. New York: Free Press, 1964, 93-127.

Schaechter, Mordkhe. "The 'Hidden Standard'; A Study of Competing Influences in Standardization." *Field of Yiddish III.* Ed. Herzog, M., W. Ravid, and U. Weinreich. The Hague: Mouton, 1970, pp. 284-327.

Schmidt-Rohr, Georg. *Die Sprache als Bildnerin der Volker: Eine Wesens und Lebenskunde der Volkstümer.* Jena: Eugen Diederichs Verlag, 1932 (2nd ed., *Mutter Sprache,* 1933).

Schorske, Carl E. "The Idea of the City in European Thought: Voltaire to Spengler." *Urbanism in World Perspective.* Ed. Sylvia F. Fava. New York: Crowell, 1968, 409-424.

Schwab, William. "Recent Developments in Applied Linguistics." *Philippine Sociological Review,* 11 (1963).

Sen, Mohit. "Role of the Mother Tongue." *Seminar,* 76 (Dec. 1965), 18-20.

Senghor, Leopold Sedar. "What is 'Negritude?" *West Africa,* 4 Nov. 1961, also in *The Ideologies of the Developing Nations.* Ed. Paul E. Sigmund, Jr. New York: Praeger, 1963, 248-250.

Seton-Watson, Hugh. *Nationalism Old and New.* Sydney: Sydney Univ. Press, 1965.

Shafer, Boyd C. *Nationalism: Myth and Reality.* New York: Harcourt, Brace, 1955.

Sharabi, Hisham. "The Transformation of Ideology in the Arab World." *Middle East Journal,* 19 (1965), 471-486.

——. *Nationalism and Revolution in the Arab World.* Princeton, N. J.: Van Nostrand, 1966.

Shepperson, G. "Ethiopianism and African Nationalism." *Phylon,* 14 (1953), 9-18.

Sherrard, Philip. *The Greek East and the Latin West.* London: Oxford Univ. Press, 1959.

Shils, E. "Centre and Periphery." *The Logic of Personal Knowledge: Essays Presented to Michael Polanyi.* London: Routledge, 1961, 117-130.

―――. "Tradition." *Comparative Studies in Society and History,* 13 (1971), 122-159.

Shouby, E. T. "The Influence of tha Arabic Language Upon the Psychology of the Arabs." *Middle East Journal,* 5 (1951), 284-302.

Sigmund, Paul E., Jr., ed. *The Ideologies of the Developing Nations.* New York: Praeger, 1963.

Siegman, Henry. "Arab Unity and Disunity." *Middle East Journal,* 15 (1962), 48-59.

Silvert, Kalman H. ed. *Expectant Peoples: Nationalism and Development.* New York: Random House, 1963.

Simmel, G. "The Metropolis and Mental Life." *Cities and Society.* Ed. P. Hatt and A. Reiss. New York: Free Press, 1957, 635-646.

Singhal, D. P. "Nationalism and Communism in South-East Asia." *Journal of Southeast Asian History,* 3 (1962), 56-66.

―――. *Nationalism in India and Other Historical Essays.* Delhi: Oriental Publishers, 1967.

Sìothchaín. Micheál O. *A Call to Ireland.* Dublin: Gaelic League, 1911.

Sithole, Ndabaningi. *African Nationalism.* Cape Town: Oxford Univ. Press, 1959.

Sjahir, Soetan. *Out of Exile.* Trans. Charles Wolf, Jr. New York: John Day, 1947.

Skinner, G. William. "The Nature of Loyalties in Rural Indonesia." *Local Ethnic and National Loyalties in Village Indonesia.* Ed. G. William Skinner. New Haven: Yale Univ. Southeast Asia Studies, 1959.

Smith, David H., and Alex Inkeles. "The OM Scale: A Comparative Socio-psychological Measure of Individual Modernity." *Sociometry,* 29 (1966), 353-377.

Smith, Wilfred Cantwell. *Pakistan as an Islamic state.* Lahore: Ashraf Press, 1954.

Snyder, Louis L. "Nationalistic Aspects of the Grimm Brothers' Fairy Tales." *Journal of Social Psychology,* 33 (1951), 209-223.

―――. *German Nationalism: The Tragedy of a People.* Harrisburg, Pa.: Stackpole, 1952.

―――. *The Meaning of Nationalism.* New Brunswick, N. J.: Rutgers Univ. Press, 1954.

―――. ed. *The Dynamics of Nationalism.* Princeton, N.J.: Van Nostrand, 1964.

―――. *The New Nationalism.* Ithaca: Cornell Univ. Press, 1968.

Sommer, Hans. *Von Sprachwandel und Sprachpflege.* Bern: Francke, 1945.

Sopher, David E. *Geography of Religions.* Englewood Cliffs, N.J.: Prentice-Hall, 1967.

Sorel, Georges. *Reflections on Violence.* New York: Collier, 1961.

Southall, John E. *Wales and Her Language.* London: D. NUH, 1893.

Spiegel, Shalom. *Hebrew Reborn.* New York: Macmillan, 1930.

Spring, Gerald M. *The Vitalism of Count de Gobineau,* New York: Columbia, 1932.

Staal, J. F. "Sanskritization." *Journal of Asian Studies,* 22 (1962), 261-275.

Stalin, Iosif (Joseph). *Marxism and the National Question.* New York: International Publishers, 1942.

Strayer, Joseph R. "The Laicization of French and English Society in the Thirteenth Century." *Speculum,* 15 (1940), 76-86.

–––. "The Historical Experience of Nation-building in Europe." *Nation-Building.* Ed. Karl W. Deutsch and Wm. J. Foltz. New York: Atherton, 1966, 17-26.

Stubbs, William. *Select Charters and Other Illustrations of English Constitutional History from the Earliest Times to Reign of Edward the First.* 2nd ed., Oxford: Clarendon Press, 1874.

Sturzo, Luigi. *Italy and Fascismo.* London: Faber and Gwyer, 1927.

Sullivant, Robert S. "The Ukrainians." *Problems of Communism,* 16, No. 5, (1967), 46-54.

Sulzbach, Walter. *National Consciousness.* Washington: American Council on Public Affairs, 1943.

Sutton, F. X. "Languages and Linguistics." Ford Foundation Representatives Meeting, Nairobi, June 6-8, 1968. (Mimeo.)

Symmons-Symonolewicz, Konstontin. "Nationalist Movements: An Attempt at a Comparative Typology. *Comparative Studies in Society and History,* 7 (1965), 221-230.

–––. *"Nationalist Movements: A Comparative View.* Meadville (Pa.), Meadville Press, 1971.

–––. *Modern Nationalism: Towards a Consensus in Theory.* New York: Polish Institute of Arts and Sciences in America, 1968.

Szabe, L. "Regression or New Development? Twenty Years of Linguistic Reform in Turkey." *Civilizations,* 2, No. 1 (1952), 46-54.

Tachau, Frank. "Language and Politics: Turkish Language Reform." *Review of Politics,* 26 (1964), 191-204.

Tagore, Rabindranath. *Nationalism.* New York, Macmillan: 1920.

Talmon, J. L. *The Rise of Totalitarian Democracy.* Boston: Beacon, 1952.

–––. *The Unique and the Universal.* London: Secker and Warburg, 1965.

Tambiah, S. J. "The Politics of Language in India and Ceylon." *Modern Asian Studies,* 1 (1967), 215-240.

Tiedemann, Arthur. *Modern Japan.* Princeton, N.J.: Van Nostrand, 1955.

Tilly, Charles. "The Forms of Urbanization." *American Sociology.* Ed. Talcott Parsons. New York: Basic Books, 1968.

Toynbee, A. J. *The Western Question in Greece and Turkey.* London: Constable, 1922.

————. *A Study of History.* Vols. VII-IX. London: Oxford Univ. Press, 1935-54.

Trevor-Roper, Hugh, *Jewish and Other Nationalism.* London: Weidenfeld and Nicholson, 1962.

Turner, R. H., and L. M. Killan, eds. *Collective Behavior.* New York: Prentice-Hall, 1957.

Vambery, Rustem. "Nationalism in Hungary." *Annals of the American Academy of Political and Social Science,* 232 (1944), 77-85.

Van den Berghe, Pierre L. "Language and 'Nationalism' in South Africa. *Language Problems of Developing Nations.* Ed. J. A. Fishman, C. A. Ferguson, and J. Das Gupta. New York, Wiley: 1968, 215-224.

Vendryes, J. *Language: A Linguistic Introduction to History.* New York: Knopf, 1925.

Vico, Giambatista. *The New Science.* Trans. Thomas G. Bergen and Max H. Fisch. Ithaca, N.Y.: Cornell Univ. Press, 1948. (First Published in Italian, 1725.)

Vogt, Hanna. *Nationalismus: gestern und heute; Texte und Dokumente.* Opladen: Leske, 1967.

Von Finke, Heinrich. "Die Nation in den spätmittelalterlichen allgemeinen Konzilien." *Historisches Jahrbuch,* 57 (1937), 323-38.

Von Grunebaun, G. E. "Problems of Muslim Nationalism." *Islam and the West.* Ed. R. N. Frye. The Hague: Mouton, 1959, 7-29.

————. *Modern Islam: The Search for Cultural Identity,* Berkeley: Univ. of Calif. Press, 1962.

Vossler, Karl. *The Spirit of Language in Civilization.* London: Routledge, 1932.

Wallerstein, Immanuel. "Ethnicity et integration nationale en Afrique Occidentale." *Cahiers d'Etudes Africaines,* 3, No. 1 (1960), 129-139.

Walshe, A. P. "Black African Thought and African Political Attitudes in South Africa." *Review of Politics,* 32 (1970), 51-77.

Ward, Robert E., and Dankwart A. Rustow eds. *Turkey and Japan: A Comparative Study of Modernization.* Princeton, N. J.: Princeton Univ. Press, 1964.

Waters, Alan R. "A Behavioral Model of Pan-African Disintegration." *African Studies Review,* 13 (1970), 415-433.

Weinreich, Uriel. "Di velshishe shprakh in kamf far ir kiyem." *Yivo-Bleter,* 23, (1944), 225-48.

————. "Di shveytser romantshn Artetn farn kiyem fun zeyer shprakh." *Bleter far yidisher dertsiung,* 5 (1953), 68-76.

————. The Russification of Soviet Minority Languages. *Problems of Communism,* 2(b) (1953b), 46-57.

Weisgerber, Leo. "Wesen und Kräfte der Sprachgemeinschaft." *Muttersprache,* 48 (1933), 225-232.

———. "Martin Luther und das Volkwerden der Deutschen." *Mecklenburgische Monatshefte,* 9 (1933), 552-554.

———. "Die Macht der Sprache im Leben des Volkes." *Mitteilungen des Universitätsbundes Marburg,* 1938, 43-51.

———. "Die Haltung der Deutschen zu ihrer Sprache." *Zeitschrift für Deutschwissenschaft und Deutschunterricht,* 1 (1943), 12-18.

Welch, Claude E. *Dream of Unity.* Ithaca: Cornell Univ. Press, 1966.

Wells, G. A. *Herder and After: A Study of the Development of Sociology.* The Hague: Mouton, 1959.

Wheeler, Douglas L. "Angola is Whose House? Early Stirrings of Angolan Nationalism and Protest, 1822-1910." *African Historical Studies,* 2 (1969), 1-22.

Whiteley, W. H. "Language and Politics in East Africa." *Tanganyika Notes and Records,* Nos. 47-48 (1957), 159-173.

———. "Ideal and Reality in National Language Policy: A Case Study from Tanzania." *Language Problems of Developing Nations.* Ed. J. A. Fishman, C. A. Ferguson, and J. Das Gupta. New York: Wiley, 1968, 327-344.

———. *Swahili: The Rise of a National Language.* London: Methuen, 1969.

Wildenman, R. and H. Parkalla. *Nationalismus in Entwicklungpolitik.* Berlin-Mainz, Handbuch und Lexicon, 1966.

Williams, Lea E. *Overseas Chinese Nationalism.* Glencoe, Ill.: Free Press, 1960.

Windmiller, Marshall. "Linguistic Regionalism in India." *Pacific Affairs,* 27 (1954), 291-318.

Wirth, Louis. "Types of Nationalism." *American Journal of Sociology,* 41 (1936), 723-37.

———. "Urbanism as a Way of Life." *American Journal of Sociology,* 44 (1938), 1-24.

Woodward, E. L. *Christianity and Nationalism in the Later Roman Empire.* London: Longmans, 1916.

———. "The Patriarchate of Alexandria: A Study in National Christianity." *Church History,* 15 (1946), 81-100.

Woolner, Alfred C. *Languages in History and Politics.* London: Oxford Univ. Press, 1938.

Wuorinen, John H. *Nationalism in Modern Finland.* New York: Columbia, Univ. Press, 1931.

———. "Scandinavia and the Rise of Modern National Consciousness." *Nationalism and Internationalism: Essays Inscribed to Carlton J. H. Hayes.* Ed. Edward Mead Earle. New York: Columbia Univ. Press, 1950, 454-479.

Wurm, Stefan. *Turkic Peoples of the U.S.S.R.* London: Central Asian Research Center, 1954.

———, Natalie Waterson, and C. G. Simpon. *The Turkic Languages of Central Asia: Problems of Planned Culture Contact.* London: Central Asian Research Center, 1960.

Yadav, R. K. *The Indian Language Problem–A Comparative Study.* Delhi: National Publishing House, 1967.

Yang, Ching Kun. *Religion in Chinese Society.* Berkeley, Univ. of Calif. Press, 1961.

Zangwill, Israel. *The Principle of Nationalities.* London: Watts, 1917.

Zarevand (= Nalbandian, Zavan, and Vartouhie). *United and Independent Turania; Aims and Designs of the Turks* (translated from the Armenian by V.N. Dadrian, 1971).

Zartman, I. Wm. "Problems of Arabization in Moroccan Education." *Confluent,* 26 (1962) (in French), in *The Contemporary Middle East.* Ed. Benjamin Rivlin and Joseph Szyliowicz. New York: Random House, 1965, 328-338.

Zatcheck, Heinz. *Das Volksbewusstsein: Sein Werden im Spiegel der Geschichtschreibung.* Brünn: Rohrer, 1936.

Zernatto, Guido. "Nation: The History of a Word." *Review of Politics,* 6 (1944), 351-366.

Znaniecki, Florian. *Modern Nationalities.* Urbana: Univ. of Illinois Press, 1952.

Index

(of nationalities and ethnic groups, places, and persons)

Sorel, Georges, 104
South Africa, viii
Southall, John E., 41, 48, 49, 83, 137
Spain, 26, 93, 105, 124, 125
Spanish, 1, 50, 75, 78, 124, 144
Spiegel, Shalom, 72
Sporschil, Johann, 99
Spring, H. L., 42
Stalin, Joseph V., 91, 98, 127
Stefan of Perm, Saint, 68
Strayer, Joseph R., 23, 24
Sturzo, Luigi, 110
Sukarno, Achmed, xiii, 120-121, 132, 136
Sullivant, Robert S., 19
Sulzbach, Walter, 17, 45, 96, 122
Sutton, F. X., 92
Swahili, 65-66, 71, 76
Swede-Finns, 105, 122, 134
Sweden, 19, 105
Swedish, 67, 105, 122, 134, 138
Switzerland, 126. *See also* German
Symmons-Symonolewicz, Konstantin, 8, 11
Syrians, 95, 120
Szabe, L., 75, 132

Tagalog, 60, 136. *See also* Pilipino
Tagore, Rabindranath, 51, 106, 114, 116
Talmon, J. L., 14, 27, 77, 97, 105
Tamil, 129, 132
Tanganyika, 34, 112, 118
Tanzania, 37, 77
Tartars, 38, 120
Thailand, 132
Tiedemann, Arthur, 30, 31
Tilly, Charles, xiii
Tocqueville, Alexis de, 92
Tokyo, 35
Tory, Geoffrey, 123
Toscano, J. V., 89
Toynbee, A. J., 44, 140
Trele, 121
Trevor-Roper, Hugh, 19, 27, 100
Turgieneff, Ivan, 55

Turgot, Anne Robert, 127
Turkey, coterminous with language, 2; and Greece, 95; and Hungary, 48; and Iran, 54; and pan movements, 111, 120, 121; religion of, 115; and tradition, 34; and Turkish Empire, 31
Turkish, 79-80; and Arabic, 67, 74; and authenticity of, 70, 74, 75, 89, 107, 109, 132; coterminous with nation, 2; and Persian, 54, 67, 74; and tradition, 143; as vernacular, 60, 67

Ukraine, 19, 36, 60, 80, 109, 122, 142
Urdu, 67-68, 81, 82, 132, 138, 142
Uzbeks, 54

Valencia, 112
Vico, Giambatista, 46
Vienna, 19, 109
Vietnam, vii, 30, 36, 119, 132
Virgil, 50
Voltaire, François Marie Arouet, 130
Vossler, Karl, 54, 55, 59, 68, 127, 128, 144

Wales, 42, 48, 107, 108, 123, 126
Walshe, A. P., 111
Waters, Alan R., 111
Waterson, Natalie, 129, 143
Watt, Ian, 20
Weber, Max, 18
Webster, Noah, 67
Weinreich, Uriel, 98
Wells, G. A., 127
Welsh, 39, 48, 72, 123, 126, 137
Wheeler, Douglas L., 114
Whiteley, W. H., 56, 59, 63, 66, 71, 76, 77, 125
White Russians, 109
White Ruthenians, 6, 142
Whorf, Benjamin, 127
Wildenman, R., 118
Williams, S. Wells, 134